On the Run

# THE NEVER DULL AND OFTEN SHOCKING LIFE OF MAURY WILLS

MAURY WILLS & MIKE CELIZIC



A Gallen/Golenbock Book

Carroll & Graf Publishers, Inc.
New York

First Carroll & Graf edition 1991

Carroll & Graf Publishers, Inc.
260 Fifth Avenue
New York, NY 10001

Library of Congress Cataloging-in-Publication Data

Willis, Maury, 1932-
On the run : the never dull and often shocking life of Maury Wills / by Maury Wills and Mike Celizic.
p. cm.
ISBN 0-88184-640-6
1. Wills, Maury, 1932- . 2. Baseball players—United States—Biography. 3. Narcotic addicts—United States—Biography. 4. Los Angeles Dodgers (Baseball team) I. Celizic, Mike. II. Title.
GV865.W55A3 1991
796.357'092—dc20
[B] 90-28800
CIP

Manufactured in the United States of America

**To all those men and women who helped me with my disease, the Dodger organization and finally to my wonderful family.**

**—M.W.**

**To Louise Curach-Tich, who said so long ago this day would come.**

**—M.C.**

ACKNOWLEDGMENTS

Among the many I owe thanks: Peter Golenbock and Richard Gallen for their faith and patience; Jon Gallen for services too numerous to mention; Jim Wright for professional advice and friendship; Barbara for her hospitality and forebearance; Frank C. for his inspiration; and Gabe Buonauro and Rob Tanenbaum for their patience. Thanks also to Michael Williams and the Dodgers public relations department and to the sports information staff at Syracuse University.

If there is any grace to my prose, I owe it to Ellen Chase, as good an editor as you'll find.

Finally, thanks to Margaret, Carl, Jim, Jane and the Zack-Man for never failing to provide the comic relief.

M.C.
Warwick, N.Y.
November, 1990

# Prologue

This isn't a kiss-and-tell book. I like to think that at no time in my life was I the kind of guy to go around taking someone else's inventory. And now, I've grown to the point where it's just not right going around talking about people's character defects, their shortcomings, their minuses, when there are so many pluses to talk about.

People aren't really that bad. We do bad things for various reasons. Maybe it's the economy. Maybe it's the times. Maybe it's the era—peer pressure, what's fashionable. We're like sheep, most of us.

One day when I was near the end of my career with the Dodgers, we got off the plane in Philadelphia. The Dodgers had their own plane, so we used a ramp that was at the end of a long concourse, and the Philadelphia airport has some long ones.

I told my buddy Duke Sims, "C'mon, Duke. Let's take these guys for a walk."

When you have your own plane, you have a lot of carry-on luggage. We always took a lot of clothes on the plane in garment bags rather than fold them in suitcases. Just about everybody took a duffel bag, too.

So we're walking with these garment bags and duffel bags and everybody's stopping every now and then to change hands. And they're following Duke and me.

We took them down one long concourse towards the front of the airport. I whispered to Duke, "To the right," and we went down another long concourse and away from the bus, which was only about 50 feet away. We turned down another concourse, down a flight of stairs, out of the airport, across a lawn, and then down to a chain-link fence that bordered a freeway before anybody bothered to ask, "Where the hell are we?"

"I don't know," I said.

"Me neither," said Duke. "Didn't you say the bus was right here?"

They had all followed one another—25 players, a manager, four coaches and about five sportswriters.

There were some cussing ballplayers. Everybody wanted to find out who led them down that way and whether it was on purpose because whoever it was was going to get it. Duke and I decided to keep it a secret.

It just shows you how people follow. You see a flock of geese flying in tight formation. Wherever that lead goose goes, the rest follow. If you're hunting geese, you only have to get that first goose to come to your call, and the rest will follow.

We're just like that. We're just sophisticated animals. And that's what I thought whenever I saw people do odd things during my career. They were just following the leader.

I want this book to be a story that people can benefit from. I touched a lot of people's lives through my baseball playing. I became an inspiration to people to persevere in whatever endeavor. They saw this little guy down there in Dodger Stadium scurrying around. That's why they named me Mouse—I succeeded against the big boys.

I played with guys like Frank Howard, Tommy Davis, John Roseboro, Willie Davis, Don Drysdale, Sandy Koufax. Big, strong guys. And there was little Maury, or as Vin Scully and others used to refer to me, Little Maury Wills, the Darling of the Dodgers.

I spent 8½ years in the minor leagues. One day, it must have been at the 1975 World Series between Boston and Cincinnati, when I was a broadcaster for NBC, a Cincinnati player came up to me. He was having a successful year in the major leagues. He said, "Maury, I want to thank you for helping me get to the big leagues. It was because of how you persevered in the minors that I never gave up. I spent 12 years in the minors before the Reds called me up. But I always figured I had a chance because you had done it."

One more story: Before a ballgame in St. Louis one day, some of my teammates told me that a couple in the stands were trying to get my attention. I looked up and saw a white couple with a baby.

"Maury," they said, "we just wanted you to know that our last name is Wills and we named our little boy Maury after you." Then they said, "We want to thank you, Maury."

A young, white couple named their baby after me. Oh, God, what a feeling for me!

That's the way I touched lives through my playing. Now I can't play anymore, but I still want to be of service. I still want to touch lives.

And that's why this isn't only a book about baseball. It's also a story about a man who was considered extraordinary and fell prey to a terribly ordinary disease.

—Maury Wills

## Chapter 1: Bump and Judy

I guess my mistake was trying to be happy all the time. That's a false world. It's like the world I created every time my son Bump came to Los Angeles with the Texas Rangers.

Bump came up to the big leagues in 1977. Every time the Rangers came to town to play the Angels, I'd get all my friends, rent a 12-seat van, buy a great, big, brand-new trash barrel and fill it with ice and soda. I'd go down to the local deli and get piles of sandwiches and other things to eat and we'd go to the ballpark and root for Bump and the Rangers. Then Bump would come home and we'd have a special dinner every night.

I had never been there for Bump—or for any of my children. I wasn't home when he was born. I wasn't home to watch him play ball or graduate from school or celebrate his birthday. I was always playing ball.

I gave up a lot to play ball. I gave up human relationships. Baseball was my relationship. That relationship lasted until I was 40 years old and the Dodgers decided they wanted to go with a new generation and didn't need my services any longer.

After I retired, I wanted to make up for all the years I had neglected my family by making life perfect when my son came to town. But Bump didn't feel comfortable in that false world. When he went to the ballpark, he was expected to perform up to the level of excellence I had established. No wonder he couldn't play well when I was watching.

Bump had contempt for his dad. Looking back, I know that he wanted to do everything better than I did. He didn't want to steal bases and play shortstop and wear number 30 and get little banjo hits like I did. He wanted to play second base. He wore number 4. He wanted to "juice" the ball.

And when he came to California in 1977 as a rookie and stayed with me, he met this new person in my life. He met Judy.

Judy was special to me. She was the human relationship I had never had during the years I was pursuing my love affair with baseball.

I had married right out of high school because I got my girlfriend pregnant. But I had never been in love with my wife. It was a marriage that produced six children, but for me no deep emotional bonds. In those days, baseball was my all-consuming love. As I worked my way through the minor leagues and into the big leagues, I didn't have the time or the capacity for anything else.

I had met Judy in 1975. She was as pretty and exciting a woman as you'll ever find. And when I met her I jumped into this new kind of relationship with both feet and grabbed hold of it and clenched it until, finally, I smothered it.

I was living the good life with Judy when Bump first came to visit. I still had a dream of becoming a manager in the big leagues. In the meantime, I had stepped off the field and into an announcing job with NBC. I bought a beautiful house overlooking the ocean in Playa del Rey and filled it with antiques. I managed teams in Mexico in the winter and trained major league teams in the spring. I went hunting and played a lot of golf. I had it all. And Judy, too.

But I didn't know how to have a human relationship. I overhustled. I gave it all the gusto I had put into baseball to become a good player. I had fallen in love for the first time in my life. And I wouldn't give up.

For three years it was good. Then I lost control and my world fell apart. It would be more than a decade before I could begin to put it back together.

The beginning of the end of everything I had worked for came when Judy fucked Bump. Or he fucked her.

The seeds were there all along. I had planted them. But I didn't see them. I didn't want to see them. By the time I realized what was going on, I was so hooked on Judy that for the next three years I just watched her and suffered. I was aware of the truth and I couldn't do anything about it. I was powerless; I couldn't let go. And when she finally left for good, I went right on suffering.

She thought about doing it with Bump a long time. It was a year after she first met him before anything happened. But I could tell she was thinking about it. She would pass as close to him as she could to the point of touching. We'd go to the airport to pick him up and it was like, "Oh! Bump!" and she'd give him a nice, big, juicy kiss on the mouth as if they were doing a scene on the screen. When we got in the car, she insisted on sitting in the front seat with us, in the middle.

It's painful to remember. I was sitting there driving the car and right there to my right they were touching. It was taking place before my eyes.

She thought about it to the point where when she and I were together, she'd bring Bump up as a fantasy. I asked her to lay off and to give him a break, to give me a break. He was doing his best to be aloof, but I knew he couldn't resist it.

I found myself all the time making sure there wasn't an opportunity. Can you imagine that feeling? I was afraid to go to the store. I knew she was after him. When I asked her not to do it, she made me feel as if I were some kind of creep, as if I were weird.

It was something that I couldn't change and I tried to change it. If I had known the Serenity Prayer—"God, grant me the serenity to accept the things I can't change . . ."—I would not have involved myself in the craziness of it. I would have found some way to stay apart from it and I would have been free of the devastation of it all. But I thought I could fix it and make it so that it wouldn't happen.

She "had his nose open." That's a black expression the guys in my neighborhood used when I was growing up. It means he had the scent. His nose was open and she was unconcerned about how it looked. My only hope was that Bump would lock into his thoughts that I was his dad and not go through with it. But his contempt for me then was greater than his love or respect for me. He didn't back off one bit.

When the nose opens and the man gets the smell of it, the old saying comes true: "A stiff dick has no conscience."

I was upstairs in the bedroom when it started. It was as if I could see it through the walls. And when I did, I came downstairs into my den and they were going at it on the couch. They saw me. Oh, yeah, they saw me.

I walked out and went back upstairs. I was hoping that possibly they would stop. I stayed up there, laughing hysterically.

Then I came back down and they were on a second couch in a more aggressive position.

I sat down in a chair in the same room, not able to look. I wasn't going to leave this time. I just sat there and I was numb. And after he had come twice—she told me that—and she had come no telling how many times, he walked over and said:

"Dad, you want to talk about this?"

I was too numb to do anything. I didn't know about cocaine then. I had no taste to guzzle down some alcohol. I was intoxicated enough by what had happened. I was riddled with confusion and despair.

I was a lost soul. I didn't know anything about drugs and how they affect your mind. But my mind was beginning to go through the changes of anger and agony. My natural adrenaline was turning into poison.

I had lost control. My whole world was gone. But I couldn't give up. I couldn't let go of her. For three more years, no matter what she did, I figured I could correct it. I'd make it good. It was just like baseball, I thought. I could control a ballgame. I could control Judy.

It took me a long time to realize it wasn't Bump's fault. He may have fucked Judy, but I fucked myself.

## Chapter 2: In Control

I'm taking a lead off first base in the Los Angeles Coliseum. I have 92,000 people in the palm of my hand. I can make them go, "OOOOOOOH!" I can make them cheer. I can make them boo. I can make them kill the umpire.

They start chanting, "Go! Go! Go!" And, yes, I hear them.

I actually controlled people. I controlled ballgames. I always wanted that. I wanted things to be my way. I never wanted to consider anyone else if it interfered with my rhythm.

So I take my maximum lead off first, a lead big enough to make the crowd go, "OOOOOOOOOH!"

I build up to it. I know the pitcher is going to throw over. When I can get back standing up, that means I can take another step off the bag. When I have to dive head first to get back, that means I have my maximum lead.

Then I'd take another half step beyond that, so that when I dive back head first with my hands, I'm too far off to get back safely.

But I can take that extra half step and still be safe. I do it by taking my lead from the back edge of first base. I don't know how many ballplayers know this, but first base is 15 inches wide. If I take my lead from the back edge and the first baseman is standing at the front edge, that gives me an extra 15 inches to get back. That gives me the extra half step.

And I take that extra half step just so when I dive back the umpire has to get down on his knees—get down almost on his belly with both hands on the ground—to get down low enough to see if I'm safe. When I came up to the big leagues in 1959, the stolen base wasn't a big part of the game. Umpires stood with their hands on their knees a couple steps behind first base in a half-crouch. I got them so that they were right on my butt, right behind the bag and down on the ground. They got down like that in order to tell if the first baseman was just missing me by a fraction of an inch. That's the only way they could give me a fair shot. Otherwise, they had to guess.

And that just made the fans gasp.

There were times the play was so close that when the umpire got down to see it, he paused before he made his call. "——SAFE!" The margin between my hand hitting the base and the mitt tagging me couldn't have been more than one light block—you know, the time it takes for light to go one block.

Umpires like Ron Luciano loved it. Luciano was an American League umpire who got in on my act during the All-Star Game. He was a showman, too. I put him and the other umpires in the action and gave them a chance to be animated and on stage.

Now, when the throw comes and I dive back and the tag comes down, the umpire takes that little pause and you have 92,000 people not knowing whether he's going to call me safe or out. They catch their breath and then scream, "YAY!"

All I have to do is get too cocky and get picked off and maybe 92,000 people are going to feel like coming down out of the stands. They're going to boo that umpire something terrible. I mean, this is Little Maury Wills, the Darling of the Dodgers. This is the Coliseum. And I'm using all of that.

They're on the edge of their seats. The pitcher throws 10 straight times to first. Then, the first time he goes to the plate, BAM! I'm on second base.

And the crowd is cheering.

I stand up and dust myself off. The only thing that's dirty is a little patch on my knee from my bent-leg slide. Today, players have to dust themselves off because when they slide head first they get dirt inside their clothes. They have to shake it off. But I slid feet first. I didn't have to take that kind of time. But I'm dusting my whole pants off. I'm walking off the base. It all takes time.

And the fans are cheering. They keep cheering until the pitcher is ready to pitch again, and he can't do that until I get done dusting myself off and get back on the base.

That's control.

I used to make things happen. Jim Gilliam, Wes Parker and John Roseboro were guys who didn't lose the game for us. They didn't make mistakes. They held the opposition and matched them. Then Maury Wills was supposed to do something to win the game. That's the way I saw my job. That's why I was always being innovative, trying to do something to win the ballgame because some Dodger teams I played for were not good enough to match the other team talent for talent and win in the conventional way. We had to do something different.

I remember a game that Warren Spahn pitched against us in the twilight of his career. He was old but he was still winning ballgames throwing what we call slop—a screwball here, take a little off there, bust a fastball in on your fists. It wasn't a real good fastball like he had early in his career, but it was fast enough when he had us leaning out over the plate looking for the slow stuff.

Spahn had us down, I think it was 1–0, and was throwing about a one-hitter in about the seventh inning. I went up and down the bench yelling, "C'mon, guys! We're letting this old man beat us. He can't even move and here we are swinging from our heels because the ball looks big coming in. And we're walking back to the bench talking to ourselves.

"We got to bunt this guy," I said. "He can't field his position anymore. Let's bunt!"

I led off the inning with a bunt for a hit. Wes Parker came up. He laid down a bunt for another hit. Somebody else came up and laid down another bunt. Then somebody got a base hit and the next guy squeaked one through the infield somewhere. Before you knew it, we had about four runs, Spahn was out of there and we won the game.

Another time, we were playing the Giants at Dodger Stadium and Juan Marichal was pitching a 1–0 shutout going into the bottom of the ninth. It was late September, and we were fighting the Giants for the pennant. In the stands, the consensus was that every time a pitcher like Marichal, Sandy Koufax, Don Drysdale, Bob Gibson, Ferguson Jenkins, or Jim Bunning was ahead in the late innings, they were going to win the game.

The fans were booing us and getting up to leave. They were fighting, too. The Dodger fans were beating up on the Giants fans because they knew we'd lost.

I was 0-for-3 against Marichal and leading off the ninth. Jim Ray Hart, the Giants' third baseman, was playing way in to take away the bunt.

Marichal was a right-hander. He had this big motion and follow-through that took him toward the first base line. Normally, I didn't get into my bunting stance early, but this time I did. Hart saw it and came charging fast. Marichal was falling off the mound toward first. So instead of holding the bat loose to deaden the ball, I held it tight.

BAM! I bunted it hard right across the edge of the dirt past the charging Hart and to the third base side of the shortstop, Jose Pagan. I was on first.

People were coming back to their seats. The fighting in the stands stopped. There was something to watch on the field.

Jim Gilliam bunted me to second and somehow I got to third and scored on an infield out or a sacrifice fly and the score was tied, 1–1.

We finally won it in the 13th or 14th inning and I drove in the winning run. Marichal went all the way, but we beat him with that bunt.

Charlie Dressen and Leo Durocher used to say, "Hold 'em, guys, for eight innings while I think of something."

That was me. "Hold 'em, guys. I'll find a way to get us a run before it's over." A great many times I did. Those 92,000 people I had in the palm of my hand. All the cheers I heard in Dodger Stadium, the good memories. All the autographs I signed in the parking lot. They call that the big leagues. It's the highest level of baseball in the world.

For me, it was a tremendous feeling of power. It's what I always dreamed life should be. I was young enough to have the stamina and the strength. I was mature enough to have the knowledge, the wisdom and the courage.

I was in control.

And now, all of a sudden, came Judy and before I know it I'm an alcoholic and an addict. I could control 92,000 people and a ballgame, but I can't control myself.

## Chapter 3: Lonely nights

I was always a loner. I always relied on myself. Yet I hated being alone.

I was written about as a loner, but the real reason I didn't hang out with the other guys on the team was that a lot of times I didn't catch the bus. After the games, I was always getting iced down because of the beating my legs took. Sometimes, Bill Buhler, the Dodger trainer, would just ice me and leave me there in the trainer's room.

Bill's a good man. He started in the Dodgers farm system in 1952, just after I did. He came up to the Dodgers two years ahead of me, in 1957, and became head trainer in 1960. He designed the Steve Yeager throat guard that most catchers and umpires wear today on their masks. He did that in 1977. And Bill did a great job of keeping me in the lineup.

A lot of times, I got out so late after getting iced down, the gates at Dodger Stadium were locked and I had to find the security guards. They'd drive me all over the stadium in a pickup truck trying to get me out of there.

By then it was late. There weren't any fans around. They had to go to work the next day. So there weren't any people waiting to see me or wanting to hang out with me.

If we were on the road, I'd take a cab back to the hotel. I didn't hang out in the hotel bars. The guys who went to the bars were just drinkers. They'd go out to drink and hope they'd find some slutty girl who liked to drink in the bars late.

If you weren't a drinker, you weren't going to go into a bar just to pick up some old sleazy chick and lose your rest sitting around. If you went in, you're having some drinks and enjoying yourself and getting yourself poisoned and ruining your health so you can't play tomorrow.

Most of the drinkers are pitchers anyhow, I believe, because they had those days off or they were the tenth guy on the staff and they weren't about to get in the game. That's not an absolute rule, but as I recall, pitchers hung out later than anyone. If a guy was a regular and knew he had to play the next day, he got his rest. He might do some heavy drinking, but he'd do it in a shorter period.

More athletes lose their rest, though, hanging out with women late rather than drinking. Like somebody said, it's not the sex before a game that's bad; it's staying up all night trying to get it. I remember having a girl and throwing her out. We had had a good enough time and I had to get some rest. So I gave her to another ballplayer on the team and she finished the night with him.

Anyway, I didn't take the team bus back to the hotel, and a lot of times, I didn't take the bus to the park, either. I just didn't like a lot of the nonsense that went on on the bus—jokes, yelling out the window at people on the sidewalk. I felt that I functioned better being by myself. Sandy Koufax was like that, too. He didn't socialize much, either.

I just always felt I had a special job to do, a little bit more than the call of duty. In order for me to concentrate and to gear myself up, I had to be alone.

For much of my career, I felt alone even when I was on the field. I felt I had an assignment, which was to win this game, to find some way to score. Any time I could get on base, I felt I had to score. I had to figure out how to do it myself because I couldn't always rely on somebody to knock me in from first base —not even from second. And I had to score from second a lot of times with Jim Gilliam hitting behind me. Jim wasn't a power hitter and the defense could cheat and play close to keep me from scoring on a base hit. But I scored anyhow, and I felt I wouldn't be able to do all this if I was always in the group, riding on the bus.

I even liked my locker to be off in a corner of the clubhouse. The clubhouse guys on the road would put me in a corner by myself. If they had a lot of lockers, they'd leave one empty next to me.

I was always lonely. As a kid, I peed in the bed. I had 12 brothers and sisters, and that set me apart from all of them. We had to sleep four to a bed, but nobody wants to sleep with a kid who pees in the bed. So I got the bed all to myself.

I don't remember having long-term boyhood friends, kids I went through school with and stayed friends with all my life.

As I got older, I couldn't stand being alone. I got so if it took me until daylight, I had to get somebody to come over and stay with me.

Maybe I didn't have any real friendships because baseball was my priority. Being a major league baseball player made me realize major success. And I got that by practicing, practicing, practicing innovative and imaginative ways of executing plays on the field. Joe Torre, whom I played against, once said that I got more out of limited talent than anyone he ever saw. I did that by being absorbed in the game.

I loved the game. It wasn't just a desire to be great or to succeed and be seen and cheered, but to play it as well as it could be played. Not as well as *I* could play, but as well as *it* could be played. The only thing that I couldn't do was hit with power. That didn't matter. I could do all the other things. God gave me a natural physical ability to do those things, but more than that, he gave me a drive and a desire to want to persevere and work hard and be good.

I was obsessed with being a major league player. I was always trying to improve. I carried a rulebook with me. I read it at least twice a year, once in spring training, and once around the middle of the season, going through the rules, trying to find loopholes that would let me create a play or take advantage of the opposing team.

I gave whatever it took to win. If it took leaving my wife and children in Spokane in January and driving to Los Angeles to practice, I did it. If it meant arriving at the field two hours before anybody else, I did it. For a night game I left the house around 1:30 p.m. and I didn't get back until after midnight—whatever it took.

When I came to the ballpark, my mind was clear. Nothing could disturb me. If there was anything that distracted me from my playing, I would eliminate it from my life, even if it meant my family. I really believed that.

Off the field, I felt inadequate. Most of this deep-rooted pain of loneliness and feeling inadequate came after I stole 104 bases in 1962.

The 2½ years before that was all a dream. I was enjoying success you wouldn't believe. I was making $23,000 in 1961. I was on the All-Star team in 1960 and '61. I hit .295 and was in the top ten hitters in 1960, my first full year. I had a higher average than Hank Aaron that year. That same year, I stole 50 bases and broke Jackie Robinson's 1949 team record of 37. When I got my 50th stolen base, they pulled second base up out of the ground at the Coliseum and gave it to me. Stealing that many bases was almost unheard of.

The next year, 1961, I enjoyed another good season, the Dodgers' last in the Coliseum. I stole 35 bases to lead the league for the second year in a row and scored 105 runs.

Then came 1962 and I steal 104 bases and break Ty Cobb's record. I'm no longer Little Maury Wills, the Darling of the Dodgers. I'm not just a baseball player. I'm a personality.

All of a sudden I had a noose around my neck. People wanted to know what I'm doing off the field. I started getting burned from not knowing how to take care of myself. I got burned on talk shows, on sports shows, on the radio:

*FLASH! Maury Wills, Dodger shortstop, did so-and-so!*

It was nothing like Jim Brown beating a girl up and throwing her off his balcony. It was nothing like Bo Belinsky throwing a girl out of his car at five in the morning. They were just juicy little things about me. Or maybe I was quoted out of context or maybe an article was written with quotes from me insinuating that I had bad-rapped somebody on the ballclub or had second-guessed Walter Alston, or maybe I said something about Frank Robinson or Pete Reiser, who was a Dodger coach.

Joe Reichler, who later worked in the commissioner's office and is the editor of *The Baseball Encyclopedia*, was a sportswriter back then. I didn't feel comfortable with him. But Joe could talk anybody into an interview. He would come on with incredible sob stories. "You can trust me," he'd whine. "I'll let you read it first. If you want to scratch anything, you can."

So I'd say, "That's okay, Joe. I know I can trust you." And the next thing you know, here's this outrageous headline in the paper.

"Joe!" I'd yell the next day. "Look at this headline!"

And Joe would say, "I can't control what the editor does. He writes the headlines."

I know that's true, but that's the universal excuse. Meanwhile, I'm burned again.

One year I got in trouble that way. We were fighting for the pennant. Sid Ziff, a writer from one of the Los Angeles papers, came up to me on the sidelines before the game.

"Maury, look at this article here from New York," Sid said. "Jackie Robinson says he doesn't think the Dodgers will win because the Dodgers don't have a leader. You're supposed to be the team leader, Maury. What do you think about that?"

He kept nitpicking at it until I got exasperated and said, "What does Jackie Robinson know? He's more than 3,000 miles away."

The next day it's all over the papers: "Maury Wills says, 'What does Jackie Robinson know?' " "Maury Wills says, 'Jackie Robinson should mind his own business.' "

Robinson saw the stories and wrote me a letter. In it he said, "Maury, someday you'll grow up."

I felt so bad. This man was my idol. This man gave me hope and desire as a kid and a vision of someday playing in the big leagues.

Jackie Robinson died before I got a chance to tell him I was sorry that I popped off. I wanted to say, "Yes, I did say that, but it was just my arrogance. I really hope you forgive me. I'll make it up to you."

I feel I have to write Jackie Robinson a letter, even though he's dead, and just not mail it. Seal it up and just keep it. That's supposed to be one way to dump something you're carrying with you.

That's being burned. I became gun-shy, and I began to grow up. You know how sometimes they say that an athlete who has had some success gets a swelled head and doesn't want to talk? I was on the way to that.

But it's not that the guy gets a big head. It's that the more success he gets, the more attention he gets. The more attention he gets, the more the writers want to go into depth about him. They start prying, prodding and getting into his personal life.

The writers don't want to repeat each other, so they all try to take a different angle. They don't want to write the same thing everybody else wrote about a Reggie Jackson, Roger Maris or Wade Boggs. They want a different slant. Some will even be deceptive. They'll tell you they want a story about one thing and they'll get the quotes they want. But the story comes out a whole different way. They put your accurate quotes in there, but they change the context. It's taking liberties. It's journalism.

You get burned. Then you start getting a little callous. The good guys—writers with honest intentions to write a meaningful article—get trapped in the paranoia of the athlete.

You end up with maybe three or four beat writers you have confidence in and trust, and you give them the stories. Then some guy who doesn't cover the ballclub every day gets pissed off and goes after you. You can't win.

Some of the good guys were the late Milt Richman of UPI, Maury Allen, who used to work for the New York *Post,* Stan Hochman from Philadelphia. Bob Broe from St. Louis was a nice guy, too. But he never wrote anything controversial anyhow. He wrote Ferdinand the Bull stories. He wrote about the flowers.

I started protecting myself not by being a wise guy and not giving autographs and not going on shows like Steve Carlton, but by just minding my own business and being alone and smiling all the time: Sign the autographs, be the good guy. And go straight home.

I was voted Most Valuable Player in the National League in

1962. I beat out Arnold Palmer and won the Hickok Belt given to the year's outstanding athlete.

And I didn't feel good enough. I was still this little hick guy. I felt self-conscious.

In spring training of 1963, the Topps bubblegum people wanted to take a picture of the American League and National League MVPs. Mickey Mantle was the American League MVP in 1962. I refused to pose with him, because I thought, "Me? Take a picture with Mickey Mantle?"

If you see the MVP bubblegum card from that year, you'll see Mickey Mantle and Maury Wills on the same card, but they're separate pictures put together.

It wasn't that I didn't want to pose with him. I was afraid. I was still that little boy who got lucky and stole a lot of bases and played good baseball.

The guys probably thought I was stuck up and thought my shit didn't stink. They probably thought I had my nose in the air and was self-centered and cocky. The truth was, I didn't think I fit in with people like Mickey Mantle.

I'll never forget the time I was walking through the lounge of the Desert Inn in Las Vegas and there was Koufax, Drysdale and Duke Snider, my good friends and teammates, sitting at a table with Mickey Mantle. They all stood up and introduced me to him. They pulled out a chair for me.

"Hi, Mickey," I said. And I kept on walking. I would have loved to sit down with them and Mickey Mantle, but Mickey Mantle scared me.

I felt safe only on the field, in the dugout. As soon as I stepped out of the dugout to do anything other than play baseball, I felt uneasy. If the situation was strange to me I didn't like it. I didn't go into it. I didn't like being anywhere I didn't feel comfortable. And where did I feel comfortable?

On the baseball diamond. The game was my mistress. After the game, I just figured I'd rather be alone, so I went home with my guitar.

I used to go home and cry myself to sleep after having 80-some thousand people in the Coliseum or 56,000 in Dodger Stadium rooting for me. If it was an afternoon game, 2,000–3,000 would be waiting outside to get my autograph. I'd sign them all and go home by myself.

I'd play my guitar to a fifth of booze and fall asleep. A fifth of scotch was my friend. I drank good stuff—Cutty Sark. I didn't drink in the morning or anything like that. I wasn't an alcoholic. I was drinking, that's all. Drinking alone. I didn't go to the bars in the hotels where the rest of the players hung out. I went places where the other players didn't go and where the fans wouldn't see me. You see, I had this attitude about being the all-American boy. I used to burn holes in my pockets hiding my cigarettes when kids ran up to me to get an autograph. It was living a lie.

I've got reel-to-reel tapes from the time I stayed in my little apartment in Los Angeles after I left my wife and family for good in Spokane, Wash. I'm crying into the microphone, actually singing songs like "Someone to Watch Over Me."

I played Gershwin numbers. I had all these song books while I was learning to play the guitar: "Because of you, there's a song in my heart."

I used to call people at four in the morning: "I'm sorry to wake you up. Would you talk to me? I need somebody to talk to."

I was so alone. Sometimes I'd call Doris Day just to talk to her at three or four in the morning. She'd try to tell me how to fall asleep. Maybe I'd ask her to come over and sometimes she would. Then we'd make love. That was the loneliness.

## Chaptcr 4: In thc books

I knew in the 156th game of the 1962 season that I was going to break Ty Cobb's record. I knew it just as I knew when I was a kid that someday I was going to play for the Dodgers.

When I was 15, I was cutting people's lawns for spending money. They'd say, "You did a nice job."

And I'd reply, "Thank you very much. I'm going to play for the Dodgers." I'd tell them this out of the clear blue sky, and they'd say in that tone that people use when they're talking to boys with big dreams, "That's nice."

"No," I'd say, all serious. "I'm going to play for the Dodgers."

I had no way of knowing that two years later, when I was 17, I was going to sign a contract with the Dodger organization. I just knew that I had this feeling.

That's the same feeling I had in the 156th game of the 1962 season: "I'm going to break Ty Cobb's record."

It sounds strange, but I didn't become involved or interested in breaking the record until the night before I broke it. I was just interested in trying to win the pennant because it was a tight race between us and the Giants. I didn't have to put any special emphasis on stealing bases. I had to do it to win games. With our lineup, that was the only way we could score runs. So the stolen bases came automatically.

Late in the summer, when I passed 70 stolen bases, everybody started noticing. It seemed that every day the writers pulled a new record out of the book for me to break. One of the big ones was Bob Bescher's National League record of 80 stolen bases. He had set that in 1911 with Cincinnati.

I broke that with about a month to go in the season. Around the same time, I got a hemorrhage in my leg from the pounding of all that sliding. From my hip to my ankle was a purple mess. It hurt to run, but we were in a pennant race and I had to keep going.

It got so bad that I told Pete Reiser, a Dodger coach I was close to, that I didn't know if I could go on. "Get a good jump and steal it standing up," he told me.

I did that once. I stole one standing up, and I thought the guys on the other team would kill me. They thought I was showing them up. So I had to alternate sliding head first with sliding feet first—my normal style—to give my legs a rest.

By the time I got around 90 steals, a swarm of writers from all over the country was following me. You would have thought it was the World Series or a heavyweight championship fight. They were the ones who told me the night after our 155th game of the season in St. Louis that I had to break the record in the next game. I needed two steals.

I had to break it in 156 games or Ford Frick, who was the commissioner of baseball, wasn't going to recognize it. A year earlier, he had put an asterisk next to Roger Maris' name when he broke Babe Ruth's home run record, because Maris did it in eight more games than it took Ruth. In 1915, the year Cobb stole 96, he played two tie games that were replayed later. But the stats from the tie games counted. So he played 156 games that year. And that's how many games I had to break his record.

Today, stealing 50 bases might not get you in the top five, but when I stole that many in 1960, it had been done only five times in 37 years. Ironically, Luis Aparicio had stolen 56 in 1959, the year the White Sox won the American League pennant, and that was considered phenomenal. Before Aparicio, Snuffy Stirnweiss of the Yankees had been the last to do it when he stole 55 bases in 1944 when major league rosters had been depleted by World War II.

The last man to steal 60 bases was George Case of the Senators, who swiped 61 in 1943, another war year. Ben Chapman had 61 steals for the Yankees in 1931, and other than him and Case, no one else had stolen 60 since 1920.

Cobb stole his record 96 in 1915, and from 1900 to 1962, that was the only time anyone had stolen as many as 90 bases in a season. Heck, from 1916 until I came along, no one had stolen even 70.

So Cobb's record was considered safe. By 1962, it was 47 years old. Joe DiMaggio's 56-game hitting streak and Ted Williams' .406 batting average didn't celebrate their 47th anniversaries until 1988.

When I stole 50 in 1960, people thought it was a fluke. Now it's 1962 and the Dodgers are playing for the first time in Dodger Stadium, the first of the big, modern ballparks. And I'm stealing bases like crazy.

We had no one to hit home runs except Frank Howard, who hit 31 that year; Tommy Davis, who hit 27, and Willie Davis, who had 21. Tommy, who led the league with a .346 average, was our only .300 hitter. But we're winning games 1–0 because I'm getting on by an error or a walk or a fielder's choice and I'm stealing the bases and scoring the runs.

And now, after 155 games, I had 95 steals, and I had to get the record the next day or it wouldn't be recognized.

Curt Simmons was supposed to pitch for the Cardinals. I figured it would be no problem. I could get out of bed in the middle of December and steal two off Simmons. He didn't like to throw to first, so he wouldn't do it unless he backed off the rubber first. If he didn't back off the rubber, he just lobbed the ball over.

But Simmons got hurt warming up before the game, and of all the pitchers the Cardinals had to take his place, they picked Larry Jackson, who was the toughest pitcher to steal off. I never admitted that during my playing career because I didn't want him to know that. Why should I make him tougher? Instead, when people asked me who was toughest to steal off, I'd say Warren Spahn. That was safe because everybody knew Spahn was tough. But, for me, Larry Jackson was the toughest.

But even though Larry Jackson was pitching and not Curt Simmons, I knew I was going to break the record.

The first one was no problem. I got that early in the game the first time I got on base. The game was still close and Jackson couldn't afford to give me all his attention at first base. His primary job was to get the batter out. I stole second, and then I had third stolen. That would have broken the record right there, but Jim Gilliam, who was batting behind me, hit the ball and wiped out the steal. That was all right. It was a good pitch and he was doing his job—trying to drive me in.

By the ninth inning, though, the Cardinals were winning something like 11–0 and I hadn't had another chance to steal. Jackson was cruising and I was the fifth batter up and it looked as if I had no chance.

I had a good feeling, though, that somehow I was going to get one last shot at it. And sure enough, the ball started squibbling around the infield, bouncing over the infielders' heads or dropping in front of them, and before you knew it, I was at bat.

The thing that still rings in my ear and always will was that just before I went to the on-deck circle to get ready to hit, Walter Alston said to me, "Go break that record, kid."

Besides being tough to steal against, Jackson was hard for me to hit because he gave me sliders in on my fists. He was a right-hander, which meant I was hitting from the left side of the plate. I hadn't become a switch-hitter until late in my minor league career, and hitting from the left side was my unnatural side. I was in only my third full year in the big leagues, and I was still learning to hit lefty.

The infield was around to the left-field side because I always had an inside-out swing and hit the ball to the opposite field.

Julian Javier, the second baseman, was crowding the bag at second, figuring I'd hit the ball that way, and Bill White, the Cardinals' first baseman who would become National League president, was playing in for the bunt.

Jackson gave me these sliders in on my fists. Right away, he had two strikes on me and no balls, and his own fans were booing him. Somehow, I managed to foul off four or five pitches. He threw a couple of pitches close that I didn't swing at and the umpire hesitated before calling, "Ball." That really got the fans going.

Finally, I got around on one of those sliders in on my fists and, would you believe I pulled a little, squeaking ground ball between second and first for a hit?

Now I'm on first base, and Jackson wasn't even worried about Jim Gilliam, the next hitter. Carl Sawatski, who was catching, wasn't worried either. He wasn't even behind home plate. He was set up over in the other batter's box. I didn't care. I knew I was going to steal it.

Sawatski would make a great designated hitter today. He could catch, but he couldn't throw. Throwing wasn't that important for a catcher before I came up. But when I started stealing all those bases, it changed the job description of a catcher. When I brought the stolen base back, they started going for defensive catchers because teams were getting run out of the ballpark.

With a big lead, Jackson didn't have to worry about the game or the hitter anymore. He forgot about Gilliam at the plate. There was only one thing left in the game and that was the record, so he gave 100 percent of his attention to me at first base. He threw over at least 16 times to Bill White to keep me close, with his own fans booing him the whole time.

Sportsman's Park held only about 31,000 people, but there must have been 35,000 squeezed in there. I think every black person in Missouri was at that game. They were screaming, "Go, Maury! Steal that base! Go! Go! Go!"

Bill White was a very nice guy. He always talked to you on first base. All first basemen talk. They try to distract you. Orlando Cepeda did the same thing. I'd talk back, but while I was talking, I kept my eye on what's going on in the infield. Most of all, I made sure he didn't have the ball in his hand on the hidden ball trick.

As I said, White was a nice guy, but I was trying to break Cobb's record in Sportsman's Park—his park—against his team. So every time Jackson threw over, White came down on my head with the ball in that big mitt. Being left-handed, the mitt was right there by the bag and he was pounding it on my head—WHAM! WHAM!—trying to discourage me from stealing the base. Even though it's Ty Cobb's record and he doesn't know Ty Cobb—neither did Larry Jackson, for that matter—no player wants to go down in the books as the guy who let somebody break a record like Al Downing, who gave up Henry Aaron's record 715th home run or Tracy Stallard, who gave up Roger Maris' 61st.

So even though I think that Bill White would have liked to see me steal the base, he's pounding me on the head with his mitt. He wasn't going to give it to me. Neither was Larry Jackson.

It seemed impossible. That's when, all of a sudden, it was like I heard a voice whispering in my ear: "Delayed steal. Delayed steal."

Al Campanis, the former Dodger vice president in charge of player personnel, taught me how to steal bases. He was scouting director back then, and I used to go up to his office in Dodger Stadium before the games and talk running with him. A couple of weeks earlier he had shown me the delayed steal in his office. I knew about the delayed steal, but I never used it. I didn't need to. I was so strong with the straight steal, I could just overpower them.

I told Al, "It's a trick steal and there's a greater degree of risk involved than with a straight steal. If you have alert infielders and a catcher who's on the ball, it won't work. I don't need it."

"Someday you might," Campanis replied.

Someday had arrived.

The delayed steal normally comes into play when you have a guy who's not an outstanding base stealer or when you have a pitcher who's really tough—a guy you can't get a good lead off—and a catcher who has a gun of an arm. That's when all the odds are against you and you have to steal it on the infielders instead of on the pitcher and catcher.

On the delayed steal, you don't take off when the pitcher makes his move home. Instead, after the pitcher decides to go home, and just as he releases the ball, you make a few shuffle

# Chapter 5: Changes

If I had not stolen 104 bases in 1962, I do not believe there would have been a Lou Brock or a Rickey Henderson or a Vince Coleman as we know them today because no one would have believed that a ballplayer could do it. They wouldn't have gotten the opportunity. They would be playing baseball in a different way.

I revolutionized the game. Being with the Dodgers and Walter Alston had a lot to do with it. The Dodgers always had a great appreciation for speed, especially when they moved into that big ballpark in 1962. The playing field in Dodger Stadium is big today, but in 1962 it was even bigger, because home plate was closer to the backstop and farther from the fences. It was the first big, modern park.

The make up of the team had a lot to do with it, too. The '62 Dodgers didn't have a lot of home run hitters. And I had Jim Gilliam, who would take a lot of pitches, hitting behind me. Look at Rickey Henderson. He stole more bases with the Yankees hitting ahead of Willie Randolph, who took a lot of pitches, than he did hitting ahead of Steve Sax, who didn't.

So I don't know if there would have been another manager with the disposition of Walter Alston managing a team with the same combination of talent the Dodgers had—*great* pitching, adequate defense, not much power, and *great* speed. Alston was open-minded—you can say he had courage—and was established enough to take a chance and let the guys run. I can't say all those circumstances would have come together someplace else. I don't know but I doubt it.

In 1959, Detroit picked me up from the Dodgers for a look-see in spring training. They decided not to purchase my contract and sent me back to the Dodgers. But say I had gone to Detroit under manager Bill Norman. They had hitters like Eddie Yost, Al steps and then cross over to go for second. By the time you start running, everybody is focused on the flight of the ball. When the catcher gets the ball, he looks up and you're halfway there. He cocks to throw the ball, but nobody's covering the bag, and the catcher does not like to throw to an uncovered bag. Meanwhile, the second baseman and the shortstop are running over there full speed and at an angle, trying to catch the ball and tag me at the same time. The delayed steal is a great steal.

So I stopped taking that maximum lead and shortened up a little bit. Larry Jackson saw me do that and figured, "Ahah! I got him now." He gave up on me and decided to go home with the ball.

Just as he released the ball, I shuffled a couple of steps, crossed over, and took off. Javier, the second baseman, and Dal Maxvill, the shortstop, were spread out.

I was so anxious to make it I dove head first—Rickey Henderson style—and came up about five feet short of the base. I crawled the rest of the way and when I got there I just hugged second base as if it were a pillow with my head on it. And the ball? Sawatski was so anxious to get me, he double-clutched waiting for an infielder to get to the bag and finally just threw the thing without anybody there. The ball took about four hops and rolled into center field.

With all the hoopla, the media following me, the ballclubs advertising my appearances, and the fans looking for it, it had really worn on me. As I hugged the bag, it was like, "Thank God it's over." They stopped the game, pulled the bag out of the ground, and gave it to me. I had broken one of the greatest records in baseball.

The bag's in Cooperstown. I gave the shoes to my best friend, Mel Exber, who owns the Las Vegas Club Hotel and Casino.

Kaline, Charlie Maxwell and Harvey Kuenn. I don't know whether they would have played a running game if Maury Wills had made that club.

With Detroit, I probably would have been an eighth-place hitter. They probably would have played a normal game of letting me get on base and have the pitcher bunt me over, or have me bunt the No. 7 guy over and bring in a pinch hitter for the pitcher to try to get him in.

Even with the Dodgers, I didn't start to pile up the stolen bases until Walter Alston came to me in July of 1960, my first full year in the big leagues. We were playing an exhibition game against our Triple-A farm team in Spokane, where I made my home. That was the first time I led off for the Dodgers.

Walter Alston told me that day, "Maury, I'm putting you in the lead off spot starting today. You're on your own. You can go when you feel like it. You've got the green light."

I said to myself, "Wow! In front of the hometown fans!" I got two or three hits that day and just stole bases like crazy. I was on my own for the rest of my career.

I don't know if other players before me were on their own. I don't know if Jackie Robinson had that freedom.

Others before me stole bases only when they had to. I was the first to make full use of the stolen base. Walter Alston never told me anything. He just said, "If you get on, I want you to get over as soon as you can." It was understood that as soon as I got on I was going.

There are different types of courage. Some people have the courage to go out and be in a physical battle and yet they can be horribly afraid of a dentist.

I had the courage and the maturity to go out there and try to do things that weren't in the book to win a ballgame. I thought it out well. It was logically sound. I calculated the odds and said, "Why not?"

I was good enough to take that extra half-step. I was good enough to change the way the game was played. I had the imagination and pride and confidence that there was no reason to give up, that no matter what the situation, I could win.

There's another kind of courage. That's being willing to take the chance of being embarrassed. Failing didn't discourage me. I figured the next time it would work.

Control is confidence and knowledge. It's going into the bottom of the ninth inning at home down a run. I'm leading off, and before I go up Walter Alston asks me, "Can you steal on this guy if you get on?"

I've got to say yes or no. If I show any hesitation, Jim Gilliam, who's batting second, has to bunt me over and then we have only two chances to get me in. If I can steal it, we have three chances to get me in from second. Maybe Gilliam can sacrifice me to third. Maybe he can hit a ground ball to the right side and get me to third. If he can, now we have two chances to get me home.

Those situations take courage. That's more than self-confidence, because I know I'm dealing with the human element. Even though I know I can take the pitcher, there's a chance I might slip taking off. There's a chance perspiration could flow down into my eyes, or something could happen in the ballpark to distract me. Or the first baseman could be talking to me like Ernie Banks of the Cubs used to, trying to distract me to keep me from getting my best jump. Or maybe the pitcher throws a perfect pitch—a fastball on the outside corner—and the catcher makes a perfect throw.

So if I say, "Yes, I can make it," I'm taking into consideration that the catcher is going to make a perfect throw and the pitcher is going to do a good enough job holding me close. Those are things I can't control.

What I can control is getting my best lead, not slipping, having good enough concentration to block out Ernie Banks trying to distract me. I know I can block out the bench. So many times the opposing dugout is on the first base side of the diamond. Guys on the bench are yelling, "PICK HIM OFF! PICK HIM OFF!" I know I can keep from being distracted by that. I can control any kind of noise in the ballpark that might be distracting.

So I can control everything except the catcher making a perfect throw or the pitcher pitching out. And the more bases I stole, the tougher things got. So I eliminated one thing I couldn't control—the pitchout sign.

I started getting my lead off first base early while the pitcher was getting the sign from the catcher. I've got terrific peripheral vision, so my head could be facing the pitcher while my eyes were looking at the catcher and stealing the pitchout sign.

You see, in order to be able to dominate those guys, I had to continue to improve and maintain this feeling of superiority. That just made them feel powerless out there. If I had stayed at the level of 1962, I would not have been good enough to continue to dominate the National League. I would not have been good enough to steal 94 bases in 1965. I would have stolen 150 bases that year, but I got a hemorrhage in my leg and had to stop. The point is I was a better base stealer in 1965 than I was in 1962 because I had to continue to improve. By then, I was taking my lead early and stealing the pitchout sign from the catcher.

That's another way I changed the game. I made catchers go from using the fist for the pitchout in the early Sixties to using three of the same thing for the pitchout—like two, two, two, or three, three, three. I didn't have to see his hand. I watched his wrist. If he was holding a fist down, the tendons in his wrist didn't move, so I knew it was a pitchout.

My mistake was I talked too much. The writers and reporters wouldn't settle for anything less than the truth about what I was doing. They wouldn't let me skate over it with some jive answer, and the people I played against read the papers and magazines, too. They improved their technique. They changed the signs.

The more I stole, the better they would defense against it. They're not robots. They're not going to let me continue to run crazy all the time. The better I got, the better they got, the better I had to get.

It was the same with bunts. Every time I improved my bunts, they would defense it and I had to devise another bunt.

That is the fun of being a successful player. It's seeing everybody else improve with you. Before you know it, the whole game is better.

I helped accelerate that process. Nobody considered stealing 50 bases as a regular thing before Maury Wills. It was assumed that stealing bases was from the dead-ball era and it wouldn't happen again. Before I came along, Ty Cobb's record was considered unbreakable.

It wasn't just base stealing. We're also talking about base running. The two go hand in hand. Not everybody has the speed to be a base stealer, but when players are stealing bases it rubs off. All of a sudden, the slow man finds himself turning a long single into a double. And he's sliding head first because he saw Rickey Henderson or Pete Rose sliding that way.

It's contagious. It makes the game better.

## Chapter 6: The projects

I was born Oct. 2, 1932, in the Anacostia section of Washington, D.C., the seventh child of the Rev. Guy O. and Mabel Wills. Six more would follow—13 of us in all, eight girls and five boys. We were close in age, but I can't say what the range was from oldest to youngest. I don't even know my family background. My mother couldn't go any further back in the family than her mother.

My family called me Sonny, and I was always the favorite. I had a baby face, a big smile and wavy hair. My sisters' girlfriends all loved me, too. I'll never forget, I was five or six years old when one of them put me on top of her. She was naked. I don't know how old she was, but she had pubic hair. It really bothered me.

The first place I remember living was in the Garfield section of Washington. That's up close to the Maryland state line, near Laurel. We moved there from Anacostia. I went to kindergarten in Garfield, and I guess we stayed there until I was about 10 or 11.

We lived in the second story of a big barn-like wooden building. There were no stores nearby. It was just a little string of houses along the road. Across from us was nothing but apple orchards.

Downstairs was a dancehall and one other family living off in a corner of it. The dancehall was empty, though. Nothing was there but rats. And roaches. I was raised with roaches. You hated to turn the light on in the kitchen area because there were armies of roaches there. The house was nothing but a shack, but it was huge, maybe 30 feet by 40 or 50 feet. There weren't any rooms.

My father put up cardboard partitions and ropes with sheets hung over them to divide it into rooms.

Electricity was a bare light bulb in a socket with a string hanging down. The other thing hanging from the ceiling was flypaper.

We cooked on a wood-burning stove. That was the heat, too. You went out and found wood to burn anywhere you could. We had to go to a pump down the street for water and we had outhouses. We bathed once a week, on Saturdays. We had to heat the water on the wood stove, and several people used the same water. I was the third in the bath. And if somebody stayed in too long, the water got cold. All this slime and grime was floating in it, and I had to get into it. I didn't want to bathe in that, but I was forced to.

My folks were gone all the time. They both worked. My dad was a full-time minister, but he didn't get enough from his little church to feed us. He also worked for the government in the Navy yard. He was a machinist. He was always selling things, too. He had a Watkins route. Watkins had everything—hair stuff, spices, and everything else. I don't know how well he did.

We took care of ourselves, and I guess we could easily have gone bad. Everybody—all 13 of us—made it through, though. I'm the only one who made it big, and yet I'm the only one who turned out to be an addict. My brother Duke got drunk a lot, but that was accepted. In fact, he was popular because of it.

I learned to wash and iron my own clothes and cook my own food at six or seven years old. With all those kids and those flimsy partitions, we had no privacy at all, and, yet, I can never remember seeing my parents' bodies. I never saw my sisters or my brothers naked. It's black culture not to show the body. I had no idea what a naked woman looked like. In fact, I got married and had six children and never saw my wife naked.

My father had a radio, and I used to listen to The Shadow. That was during World War II when we had blackout rehearsals for air raids. The door would be squeaking—"Who knows? Ha Ha Ha Ha. The Shadow knows"—and all of a sudden the lights would go out. They didn't give you any warning. They just turned the lights out on us when they were ready to.

From there, we moved to the Parkside project, in northeast Washington on Kenilworth Avenue. The project had to be at least six city blocks long with a big field and the Anacostia River on one side and a big, polluting power plant, which is still there, on the other side, right across from RFK Stadium. If you're at the stadium, you can see some big smokestacks. That's where the projects were.

Each building in the project had two stories and two apartments. On each end was the only door that each unit had. There was a little yard around each building. You came out of the door and there was a big coal bin on the left side. We had a coal stove for heating—I remember my father stoking it all the time—a gas stove for cooking, and an indoor bathroom.

Moving into the projects was like moving from Watts to Beverly Hills. We had rooms. We had running water inside. It was two stories. That sounded nice.

All 13 of us were together in that house. There were four bedrooms, a living room, and a kitchen. Mom and Dad had one room. I don't know how we were all piled up with one another, but I know I slept in a single bed with at least four others.

I had a problem with wetting the bed. I just peed all over everybody all the time so nobody wanted to sleep with me. If they wanted to get on me about something they called me "Pee-Boy." That was humiliating. Nobody in the family had any problem with me playing tricks on them because I knew that they would call me "Pee-Boy" in front of my friends. I'll never forget the time my favorite aunt took me home to spend the night at her house. I slept on her brand-new couch in the living room and I peed all over it. I lay there in the morning as if I were tired or hurt. I didn't want to get up. I was waiting for it to dry right around me.

I remember my father used to try to break me of it. He used to wake me up, take me to the bathroom, run the water, make "sssssss" noises. But it wouldn't come. I couldn't pee. So I'd get in bed and—whoosh!—I went all over everybody.

Maybe it was a subconscious way to get some space for myself. I must have been 33 years old before I stopped. It was every night, and every time I did it I was dreaming that it was all right. And then I'd wake up and it wasn't my imagination.

I was the National League MVP and I was still peeing in the bed. In spring training, when we slept in dormitories in bunk beds, I'd always sleep on the bottom. In the morning, I'd turn the mattress over. One time, I did sleep on top and it dripped. Oh, Jeezus!

Sometimes, I would wake up in the middle of the night and I would feel a cold spot under me. I'd open my eyes and pray to God that I hadn't peed all over myself. I'd look down and there it was. I never wanted to stay over at someone's house.

I stopped in 1965. I stole 94 bases that year. We won the World Series and I got 11 hits. Some kids from the University of California-Santa Barbara came down to Los Angeles for the games and I signed some autographs for them and became their favorite player.

When they found out I drove through Santa Barbara on my way home to Spokane every fall, they asked me if I'd drop by the campus and see them at their fraternity. I told them I would.

The whole campus was excited when I arrived and these kids were excited that I was going to stay with them. They had chipped in and bought a brand-new couch for me to sleep on.

I peed all over that brand-new couch. They had some big things planned for me the next day, but I couldn't get up. They were all around me talking, and I was under the covers. They were saying, "C'mon, Maury. Get up."

"I want to rest a little longer," I said.

Finally, I had to admit that I had peed on their new couch. It was one of the toughest things I ever had to do.

They were so nice about it. "Don't worry about it, Maury," they said. I insisted that I would clean it myself even though they said not to worry about it. They went out and got some cleaning fluid and we all cleaned the couch together. That broke me out of it. I haven't had the problem since.

Just last year, I saw a doctor for something else and ended up telling him about that. He said I'd be surprised how many people have that problem. He said I should tell the story of how I stopped because it might give hope to others.

There wasn't enough room for everybody to sit at the same table, so we never all ate at the same time except on Thanksgiving and Christmas. The dirty dishes stayed in the dishwater until we ate the next meal. That's when we cleaned the dishes—before dinner. The sink was always loaded with dishes.

It was survival of the fittest. With 13 kids, whoever got there first ate. I was always off playing ball, and I knew that when I came home and they had had dinner four hours earlier, there wasn't going to be anything left. But I'd rather play ball than rush home to eat. I could always find some scraps. I lived on scraps.

The only times I could sit down and have a real good meal from beginning to end was on Thanksgiving and Christmas. I mean, sit down, be ready, and be served a big, full plate. Otherwise, it was something I cooked myself—usually potatoes.

I had fried potatoes, baked potatoes, boiled potatoes. And beans—boiled beans, fried beans, beans for dinner, beans for breakfast, beans for lunch. And I always said, "Dad, do I have to eat beans again?"

And he'd say, "You better eat those beans, boy."

My father would buy food by the bushel basket. He'd buy a basket of cabbage, basket of potatoes, basket of corn, and navy beans and lima beans in a big bag. And always a big container of lard. Damn, but we black people used lard.

When company was around, we could never open the door to the closet because if you opened it, everything tumbled out. I'll never forget the horrible fear that with somebody visiting a roach might run across the furniture or across the person. That's not to mention the rats. We had rats a foot long. My father used to set traps that they would actually carry off. You could put saddles on those rats. You could hear them at night going through the trash cans. It wasn't a big deal, though. It was all part of life. Everybody lived that way. That was the world. Rats weren't something that horrible. They were disgusting, but rats were rats. They lived there, too.

I didn't have my own shoes until I was 11 or 12 years old. I only had shoes at all because I needed them for school. They were hand-me-downs, and I put cardboard in the bottom to cover the holes. It was a big deal if we went to Thom McAn's and got a pair of shoes for Easter.

I didn't see my folks too much. When I was six, I used to go to evening church services seven days a week with my dad. The only reason I went was that I wanted to ride in the car with him. As soon as I got to the church, I got up in this big chair by the pulpit and went to sleep. My father's car was an old Nash with wooden spoke wheels. I'll always remember that car. The whole family didn't go. Only I went, and sometimes one of brothers. On the way back, my dad would stop and get us hamburgers at the White Tower. That's why I went—to get those hamburgers.

My dad's Baptist church was a little storefront, not much bigger than an efficiency apartment. The congregation was small. But my father never went out without his Bible in his hand. He took the Bible all the time. That was the source of strength to get through life in the black community. You've got to have that religion. I have my dad's Bible now. But I can't say I've read it much. What I've learned about religion is through conversation and feelings I got from preachers' sermons.

My father was loud when he preached. He'd be screaming and yelling and people would start crying and shouting. He had a brother, Raymond, who could yell even louder. Uncle Raymond would scare the daylights out of us.

When I got to the age where I started playing ball in the playground on Sundays, I couldn't go to church anymore because the games would start at 10 o'clock and the services didn't start until 11. My father was so nice about it. He used to hold services in the living room at home so my brothers and I could go to the baseball diamond and he'd go to his church. We didn't want to disappoint him by not attending services and he didn't want to disappoint us by taking baseball away from us.

He started having Uncle Raymond come over to our house to hold the services, and he'd preach the fear of God into us. He'd start yelling and we'd start crying. When Uncle Raymond started coming, we didn't want to sit in those services. So we'd sneak out of the house and run to the field rather than sit in those sessions with Uncle Raymond.

If I hadn't had baseball, I might have been a preacher. A preacher doesn't make a living, though. I have more in my pocket on a bad day than my father collected in a month. But of all the boys I was the one they said would be a preacher. I'd laugh and say no. But here I am now, preaching the gospel of being clean and sober.

It seems all my life I was crossing railroad tracks to get somewhere. As a kid, I had to cross the tracks to go to the store. I lived two doors from the tracks by Howard Road. I imagine they're still there.

The freight trains that used those tracks were so long that when we wanted to get across the tracks, we would jump on the train and then work our way between the boxcars to the other side. Then we'd jump. We might end up a half block down the tracks, but at least we got to the other side, because the train was a mile long and moving slowly. It seems they were always freight trains. I remember the Chesapeake logo on the cars because we used to throw stones at the boxcars. I guess kids still do that. We used to hear the noise on the tracks when a train was coming and we'd get a load of rocks and stand there on the bank and wait for it. We just threw at boxcars. Once in a while, the doors on a boxcar would be open on both sides. If you could throw a rock all the way through, that was a big deal. We didn't throw rocks at the caboose. We didn't try to hit anybody. We weren't into that kind of stuff.

There was a big refinery by the Anacostia River. The river was polluted. You couldn't even see under the surface, it was so dirty. That was our swimming pool. We went out only about 15 feet because there were currents and a deep hole.

I saved somebody's life in that river. A kid who couldn't swim slipped into that hole and went under. I couldn't swim, either, but I went down and put myself on the bottom so I could push him up and get him out. The bottom was slimy and my toes sank into it. I can feel it now. I couldn't have been more than 10 years old. We were all so scared. I pushed the kid out and then I pushed off the bottom and came out, too. I came up gagging with a mouthful of water.

We were afraid to tell anybody what happened. We didn't want our parents to know because they might get mad at us. That's the last place you were supposed to be—down at that river swimming.

If we wanted to go to a swimming pool, we had to go from the projects past where RFK Stadium is now up to Griffith Stadium. The pool was in northwest Washington on Georgia Avenue. We had to catch a streetcar just to go swimming.

I used to like to go down to the playground at our project when the girls were playing. If they were playing dodgeball, I liked to get in their way. If they were skipping rope, I used to jump in and show the girls I could do it better than they could. I was always mischievous. I always wanted to get into someone else's game. I wouldn't start my own. I wanted to jump into somebody else's and show everybody up.

Sometimes, kids would be throwing rocks up into a tree, trying to knock an apple down in an orchard. I'd come along and say, "Watch this." I'd take a stick or rock and knock the apple down. Then I'd grab it: "It's mine!"

Somebody had been trying to get that apple for 20 minutes. They had got the branch and stem weak. Then I came and knocked it down with one blow and took it away.

When I was 14, I jumped into a girls' dodgeball game. They told me to get out but I wouldn't. So one girl picked up a piece of brick. I started running and she threw the brick way up in the air at me. It came down right on top of my head. It damaged something in my scalp, because I got a gray streak in the middle of my hair from that. I've had it ever since.

Doing things like that kept me from thinking about the problems of life, kept me from thinking about not having enough money. It didn't seem that there was anything wrong with having only a couple pennies in my pocket when I needed a nickel to get a Popsicle. I wouldn't steal. I never thought of stealing something from a store. I don't know how that got started with kids. We didn't go around stealing. I never heard of doing such a thing.

Even when my life went to hell after my baseball career and I was hanging out with thugs and thieves, I was always out of place. I was always a tenderfoot in that culture and I got taken advantage of like you wouldn't believe. I never knew how to be cold and heartless. I was a soft touch. That's why people were always around me, wanting to keep me into the drug when I was trying to clean myself up. I was such a lamb.

Was my childhood fun? Yes. But there was not enough direction, not enough preparation to become an adult. We lived a day at a time. I wasn't raised with a future.

I went to black schools all my life and, with all due respect, I was cheated. I got what education I have through traveling, baseball, meeting people and doing things. I didn't get it in school. I didn't learn squat.

Nobody ever gave me direction. Nobody ever asked me, "What do you want to be when you grow up?"

We weren't expected to go to college. The method of teaching wasn't able to get a student like me to apply himself. I can only remember five students out of about 1,300 in my whole high school who were considered students. One of them played on the football team and we admired him. The others couldn't play football. They were cadets on the drill team—pansies. They were going to college.

I went to Cordoza High School, but I wasn't much of a student.

The one class I did really well in was English grammar. That was taught by the toughest teacher in the school, and we considered her the meanest, too. All the coaches kept their athletes out of her class, but I wanted her because I liked that subject. My football coach tried to take me out of that class because he was afraid I wouldn't get by that teacher and I wouldn't be able to stay on the team. She wouldn't excuse me and she wouldn't let me transfer. She made me stay there and I learned something.

I was quarterback on the football team and knew 150 plays and the assignments for everybody. One of my buddies on the team was an outstanding halfback. He knew all the assignments on all the plays but he couldn't find an inch mark on a ruler. That was education in the projects.

I learned in my major league career that an education is something they can't take away from you. I've always preached that if a kid coming out of high school has a chance to go to college or play pro ball, he should go to college first. Get that education. You still have time to play baseball. I realized that when I started traveling around the world. I found out how much I didn't know, simple things that come from a little formal education. I began to reflect on the teachers who let me slide in school because I was a good athlete. And I grew to respect the teachers who were tough because they taught me something.

The projects were all black. The school was all black. Everything was that way.

We lived in the projects and stayed there. I grew up in Washington, D.C., but I never went downtown to see the Capitol, the White House, the Smithsonian, the Lincoln Memorial. That part of the city might as well have been on a different planet. We used to see it all in the distance, but we never had any interest. When I came to Washington, D.C., in 1962 to play in the All-Star Game, my brother, a school teacher who had a tour business on the side, took me around. He told me about Arlington National Cemetery and gave me the background on the Capitol and the monuments in the town where I grew up.

It was separation then instead of segregation. We didn't call where we lived the ghetto. It was the projects. We felt we had everything we wanted. It was nothing like the racial consciousness that flowered in the Sixties. The racial issues didn't even begin to surface until the Fifties when Rosa Parks kept her seat on that bus in Montgomery, and when they ordered the schools desegregated in Little Rock.

All my young days were full. We had our own little rivalries in school and everything was great. Virginia State played Morgan State, Howard University and Hampton Institute. We thought those were the greatest rivalries in the world. We didn't care about Southern Cal or Notre Dame.

We didn't have black role models. We didn't yet have Jackie Robinson. Washington had the Homestead Grays in the Negro League, but we were too busy playing to go down and watch them. I wasn't aware of Satchel Paige and Josh Gibson—not until 1947.

They tried to teach us about Paul Robeson in school. He was an opera singer. But he went communist. I remember that. He wasn't our hero.

I remember Joe Louis as a kid. Every time he was in a fight the whole family gathered around the radio. I was just a kid and I remember everyone going crazy listening to the fight. When Joe Louis fought, the whole black neighborhood came to a standstill. Nobody was in the streets. But I was too young to grasp it all. The older generation admired Joe Louis. Sugar Ray Robinson was the one I liked as a champion, a man of greatness. But I couldn't really relate to being a fighter.

My hero was Barry Sullivan. He was a white movie actor. I named my first son after him. But how in the world could I hope to be like Barry Sullivan? There was no chance. That's what it was like growing up as a black kid in the projects. That's what kind of future there was for me—none.

My other hero was Bump Elliott, who was a star football player at Michigan at that time. I used to sit in front of the radio every Saturday in the fall and listen to Bill Stern announce the Michigan games. My son Bump is named after Bump Elliott.

In this black neighborhood with all the separation, I listened to Bill Stern. My brothers—all of them athletes—didn't listen to Bill Stern. They didn't know about Doc Blanchard and Glenn Davis. Another of my football heroes was Kyle Rote at Southern Methodist University. I'm sitting in this project and these are my heroes.

Not until Jackie Robinson came into baseball could a kid like me have anybody to emulate. Jackie Robinson created the burning desire in me to put all my efforts into becoming a professional baseball player—he and Larry Doby of the Cleveland Indians. Then, before you know it, there's Joe Black, Roy Campanella, Don Newcombe, Monte Irvin. Shucks, with all those black players in the major leagues, I knew I was going to make it. That was my inspiration.

## Chapter 7: Boot black, nacky sack

I didn't have any money. I didn't have a dime, a nickel or a quarter to get an ice cream. The ice cream man—Good Humor it was—would come around in a truck. I'd ask my folks if I could get some, but they didn't have the money to get a Popsicle. I carried my lunch to school and didn't have a nickel for a little container of milk or a piece of fruit.

I was 13 when the Dodgers signed Jackie Robinson to a contract and assigned him to their AAA team in Montreal. All of a sudden I heard all the adults in the neighborhood talking about Jackie Robinson. I said, "Who's this Jackie Robinson?" I'd hear "Brooklyn Dodgers." "What kind of team is that? Where's Brooklyn?" All of a sudden I realized there's the Washington Senators, a major league baseball team, in my city. I started listening to Archie McDonald, the Senators' announcer. I started hearing about the Homestead Grays and Josh Gibson, Luke Easter and guys like that.

I started to grow just because of Jackie Robinson. I started applying myself. I started getting away from the project mentality and started to branch out on my own. I started to realize that something better was going on.

I started going into the white neighborhood. Would you believe it was on the other side of the railroad tracks? I'd go up and knock on somebody's door and ask if I could cut their lawn.

It was a working-class white neighborhood. The row houses were two-story brick with tiny lawns and a porch or stoop in front. An alley ran behind the houses and that's where the driveways and garages were. These were rich people to me. Black people live in those houses now.

It took nerve to knock on those doors. Some of those people had dogs—big dogs—just because somebody like me might come around at the wrong time. A lot of times a big dog would come after me and I'd scale fences to get away. That didn't stop me, though.

When the lady answered the door, I'd say politely, "Excuse me, ma'am. Can I cut your lawn? Please? I just charge a nickel." Or a dime or quarter. Whatever it was.

The people were so nice. Sometimes they didn't really need the grass cut, but to have me come over and ask—"Only a dime . . . Only a nickel"—it was like they wanted me to have the money more than they needed the grass cut. So they let me do it. And they'd bring me a glass of Kool-Aid or they'd ask me if I wanted to come in for a glass of water.

I'd say, "No, thank you. I'll wait here."

I couldn't even conceive of going in the houses at first. But it gave me confidence to knock on more doors. I even got some tools so I could snip the grass around the edges of the lawns. I liked that work.

I went down the alleys behind the houses where the white people lived. They threw their trash back there and they would throw scooters and tricycles away. I took the wheels and axles off and went home and made a wagon. I nailed some boards together and put sides on it. Then I took a two-by-four and nailed it across the bottom. I put the axle down the middle of the two-by-four and bent some nails over it to hold it on. Then I put the wheels back on the axle. They even had little hubcaps.

Then I'd go to the Safeway store where people bought their groceries. I would stand outside the store with my wagon.

"Carry your groceries, ma'am? Only a nickel."

They'd put the groceries in and I would take their groceries home. Or if they had driven to the store, I'd ask if I could take the groceries to the car.

"Only a penny." They'd give me some change, five or ten pennies. Maybe even a quarter.

Then I saw some guys—grown men—coming around the projects in a truck selling wood to burn. So I started going down to the riverbank where we used to swim. I'd find old driftwood and pull it in. I'd put the wood in my wagon, take it home, cut it up and stack it in bushel baskets. I'd do that all week long and on Saturdays, I'd take the wood through my project neighborhood and sell it.

I had a shoeshine box and my brothers and I would walk to a bus and travel a long way to get to a white neighborhood to shine shoes. We went to a little area that had about four stores in a strip. That was a shopping center back then.

I'd stand in front of the stores, pop the shoeshine rag and chant real fast: "Hey! I'll give you a New York shine and a Baltimore gloss. Step in the mud and it won't come off!" POP! POP!

Or: "Boot black, nacky sack. Make it crack or get your money back! How about it, good looking?"

And: "Shine your shoes, not your socks. Don't believe, put your foot on the box!" CRACK!

The men found that clever.

I charged a nickel or dime a shine. I'll never forget when a man paid me 50 cents and I quit for the day and saw three movies. I bought all kinds of leftover, day-old doughnuts from a store next to the movie theater. I had a ball. All that on 50 cents.

I was in the big money now, so I didn't do any more wood. I didn't cut any more lawns.

I was always the only one, alone, cutting those lawns and doing those things. None of the other little black kids went into those white areas. And when I was cutting lawns in the beginning and people asked me if I wanted to come in for a drink, I thought, *"Go inside?!"* It was the same way I felt when they asked me to take a picture with Mickey Mantle. I said I'd wait outside.

It must have been the same for Roy Campanella and later John Roseboro when they got to the big leagues. They never wanted to make a fuss. Roseboro didn't like to go down to the dining room or coffee shop to eat. He preferred to order room service.

Eventually, though, after two or three times of being invited to go in to one of those houses and have a glass of water, I got enough courage to go in.

I remember it being cool inside. I remember hardwood floors. We had linoleum but they had hardwood floors, nicely shining—something like the table I ate on at home, if the table were clean. Wall-to-wall carpeting wasn't in then. But there'd be a Persian-type rug on the floor with all these designs in it. And everything in the house was . . . just clean. Everything was in place. You could open a closet without running into a booby trap where everything would fall out. In the kitchen, the sinks were clean. I didn't see roaches running all over the place. It was something just looking around.

It has been written that if Maury Wills hadn't played baseball, he would have been something else great in life, but I don't know. I think the culture might have prevented me.

I was the chosen one. None of my brothers cut that wood or mowed those lawns. It was frightening with those dogs. But I had drive. I think I had a vision and a dream that nobody else in my family had, a dream that not even any of my friends in the projects had. I walked through that door. You can't see through those screen doors from the outside. I could only imagine what it was like in there. Then that screen door opened and I walked into that house for the first time and I saw those hardwood floors just immaculate, and the house clean and cool. No flies. No flypaper. And not a roach around when I went into the kitchen.

I knew there was a difference in the races. We did think that, of course, white people were better.

But in those homes I felt I was in the real world. I knew that's the way life should be.

# Chapter 8: Jerry Priddy

Sometimes when I'm with a friend who's in a hurry, a little kid will ask me for an autograph or want to talk to me. It really bugs whomever I'm with because I sign the autograph and talk to the kid.

"Maury," they'll say in exasperation, "you can't please the whole world." When they say that, I think of Jerry Priddy and what he did for me when I was 10 years old. When you see me sign an autograph for a kid, you're actually seeing Jerry Priddy.

Jerry Priddy played second base for the Senators in 1943. He came from the Yankees. He was a journeyman with good hands. He couldn't hit, but he could turn the double play.

He came to my playground in the projects. He probably didn't want to be there, but the Senators ordered him to go. They probably gave him 20 bucks or less, because when I was going to playgrounds for the Dodgers 30 years later they gave us only $50. He probably would have given $20 not to go.

There are all these little black kids standing around in the playground and here comes this guy from the Washington Senators. This was long before blacks were in the major leagues, and I remember thinking, "Where does he come from? 'The Senators.' What's that? 'Major leagues.' What's that mean?"

I was used to seeing black people all the time. But we didn't know anything about the Washington Senators. We didn't even know about the Homestead Grays. The local sandlot semi-pros were our heroes. They were big, drunken men who carried a half pint of whiskey in their back pockets. That's why a lot of black kids grew up and carried a half pint in their back pockets, too. Except now, they carry crack.

Jerry Priddy had his uniform on. It was the uniform that got me to listen and opened my ears and eyes to what he had to say. The name didn't mean a damn thing to me. Without the uniform, he was another man off the street. He was supposed to stay for just an hour, but he stayed two at least, and he had the attention of us all. It was little kids standing beside Santa Claus, tugging at his boots.

He looked me in the eye and singled me out. He told everybody, "Watch this kid! Watch how he gets the hop!"

I didn't have any shoes and I had borrowed somebody's glove. Four or five of us used to use one glove. When we were younger, I used to take what they called a two-pound paper bag, pull it over my hand, bunch it around my wrist, pound a pocket in it and catch the ball in there. It worked, too.

Anyway, Jerry Priddy saw I could play. "Don't you have any shoes?" he asked me.

"No, sir," I said.

"You go home and tell your folks to get you some shoes," he said. "You have a chance to be a good player." He said that to me, this man, this white man.

After he came to the playground, I got my brothers to take me to Griffith Stadium to see him. It was like being in an oasis. I started listening to Archie McDonald announce the Senators' games. I learned about guys like Stan Spence and Chick Pieretti, a little left-hander like Bobby Shantz. I was little and a pitcher so Chick Pieretti became my idol until Jackie Robinson came along. Then it became Chick Pieretti and Jackie Robinson. I never gave Chick Pieretti up. Nor Jerry Priddy.

I met Jerry Priddy in California after I became a major leaguer and I told him that story. He couldn't remember it from that long ago and that obscure place. Then one year, Jerry Priddy got in trouble with the law over something he did with a trucking company he owned. It was a big case. Gene Mauch, who was managing the Angels, was a friend of Jerry's and Gene asked me to write to the judge in the case in an effort to lessen Jerry's sentence. I wrote that letter with great pride and gratitude.

When I make appearances even today I wear a Dodger jacket and cap because I remember how Jerry Priddy's uniform got my attention. It's amazing how something in your formative years can have such an impact on you. That's why it's important that athletes conduct themselves properly, because they're the heroes and role models of youngsters.

Jerry Priddy did that. He's followed me all through my life.

## Chapter 9: Half pints

Growing up where I did helped a lot when I became a professional ballplayer. Guys tried to intimidate me, but that was kindergarten stuff compared to what I went through on the playground in the projects.

I was always good enough where I didn't have to do anything extra to get a chance to play. They could be choosing up sides at the playground and I would get there late knowing that somebody would choose me before I got there in the hope that I would show up. Guys who didn't play so well had to get there early and hope that somebody would choose them.

Sometimes when I was doing the choosing, I showed off by picking the lesser players first. I wanted the weaker team so I could do enough to overcome that handicap and beat the other team anyway. That was just cockiness.

There was great competitiveness on the playground, and I wanted to be the best of the Wills boys. I wanted to be the best on the playground and I succeeded. I think the drive came from being buried in the middle of a big family. The only way I could get any recognition was to persevere on my own. I was the smallest in the family. Even with the Dodgers, I was Little Maury Wills.

When we went to the playground, they had bats and softballs, but when we were playing on our own, we used a tennis ball and a broomstick. My brothers could hit that ball so far. I remember I never could hit the ball high and far, but I was one of the best hitters on the team because I hit line drives. I didn't want to hit line drives, though. I wanted to hit the ball high and far like my brothers.

When I got to play what we called semi-pro ball, hitting wasn't the big thing. I hit .400 everywhere I played. Defense was what made you shine in semi-pro. My brothers and I used to run backward on the bases sometimes. And on defense, sometimes a guy would hit the ball to shortstop when nobody was on base and I'd throw the ball to the third baseman. He'd throw it to the second baseman and the second baseman threw it to the first baseman to get the guy out. That's where we had all the fun.

I was also a pitcher, and sometimes the outfielders would come in to the infield and sit down, and I would pitch and nobody would touch the ball. That's really showing off. Satchel Paige used to do that when he barnstormed around the country. One of the guys must have heard about that and that's why he suggested it one day.

"Call them in!" he said.

"Huh?" I said.

"Call them in."

So they called the outfielders in and I struck everybody out. After that, when I started getting really cocky, I'd call the outfielders in myself.

That was really cruel to the batter to humiliate him like that. That man probably had a girlfriend or sweetheart, or maybe a dad or a son there to see him play. And I called everybody in, struck him out, and everybody's laughing. That was black humor in those days—torturing somebody.

I was playing with grown men on a semi-pro team when I was 14 years old. Semi-pro didn't mean you got paid. It meant you had uniforms and equipment. If you played pickup games with whatever you had on, that was sandlot ball. The semi-pro games were on Sundays, when we used to climb out the upstairs window to get out of going to Uncle Raymond's services. We used to wash our uniforms and press them with an iron. We'd put a sharp crease in the front of the pants like you would on a pair of slacks. That was a big thing, to have a crease.

The guys came to the semi-pro games with a half pint of whiskey in their pockets. They would take a nip between innings and between times at bat. I believe they even took a slug between pitches when they were up there hitting. They slid like Pete Rose, on their bellies, so they wouldn't break their bottles. My brother Duke was one of those guys. And he was a leader.

Duke was the kind of guy you had to get out of bed Sunday morning so we could leave to play ball in Maryland or Virginia or wherever we were playing. He'd come down in the morning still drunk. He couldn't even see the ball, but he was a natural hitter—the only left-hander in the family.

Mickey Mantle tells a story about how he didn't expect to play the next day because he was injured. So he got plastered that night and came to the ballpark half blind. The game was tight and Casey Stengel sent him up to pinch-hit. They pointed him toward the plate and he hit the ball out of the park and won the game. When he got back to the dugout, they asked him how he did it.

"I just hit the one in the middle," he said.

Duke was like that. They'd pour him into the bus and let him sleep all the way to the game. He'd still be on the bus, sloppy drunk, while we were playing. Then in the last inning, when they needed a pinch hitter, they'd point him at the plate and he'd hit the damned ball into the woods. As he was rounding the bases, he'd fall between third and home and drag himself to the plate. But he won the game and because of that everyone would buy him another half pint.

I wasn't one of those guys with the half pints, but I did drink sometimes. I can remember in high school I threw up all over the back yard coming home from a party. I was the big star on the football team and I had to drink to be one of the guys. These guys had got this 49-cent fifth of wine—Spodey-Odey. Real cheap stuff. And I turned that bottle upside down and guzzled it. If you're going to drink wine like that, you'd want to put it in a half gallon of soda-pop to kill the taste, but we drank it straight.

And I threw up all over the back yard.

I'll never forget my father getting me out of bed and taking me down to the back yard and showing me the stuff on the ground. He said if he ever saw that again, he was going to whip my butt forever. He didn't whip me that day, but when I was younger, my daddy whipped me with some switches like I never want to be whipped again.

The guys who had the whiskey also had knives. Some of them may even have had guns if they were old enough. But everybody had knives. That must be how that old racial stereotype originated that every black guy had a knife in his pocket. Redd Foxx said that wasn't true, though, because his brother Harry didn't carry a knife. He carried an ice pick.

I didn't carry a knife and I didn't carry a half pint. I was never a rough-and-tumble guy who was always in the middle of things. I was tricky. I was always on the outskirts of it. Guys used to get frustrated because they couldn't really tee off on me on the football field. They couldn't get a clean shot at me. And when we had fights, I was always the guy on the perimeter looking in. I may even have started it. But I didn't have the disposition to be in the middle of it.

You could get as physical with me as you wanted in the course of a football game, but when it came to the riff-raff stuff, I didn't want to participate. I lost a girl one day because of that.

We were getting ready to play a semi-pro football game. We used to hold raffles and dances to raise money to buy equipment for our teams. We had a regular season and everything. So the game's close to starting, and I have this cute little girlfriend. I'm standing behind her at the sidelines behind the ropes we put up around the field. And I'm talking some good stuff to her. Or, as we used to put it, I was talking holes in her clothes.

Reggie Green, my archrival from Armstrong High, was after this girl, too. As I was talking to her, he came over to her from the side, tripped me, and knocked me away from her. The only thing for me to do was go back and reclaim my position. If I had, all hell would have broken loose and one of us would have got our butt kicked. But I just looked at him and walked off, leaving him with the girl. That's how far I'd go to avoid a confrontation.

Gamesmanship was important. In a football game we'd razz the guys on the other side of the line: "We're comin' after you! We're comin' right over you, y'hear? We're gonna get your ass!"

And then the guy tackled you, and he stepped on you as he got up, just trying to intimidate you.

One of the biggest compliments I ever had in my life came when I was playing on a semi-pro football team. The guys from the other team came over to me and shook my hand after the game. "You're all right," they said. "We tried to intimidate you and you didn't give in."

## Chapter 10: You've got to be a football hero

There were three black high schools known for sports in Washington, D.C.: Cordoza, Armstrong and Dunbar. I went to Cordoza. Cordoza was known for football, baseball and track. Cordoza's track teams were famous all the way up to New York, where we used to race against Boys High, which had some very famous athletes, including Tommy Davis and Lenny Wilkens, the former basketball star who's now a coach in the pros. Armstrong was known for its basketball teams. Dunbar was known for getting beat up on all the time. The only thing they were real good at was tennis.

I was a star in football, baseball and basketball. I won an award that was given to the best athlete in my class in Washington, D.C. The award was given for what you accomplished in high school. All the coaches and athletic departments in the black schools got together to pick the winner. Even though the white schools weren't involved in it, we said that the award was for the whole city.

We claimed to be city football champions and the white schools made the same claim. One year there was big talk about playing the champion white school. It was a big disappointment when the administration wouldn't allow it. They wouldn't give a reason. That was the mentality of the school boards at the time.

I was a pitcher in baseball, quarterback in football, and a guard in basketball.

I was good in basketball, but I didn't have the drive I had in football. I played because it was the thing to do. I stole passes and I did the scoring. I mean, I put the ball up a lot. We had some big rough guys getting the ball off the boards and throwing it downcourt like the Lakers and I was the guy always hanging downcourt to get the ball and the layup.

In baseball, I pitched something like nine one-hitters during my high school career. And the guy who got the hit was always Reggie Green from Armstrong. Reggie was a tall, lanky, left-handed kid. He'd always get the one hit. Then he'd pitch a one-hitter against us and I would get the one hit.

But football was the big sport in high school because all the girls came to see the games. Football was where we had the crowds. That was the appeal of it, showing off for the crowds. The alumni, parents, teachers and all the students came to see us play football, but they didn't come to the baseball games. Football was my first love.

I did everything. I played quarterback on offense and safety on defense. I kicked off, punted, and kicked conversions, too. I could kick off to the back of the end zone, so I know I had a good foot. I kicked straight on like Lou Groza of the Cleveland Browns and everyone else in those days, but unlike Groza, who took just one step before he kicked, I stood four or five yards back like present-day kickers. With timing, when the ball was snapped and spotted, I was there. That's how I generated power.

I was fast and shifty running with the ball, like Dave Meggett of the Giants. I frustrated the other teams. Nobody ever blind-sided me because I had that great peripheral vision that later would allow me to steal the pitchout sign from the catcher. The only way they could get me was to pull me down.

The most spectacular thing I ever did was during my junior year against our archrivals, Armstrong. Armstrong was an all-boys trade school. Cordoza was a regular high school. We were the power in football, but Armstrong had a chance to knock us off. They had a big, tall quarterback named Avatus Stone, who also punted. He wound up going to Syracuse, where he started two years. He went on to play five years in the Canadian Football League and one year—1958—with the Colts in the NFL. He was a great punter. He hit these high, booming spirals. He was actually happy when they didn't make a first down so he could go back and punt.

So we're playing Armstrong and both teams are undefeated. The score is 0–0 in the third quarter when Avatus Stone goes back to punt and I go back to return it. He hits one of his high, booming kicks all the way to the five-yard line.

I had already taken five or six punts from this guy during the game and gone nowhere. They were smearing me after two, five, maybe 10 yards. Now, I catch the ball and all of a sudden I'm going straight up the middle for about 10 yards, and then I'm heading for the sideline and I see daylight.

I can't believe it. Nobody's there! But all of a sudden here's this guy right next to me. His name is Chubby Lewis and he's a world-class track guy—a 100-yard dash man and a hurdler. I can still see that as if it's happening this moment. He was a little guy about my height, but built like Joe Morris. I'm running the sideline and he's side by side with me trying to close the angle and tackle me.

And I just pulled away. It wasn't as if he reached for me and I shook him off. He had the angle and I accelerated. When I got to the goal line, he was four yards behind me.

Nobody could believe it. "Chubby Lewis was two strides behind you when you got to the goal line!" they yelled.

That was the only score in the game and pictures of that touchdown were all over. We won 6–0 because I missed the extra point.

That was the championship. We were undefeated, and that play is still in the annals of high school football in Washington, D.C., as one of the all-time great plays.

I can still feel that play. It's more memorable than the day I broke Ty Cobb's stolen base record in St. Louis and they pulled the bag out of the ground and all the rafters were bending in Sportsman's Park from the noise. I can still feel that, but that punt return was better.

Until that day, my brother Bob was always the fastest runner in my family. He could *fly.* We could all run. But Bob was always the anchor on the relay team and I was somewhere in the middle. He would take the baton a step or two behind the other guy and overtake him and win while everybody was going crazy and screaming, "BOBBY WILLS! BOBBY WILLS!"

When I scored that touchdown it was if I were breaking adhesions. It was the first time I realized I could run. I never lost a race for the rest of my life. I even challenged Bob and beat him.

Outrunning Chubby Lewis and winning that game did it. After that, the scholarship offers started pouring in. I got nine offers from major schools including Ohio State, Rutgers, Syracuse and Fordham, and a ton of offers from the black schools. The scouts and recruiters all came down to Cordoza.

I didn't visit any of the schools, though. My high school coach was going to move on to Virginia State University in Petersburg and I wanted to go with him.

Then the Dodgers offered me a minor league contract and I took it.

If Bump Elliott had come along, though, and offered me a scholarship to Michigan, I would have been gone. I would have been a football player. And I believe I would have made it. I was a quarterback, but no way would they have let me play that in college. They probably would have made me a defensive back. Leo Miles, who was the star quarterback at Cordoza before me, went to Virginia State and ended up in the pros as a cornerback. He played one year with the Giants. I figured I would have been somewhere in the defensive backfield like him. I probably would have kicked conversions, too.

But Bump Elliott didn't call and the Dodgers did. I chose baseball over football. Baseball was a game of skill and I liked that. Baseball was the summertime, the beautiful time of year.

Football was my first love, but baseball was my true love.

## Chapter 11: The $500 man

The Washington newspaper had a tryout camp at Griffith Stadium in 1950. I was 17 and just finishing high school.

Some of the old guys I played semi-pro ball with—the guys with the half pints—took me to the tryout. They knew I was going to get signed.

There must have been 300 kids there. They gave me a number and told me to sit in the stands and wait for them to call me. I sat up there for hours because there were more kids than they had time to look at.

The camp was just about over when my teammates who had brought me took matters into their own hands. They took me down to the field and confronted one of the scouts.

"Hey! This kid can really throw. You gotta look at him," they advised the scout.

"I'm sorry. We've been here long enough," the scout told them. "It's over."

"No, it's not!" one of my friends declared and he got right in this white scout's face.

The scout considered the situation and decided that perhaps my friend was right. "Okay," he said without enthusiasm. "Let's see him throw."

They got a catcher for me and I threw three pitches—aired them out. Goddam! The scout looked at me and said, "Throw some more. Show me a curveball."

I ripped off a curveball. I had the guy's attention.

"Give me one three-quarters," the scout said.

I reared back and threw a fastball so hard the catcher missed it. He was expecting three-quarters speed, but I had thrown it with a three-quarters delivery.

"No. No," the scout said. "Three-quarters speed. Take a little off it."

I didn't know how to take a little off it. But it was all right because the fastball is what they look for. If a kid has speed, he has a pretty good chance. You can teach him how to do the other things, but you can't teach him how to throw harder. It's like base running. I can teach a runner how to get from first to third sooner, but I can't make him run faster. It's like John Thompson, the Georgetown basketball coach, said when they asked him why he gave a scholarship to Dikembe Mutombo, who hadn't had a lot of basketball experience in his native Zaire.

"Because you can't coach 7-foot-2," Thompson replied.

You can't coach speed, either. You can only coach technique.

Anyway, the scout asked me for my name, address and telephone number. "We'll be in touch with you," he told me.

Three weeks went by. Finally they called and invited me to another camp in Maryland. This one was a week long.

I went up there and threw on the sidelines. Finally, I got into a game and pitched two innings. I struck everybody out. Nobody touched the ball. They had me pitch another inning, and I struck out three more in a row. Again, nobody touched the ball. They had a race and I outran everybody by 20 yards.

"We'll get in touch with you," they said.

Two weeks later, they called me again and invited me to a third camp in Cambridge, Md. By now, they had broken the 300 kids who came to the original camp down to about 20 prospects. Again, they had me pitch two innings and again I struck everybody out. I pitched another inning and struck everybody out again. In the two camps, I had faced 18 batters and none of them had even touched the ball.

They took me on the side and showed me how to throw a change-up. I threw it pretty well, which showed them I had the ability to learn. They had another race and again I beat everybody by about 20 yards. Then they put me in the batting cage and I hit the ball for them.

Finally, a scout asked the magic question: "Would you like to play pro ball, son?"

"Yes, sir!"

"We'll be in touch with you."

It was early summer and I was still living with my mom and dad. I didn't have a regular job, but I already had a baby, Barry. He was living with his mother, Gertrude, in another project. Gertrude and I would get married in October, but already, she wasn't too happy with me. I was still hanging out on the corner by the pool hall with the guys with the half pints and pumping gas and shooting pool to make a little money.

The last camp was in June and they never called me back. I was so disappointed. I figured they were putting me on. Before I knew it, it was September. That's a long time to wait.

Then, just like that, a scout from the Dodgers called and said he and another scout were in town. They were coming to my house.

It was like the Pope was coming. Everybody got dressed up and squeezed into the living room—all 15 of us. The photographer for the Afro-American newspaper came to take a picture. He took one look at all the family and said, "Geez, Reverend. You've really been waling, haven't you?"

My father didn't have any idea what he was talking about. He just shook his head up and down and smiled: "Yeah. Yeah."

Rex Bowen and John Curry were the scouts who came to sign me. I had visions of getting a $6,000 signing bonus. That was how much I had read someone else had signed for, so I thought that's what I would get. Rex didn't offer $6,000, though. He started by offering me a new suit of clothes—a sport coat, slacks and a shirt.

My father turned it down.

"What are you looking for?" Bowen asked.

"Uh, a few thousand?" my father said.

"I'll throw in a pair of shoes," Bowen said.

When my father balked, Bowen got up, put on his coat and he and Curry started out the door. As he was leaving, he said, "Five hundred. Take it or leave it."

"Just a minute," my father said quickly. "We'll take it."

They gave me a check. It was the first check I had ever seen. I gave half the money to my father, and the other half to Gertrude. She put it in a shoebox under the bed. That was a big bankroll, but it was gone soon enough.

So I signed and the photographer took the picture of all 15 of us and the scouts and it ran on the front of the sports page: "Sonny Wills Signs With Dodgers."

## Chapter 12: The mother of my children

Gertrude and I never talked much when we were together. We don't talk much now that we're not together. We never had much to say at any time.

I saw Gertrude Elliott for the first time walking down the corridors in Cordoza High during my senior year. She was the prettiest thing I ever saw in my life. I just had to get to know her, but I never dreamed I would. She wasn't a cheerleader or one of those girls who are impressed by the star quarterback. She was quiet and very smart and she hung out with the people in school who had brains.

That was a challenge and I went after her. I got her, too.

She lived in a different project in southeast Washington, in Anacostia. I had to take a bus there.

Her mother worked Tuesdays, so that was the day we both cut

school and I'd go to see her at her house. Before you knew it, we were petting and doing stuff like that. I remember one day her mother came home unexpectedly and Gertrude hid me behind the couch in her living room. We thought her mother would just come in, get something, and leave. Instead, she sat down and stayed for the longest 20 minutes in my life. She wanted to talk to her daughter.

And I'm lying breathless, stretched out behind the couch with the couch pushed back against the wall as far as it would go. That was frightening.

During my senior year, we eloped. We got on a bus and took it all the way to Cleveland, where her father was. Her mother got the sheriff after us, but nobody knew where we were. We stayed in Cleveland a couple of days with one of her relatives waiting for her father to show up. We never did find him and we ended up coming back without getting married.

I went back to school and she got pregnant before she could finish school. It probably happened on a Tuesday when her mother was working. We did it on the banks of the Anacostia River. She got pregnant without taking her clothes off. I never did see her naked.

I didn't know what I was doing, and she didn't either. Neither of us had had any experience. We just did what comes naturally. You can go into such a thing with no experience for the very first time and you can wind up making a baby. It doesn't seem fair at all.

I don't remember my father getting upset. At least if he was, he didn't show it. He did insist that I marry Gertrude to give the baby a name.

The wedding party consisted of just the two of us. The ceremony lasted about 10 minutes. When it was over, we walked out and my father drove us back to her mother's place. I left her there and went down to the corner with the boys. I don't even know if I went back to her on our wedding night.

I was just following in the footsteps of my heroes, the guys I admired when I was young who hung out on the corner outside the pool hall with the half pints in their pockets.

When my son was born, I named him Barry after Barry Sullivan, my movie-actor hero. Here I am a little black kid in the projects back in the Forties. I'm 17. My wife is 16. I don't even know my way out of my own neighborhood. And I'm a father.

I call Gertrude the mother of my children. We never had much of a marriage. I was gone all the time playing ball. I'd come home for a short time in the winter and I'd get her pregnant. She was always pregnant in the summer and barefoot in the winter.

I'll never forget one time when I was playing in the minor leagues in Spokane, where we made our home, and one summer she didn't get pregnant and somebody must have given her some shoes because we went to a party. She danced with a guy five times at that party, and every goddam song was "The Great Pretender" by the Platters. I like everything in music except that song.

I played in Spokane in 1958–59, and that's when we moved from Washington, D.C., and bought a home there. When I joined the Dodgers in the middle of the 1959 season, she didn't want to leave. She thought Los Angeles was too fast and had too much crime. She would come down at times, but she didn't want to stay there. She sat home and had babies.

They were her children, not mine. I always felt certain the children, too, felt they were more their mother's children than mine.

My oldest son, Barry, had six scholarship offers out of high school in Spokane to play baseball. He turned them down. He told me later in life that he didn't want to be a professional baseball player because he saw his mom staying home while I was gone all the time. He wanted to get married and he didn't want his wife sitting there waiting for him like his mother did for me.

I was too young to know what love is when we got married. And during my baseball career, I never had time for emotional relationships. Baseball was my commitment. I had periods when I had girlfriends or somebody I was dating, but I couldn't ever get emotionally involved. I was too distracted by baseball, too obsessed with being a Dodger. It was the same obsession I would later have with being an addict.

The measure of my obsession with baseball came during one of Gertrude's pregnancies. We knew the baby was going to be a boy and I had already named it Bragan Reiser Wills after Bobby

Bragan, my manager in Spokane who got me to the big leagues, and Pete Reiser, the coach with the Dodgers who kept me there.

Something went wrong with the pregnancy and the doctor called me and said they had to force delivery. The baby was stillborn—it had been a question of the baby dying or the mother dying. After the delivery, Gertrude went into a coma and was in pretty bad shape.

I got about three telegrams saying that it was urgent that I come home. But we were playing the Giants the next day in a three-game series. I said I couldn't come home because we were playing the Giants and I had to be there.

I went to the ballpark and told myself that no such thing was taking place in Spokane. I played one hell of a ballgame against the Giants. After the game, I called the doctor.

"Don't worry about it, Maury," he told me. "You stay there and play. I'll take care of her. If I need you up here, I'll call."

"You sure that will be all right?" I asked.

"Yes," he said.

He didn't promise me anything as far as her safety was concerned. I played the second game and played my butt off again. I had that ability to eliminate anything that distracted me from playing, to eliminate it from my life no matter what it was. I played a great three-game series. When it was over, I flew to Spokane and stayed about four hours. Then I joined the Dodgers on the road. I had to get back to the team.

After the 1964 season, I came home and got Gertrude pregnant for the seventh time. That was in December. In February, she told me to leave and not come back. I didn't want to leave right then, so I stayed until March and then left for spring training. I never came back.

I don't remember having any fun sexually with her, just having babies. I never saw her body. She went in the bathroom to change clothes even when all the lights were out. That was the culture I grew up in. That was black culture.

## Chapter 13: C-O-L-O-R-E-D O-N-L-Y

Growing up in Washington, D.C., I had experienced separation of the races, but not segregation. We thought we had everything we needed. I never ran into things like I saw in Vero Beach when I went to Dodgertown in the spring of 1951 to begin my career as a professional ballplayer.

Today, Dodgertown, a former naval air station, is built up and modern, but when I joined the Dodger system in 1951 the team had been training there only three years. We still stayed in the old junior officers quarters in two-story wooden barracks. Even then, though, the spring training facility was the only one of its kind and the best in baseball.

I took a train from Union Station in Washington, D.C. I had never been in Union Station before. Heck, except for jumping on the freight trains and scrambling between the cars to get across the railroad tracks, I hadn't even been on a train.

I thought it was the greatest thing that ever happened to me. I sat there for a day and a half on the train with my nose pressed up against the window, rocking from side to side.

The train left me off in Vero Beach and the Dodgers had a bus waiting. It was a little school bus with straight-back seats. It was a good thing they had the bus because I wouldn't have known how to take a cab. I hadn't ever been in a cab before, either.

I didn't notice the "Colored Only" and "White Only" signs when I got off the train. I wasn't looking for anything like that and had no reason to. I was just looking up in the air.

When we got to Dodgertown, they stood us in line and checked us in as if we were in the army. They gave each of us a key and I think we had to pay a dollar deposit on it. I remember walking down the long barracks hallways looking for my room. The guys in the major league camp had double rooms with adjoining doors and a bath in the middle. The minor league quarters had four double bunks in each room with the toilets down the hall. Of the seven other guys in the room with me, I think I was the only one to make the big leagues.

I found that the white players and black players were all mixed together. That was a thrill for me, a brand-new experience. I mean really a thrill, because I had gone to an all-black high school and played in an all-black conference. Rooming with white players was a grand experience for me.

I could hardly wait to get into my Dodger uniform. I say Dodger uniform, but I was given some baggy, old gray flannels that didn't fit with a green number on the back. You could tell the teams in spring training by the color of the numbers. I was assigned to Hornell, N.Y., one of five Class D teams and one of twenty Dodger farm clubs. We had a battalion of people down there.

The first day on the field, they put the players in their respective positions. We had a lot of center fielders, left fielders and right fielders; a few third basemen, a few shortstops, a few first basemen, a few catchers and a horde of pitchers. And I'm a pitcher. I'm standing there looking at these great big guys, and I'm just a little guy about 5-foot-8 and 155 pounds.

I guess I was imaginative even in those days because I looked over at second base. There were no second basemen. So I went to one of the managers and said, "I can play second."

"You can?" he said.

"Yes, sir," I assured him.

"Well, get on over there," the manager said.

I stayed at second base all of spring training. I never did pitch.

We threw the ball around and then we had a chance to hit. I climbed in the cage and missed the first 15 pitches thrown to me —and I had a .400-some batting average in high school.

The Dodgers trained about two weeks in Vero Beach before going down to Miami. They'd stay in Miami the rest of the spring and play their games there. But they also played a couple of exhibition games in Holman Stadium in Vero Beach.

When the Dodgers came up to play, we minor leaguers were gawking at them.

"Jackie Robinson," someone would say in an awe-struck whisper. "Don Newcombe."

"Here comes Roy *Campanella."*

*"Pee Wee Reese!"*

"Duke Snider . . . Carl Furillo . . ."

It wasn't as if three or four guys were stars on that team and the rest were fill-ins. Everybody on the team was a star. We're talking about the same guys who would be the world champion '55 Dodgers.

So I went to Holman Stadium to see the Dodgers play their exhibition game. I wanted to go down behind the dugout because the dugouts were open without any shelter over them. I wanted to see the players up close.

I couldn't sit there. I had to go down the right field line in the section that was colored only. There was a big sign to tell where it was: "COLORED"—C-O-L-O-R-E-D—"ONLY"—O-N-L-Y.

Goddam.

Then I went to where the restrooms were and went in without looking over the door. I had gone in the white-only restroom. I got run out of there. Then I looked up and I saw it again: "COLORED ONLY."

What a slump I went into. I couldn't believe this.

A couple of years after that, Jackie Robinson complained about those signs. He put up a fuss and eventually the Dodgers took them down at Dodgertown even though they stayed up in the town of Vero Beach. Then black people could sit anywhere in the stadium they wanted. That was a big deal for me because it was Jackie Robinson who did it.

Even though they took the signs down, the black people were so accustomed to sitting down the right field line in the corner of the stadium that they still wouldn't go anywhere else. They just sat in that same section. Every once in a while you'd see a few sprinkled through the stands as the years went on.

The city of Vero Beach stayed segregated for a long time. They had separate drinking fountains and everything. The Dodgers had a bus that would take us to town. I took it a couple of times to get some things I needed. I'd walk down to the Rexall drugstore and see people sitting inside at the soda fountain. They were having ice cream sodas and great big, tall root beer floats. I looked at them thinking how nice it would be if I could sit there and have one of those things. We didn't have anything like that in camp. But I couldn't go in: "WHITE ONLY."

The black players had to go to this little black town called Gifford, across the tracks from Vero Beach. It was a little rat-infested place with one old beer joint and one barber who didn't know how to cut hair.

I hated getting a haircut in Gifford, the barber was so bad. Finally, in the spring of 1962, when I was established with the Dodgers, I told John Roseboro, my roommate, "I can't stand to get another haircut in that town. Will you cut it for me?"

"Sure," John said. I looked in the mirror when he was finished. Looking back at me was the worst haircut I ever saw. There was no fixing it.

"Cut it all off, John," I said. So he skinned it and I stole 104 bases that year. After that, I skinned my head every year in spring training.

At night, we went to Gifford if we wanted to go somewhere where there was music and dancing where we could just hang out and see what the local girls looked like.

I played ball 23 years and went to Vero Beach with the Dodgers 20 of them. I saw at least three generations of little black kids in Gifford—the fathers, their sons, and then their grandsons—grow up picking oranges. That's all they did. Pick oranges. That's the only thing they had a chance to do.

I took the bus downtown once with some Cuban players. These guys were so black they were blue. And they sat at that counter in the Rexall drugstore and they had sodas and root beer floats. And while they had them they talked Spanish and it was okay with everybody.

I looked at that and wondered: "What is it? Is it because I'm black and speak English that I can't go in? Give me some kind of reason that's feasible." I couldn't understand it. Their hair was just as nappy as mine.

The Cubans got me to go in and sit there at that counter with them. They yelled Spanish back and forth across me and I acted like I didn't want to talk. If somebody said something to me, I just said, "Si, Chico."

And all the while I sucked at my root beer float and ice cream soda. We left the drugstore and the Cubans walked through town just as if they were citizens. They went by an Italian restaurant and wanted to stop in and see the owner, who was a nice guy, and get something to eat.

"No way," I told them. I left them there and walked the five miles back to camp alone. I had the sense to know I couldn't overdo it.

Isn't that amazing? I was worried about getting exposed as being an American instead of a Cuban. I knew that it was unfair. Segregation was something I had heard of, but I had never experienced it.

I came back to camp and told all the American black guys what I did. They shook their heads in disbelief. "Boy," they said, "you're gonna get strung up one day doin' that."

I had never heard about the Klan before I went to Florida. I had heard about the South and the difference in people there. I knew there was a barrier down there. I knew that I was black and that I just couldn't do everything or go places I wasn't accepted.

It didn't do any good to be pissed off. Jackie Robinson was really ahead of his time as a prominent black standing up for his civil rights. That made him stand out all by himself. It made him that ugly word—militant.

But Jackie Robinson had guts. Even Roy Campanella didn't support Jackie. Don Newcombe didn't support Jackie. Campy was passive about it all, and Jackie didn't understand that.

In St. Louis, they used to make the black players stay in a separate hotel from the rest of the team. Jackie complained about it. Campy was on Jackie's case about relaxing and leaving it alone. But because of Jackie they got to stay in the Chase Park Plaza in St. Louis with the rest of the team. They stayed there but they had to eat in their rooms. They couldn't go to the dining room. Finally, they lifted that ban and let them eat in the dining room.

Jackie went down there to eat, but Campy wouldn't go. Campy didn't want to be a crusader and go down there and eat just because they said he could. So out of habit Campy ate in his room, just like the people who kept sitting in the right field corner even after the Dodgers had taken down the colored-only signs.

John Roseboro had that same habit. He and Campy just stayed in the room. They weren't going to do anything different.

When I roomed with John after I got to the big leagues, I could never get him to go to the dining room with me. I wasn't going there to be a crusader. I went there because I thought it was a nice place to eat. A lot of people—white people—were courteous enough to fight for the right for us to eat there. It was an opportunity to go to a nice place to eat instead of staying in a little cubicle.

So I went down to the dining rooms. I was nicely received. I really enjoyed myself eating downstairs.

## Chapter 14: "I want to pitch"

Going to Hornell in upstate New York was like going to another planet. I saw trees and parks and clean streets.

I was 18 years old, making $130 a month plus $1.25 a day for meals and about to start my first season in Class D in a little town of about 20,000 people in the Elmira-Corning area. To me, Hornell represented the real world.

The Dodgers got me a room with a white family. I think they were Greek and I had a little room in their house that the club paid the rent for. They were fine people and they were great to me. I had never driven a car before and the man let me drive his even though I didn't have a license. They didn't have any children, and I suppose they couldn't have been much older than 25 or 30, but I was so young myself. I was 18, but I was really green. I was probably the equivalent of a 12-year-old today.

I lived within walking distance of the ballpark, and for the first time in my life I was somebody in the real world. In this small town, the Hornell Dodgers were all heroes. We were just green kids right out of high school and yet we were heroes in Hornell.

I came through a year after Don Zimmer, who was a highly rated prospect in the Dodger organization at the time. Zimmer played shortstop and set a record by stealing 54 bases for Hornell in 1950.

I played second base, hit .280 in 123 games and stole 54 bases to tie Zimmer's record. Late in the season, though, I was in a horrible slump. I was distraught and didn't know what to do.

"Look," I told Doc Alexson, the manager, "I was signed as a pitcher. I want to pitch."

"No, you don't," he said. "You're a second baseman."

"No," I said, half pleading. "I want to pitch."

I begged him until Doc said, "All right, I'll let you pitch a game. Three days from now be ready."

I worked out on the sidelines to get my rhythm back. Before the game, I warmed up and my curveball was falling off the table and my fastball was really popping the catcher's mitt.

I walked out to the mound and went to work. Eight batters later, five runs are in, the bases are loaded, nobody's out, and it's still the first inning.

Doc had seen enough and he came to the mound to take me out.

"Give me a chance, Skip," I said.

*"Give you a chance???"* he thundered.

"I can get this guy out," I told him.

"Okay," he said. "You got one more hitter."

"Thank you. Thank you." I was practically kissing his feet. "That's all I need."

So Doc went back to the dugout, the batter climbed in the batter's box, and I threw my best fastball.

The batter took his best cut and hit a line drive that went through the third baseman—almost literally. It was hit so hard it almost killed him.

When Doc came back out, I went quietly. My pitching career was over.

The season ended a success, though. The Dodgers wanted to send me to Santa Barbara in 1952, which was a step up to Class C. But Santa Barbara sounded like the end of the world even if it was a promotion. I asked them if going back to Hornell would hurt my chances of getting to the Dodgers. They said if that's what I wanted to do it wasn't any problem. I could go from Class D to Class B as easily as I could go from Class C to Class B.

I didn't play winter ball that year. I went back to Washington, D.C., and stood on the corner and shot pool, watched the guys with their half-pint bottles and took a slug of bad whiskey now and then. My wife was still living with her mother in her project. I stayed with my parents in my project.

In the spring I went back to Vero Beach and then up to Hornell, where I stayed with the same family. I hit .300 and led the league in hits (160), runs (108), at-bats (533) and stolen bases (54).

It was time to move up.

The next year, 1953, I jumped Class C and Class B and was assigned to the Pueblo Dodgers in Class A. That's where I met Bobby Winkles, who was playing in the same league for Colorado Springs. Years later, after he became the baseball coach at Arizona State, I called Winkles and got a full scholarship for my second son, Bump, who went on to play for the Texas Rangers.

I learned a lesson in Pueblo, courtesy of Lacey Curry, a teammate, and George Pfister, the manager. Lacey, who's a minister now, was a journeyman minor leaguer who had been in the Dodger organization about four years. Every year he played for a different club because none of the managers wanted him on his team. Lacey was a good player, but a troublemaker.

One day early in the season, Pfister was chewing some guys out and got on me about something I was doing wrong. I had gotten off to a great start, but I was nodding my head and saying, "Yes, sir. Yes, sir. Yes, sir."

Lacey came up to me after the meeting and said, "Look, man, you don't have to take that crap! You're playing great ball! Next time he tries that, you tell him, 'If you don't like the way I'm playing, well, ship me out!' "

"Really?" I said doubtfully.

"Sure," he said with authority. "Shit, man, you're the star here. You're playing good."

Not long after that, George Pfister got on me about something, so I jumped up right in the middle of the meeting, just the way Lacey told me to, and barked back.

"Don't get all over me," I told him. "You don't like the way I'm playing, well, ship me out!"

As I was saying that, my wife was on a train coming out from Washington, D.C., to join me for the first time in my minor league career. She had at least two babies with her. And she was still on that train when I found myself flying the opposite direction to the Class B Miami Sun Sox. I was going there just 18 games into the season because Pfister took my advice and shipped me out the same day.

I learned right then and there to think for myself. Don't listen to everybody who wants you to come in with them just because they have a problem and they want somebody to help. They'll mislead you every time.

And your wife will show up in Pueblo and find you're not there.

So I finished that year in Miami, played my first year of winter ball for Leon in Mexico, then went back to Pueblo the following year. By then, I had completed four years in the minors, but nothing I had been through could prepare me for my next stop—Fort Worth.

## Chapter 15: "Where do I stay?"

I was the Jackie Robinson of the Fort Worth Cats.

When the Dodgers sent me to Fort Worth in 1955, the Cats had never had a black player. Fort Worth was in the Class AA Texas league and was one of the Dodgers' key farm teams. You could go from Fort Worth to the big leagues. That's how good the Texas League was.

They didn't tell the press I was coming. They brought me in at night and sneaked me into the black hotel in town and put me in this little eight-by-ten room. The restrooms were down the hall. Outside the window, the hotel's neon sign flashed a one-word statement all night long: "CHEAP—CHEAP—CHEAP." It was like a bad movie.

That hotel was the first sign I was going to have a problem. In Pueblo and Hornell, I had had no problem getting a place to stay.

I knew Fort Worth was going to be different. I knew I was the first black on the team. But they didn't sit me down and talk to me like Branch Rickey sat down with Jackie Robinson. I was thinking of Robinson when they sent me there, and when they sneaked me in and put me in this hotel I felt like a fugitive.

They had a press conference the morning after I got in. The

Fort Worth media weren't very sophisticated. They just wrote what they thought of the situation rather than asking me what I thought. Nobody even interviewed me. They just wrote about the new colored boy with the Fort Worth Cats.

Not long after I arrived, I got on a city bus to go to the ballpark. I saw two white boys I recognized from spring training sitting behind the driver. I sat down next to them and started talking to them. "How you doing? You guys live up this way?" That kind of stuff.

All of a sudden, I heard someone say in a nasty voice, "Hey, boy!"

I looked up and noticed that the bus hadn't moved.

"In the back!" the driver snarled at me.

I turned around and there in the back of the bus was the sign: "COLORED ONLY." I wanted to climb under the floorboards. And the driver was snickering at me.

This was in 1955. In December, Rosa Parks would refuse to give up her seat to a white man on a city bus in Montgomery and start the civil rights movement that put an end to those signs. But that event was months away. I trudged to the back of the bus and sat down. All the black people back there looked at me in disbelief, as if they were thinking: "Where's this boy from? What's he trying to do, start some problems?"

Nobody talked to me. I sat there in silence, looking at my teammates up in the front talking and laughing. The two white players got off at the ballpark and rushed inside. I got off slowly, and by the time I got to the clubhouse, the whole team was in there laughing at me and making ugly, snide remarks which they called humor.

That stayed with me. My whole attitude and disposition started changing. I started feeling different—not good enough. I was 22, an age when my values and principles were being set. It was that year that the feeling that I was different set in permanently.

It affected my play, but the manager, Tommy Holmes, didn't care about my problems. He was rougher on me than any manager ever thought of being. I ended up sitting on the bench most of the year and hit .202—by far my worst year of professional ball.

The next payday after the bus incident, I went down to a used-car lot and bought a little used car—my first car—with a broken gas gauge.

The team had a DC-3 team plane, and when we went on road trips, they let us park our cars inside the fence at the ballpark. When we got back, I hitched a ride from the airport back to the park with the equipment man, who let me sit on top of the equipment in the back of the truck. Then I picked up my car and drove back to the hotel with the sign going "CHEAP-CHEAP-CHEAP" outside the window.

The next day was Sunday and we had an afternoon doubleheader, so I got up early. The car's battery was down and it barely started. Some guy told me to take it out in the country and drive around to recharge the battery.

So I drove around in the country charging the battery and the car ran out of gas. That's how I learned about the broken gas gauge. I walked two or three miles and saw a little beer joint on the side of the road—a real cowboy bar.

I had to get to a telephone and I didn't have any choice but to go in.

"C-c-can I use th-the ph-ph-phone?" I stuttered. I knew I was walking on thin ice. All these cowboys were staring at me.

I called the ballclub and told them what had happened. I said I would get a friend to come out and get me some gas.

I called a man who had befriended me. He was a prominent member of the black community who came to the games and offered me whatever help he could give. I told him as best I could where I was, and by the time he found me with the gas an hour and a half had gone by. I got to the ballpark in the third inning of the first game.

I dressed as fast as I could and tried to sneak onto the bench, but the guys saw me and started clapping and cheering sarcastically. I tried to explain to Tommy Holmes what happened, but he just chewed me out. He thought I was out screwing around.

That was the common wisdom. Any ballplayer, black or white, who blew a play or got in late or did anything out of the ordinary was out screwing around. They always assumed that there had to be women and whiskey involved. No matter what the truth was, that was how you got labeled.

And the people who were in charge had been accused of the

same things when they were playing. They just assumed that the players in their charge were doing the same things they had done.

Danny Ozark, who was our first baseman, was also the team's traveling secretary. We went to Houston on a road trip. The bus stopped in front of the white hotel and everybody got off, including me. Ozark told me to find myself a room.

I walked and walked with my bags through Houston trying to find a place to stay, looking for some black people on the street who could give me directions.

The same thing happened in Shreveport, except it was three o'clock in the morning when the bus pulled up in front of the white hotel.

"Where do I go, Danny?" I asked.

"Didn't they tell you?" Ozark replied.

"No," I said. "What am I supposed to do?"

"I don't know. Find a room somewhere." That was his advice.

The team had a black trainer named Alex who had been with the Cats for years. Alex called the one black taxi in town and we waited an hour and a half in the dark for it. Alex had the driver take us to a black family he knew, an older couple in the black neighborhood. They put me up on a little cot on a screened-in porch. In the morning, they said, "We didn't say we were going to feed you."

So I walked a couple of blocks to the local drugstore—if you can call it that—and had hot chocolate and Oreo cookies for breakfast.

Now I had to get to the ballpark. I started with plenty of time because I didn't want to be late again. But it took even longer during the day, and by the time the one black taxi picked me up and took me to the ballpark, everyone was dressed and Tommy Holmes chewed me out again. He had no idea where I had been. He didn't want to know, either.

So I sat on the bench a lot and had a lousy season. When it was over, I had to get back home to Washington, D.C., and I knew the old junker I had been driving wouldn't survive the trip. I had something like $200 to my name. I took $100 and put it with my old car to trade up to another junker—a Buick. It blew smoke out the back. The manifold had holes in it. It burned oil. And I was pretty proud of it. I nursed that thing all the way back to Washington, D.C. While I had it, that car taught me to recognize any problem on an automobile just from the sound of it. I knew the sound of a water pump going bad. I knew the sound of an ailing fuel pump. When it wouldn't start, I could tell the difference between a stuck choke, a bad solenoid and a weak battery cable.

I drove that car a lot, but I never drove it back to Fort Worth.

## Chapter 16: Switch-hitter

During most of these years, my wife continued to live with her mother and our children in her project in Washington, D.C. When I was home, I stayed with my folks. My wife had joined me for the first time during a season in 1953. That was the year she took a train to Pueblo while I was flying to Miami. She took another train to Miami and we had our own apartment. It was the first time we had actually lived together. When we came back to Washington, D.C., after the season, I went to play winter ball to make more money and she went back with her mother and the kids.

I skipped winter ball the next two seasons, when I played in Pueblo and Fort Worth. After I got back to Washington, D.C., after Fort Worth, I didn't read the papers. I wasn't aware of what Rosa Parks had done in Montgomery. I didn't learn about that until I got to spring training in 1956 in Vero Beach. There, I was back in the area where I was restricted as a black. It was frightening down there because the backlash from the Montgomery bus boycott Rosa Parks started was at a peak. People were angry all around the country. Those were troubled times and we didn't leave the Dodger camp much.

I was sent back to Pueblo in 1956 and responded by raising my average 100 points to .302. I led the league in stolen bases with 34, scored 110 runs, and had 33 doubles, eight triples and a professional-high 10 home runs. Ray Hathaway, another fine man, was the manager and he made me team captain. I was playing well, but Pee Wee Reese and Don Zimmer were ahead of me. I just didn't impress anybody.

In addition to being team captain, I took a job as clubhouse attendant to make more money. I was washing jock straps.

Gertrude stayed in Pueblo that winter while I played in Cordoba in the Mexican league.

In 1957, I moved up to the Seattle Rainiers. I took my family. We drove all the way there from Washington, D.C.—two adults, four kids, a dog, and all our belongings in a little two-door Plymouth. We slept on the side of the road. That winter, I played for Mayaguez in the Puerto Rican League.

In 1958 I was promoted to Spokane in Class AAA. This time, I decided we should move out there instead of making another round trip cross-country. The thing that sold us on Spokane was the kindness of a black family we stayed with in 1958.

Spokane is home for my kids. Their mother still lives there. It's where they went to school. It's a great place to raise children.

Spokane is also where I met Bobby Bragan, who got me to the big leagues.

Bragan had played for the Dodgers as a catcher and utility man during the Forties. He managed the Pittsburgh Pirates in 1956–57, and started the 1958 season as manager of the Cleveland Indians. After 67 games, with the Indians in fifth place, five games under .500, he was fired. The Dodgers then hired him in the middle of the season to manage a different Indians team—the Spokane Indians.

There are special times and special people in baseball. Bobby Bragan and 1958 were both for me. I was 25 years old and in my eighth year of minor league ball, still trying to make the big leagues.

Bobby Bragan took a liking to me. I was what we called in baseball his "little Bobo"—his favorite.

When Bragan took over I was a shortstop with a good glove, outstanding speed, and a great arm. But I was a right-handed hitter going through a 7½-year batting slump. My problem was that just about every time a right-handed pitcher threw me a curveball, I would spike somebody in the dugout—that's how badly I was bailing out.

One day before a game, we were horsing around during the last few minutes of batting practice. The game was called "base hits." You got two pitches, and if you got a clean hit on the second one, you got to swing again. Since we were fooling around, the last two times around I jumped in and swung from the left side of the plate.

When it was over, Bobby called me over and said, "Maury, did you ever consider being a switch-hitter?"

"No," I answered.

"Well, I was watching you," he said, "and I think you ought to give it a shot."

I said I'd try. Before the next five or six home games, Bobby came out early by himself and threw to me for a half hour while I practiced hitting left-handed. Bobby told me not to try to hit the same way left-handed that I hit right-handed. And he told me not to try to pull the ball. "Top that sucker," he said. "Hit it to deep shortstop."

I wasn't good enough to see the top half of the ball and hit it on purpose, but I held the bat high, and with the type of swing I had, I naturally stayed on top of the ball. As for hitting to the opposite side, I couldn't pull the ball anyhow.

The advantage of hitting the ball to the left side was that the extra step I gained by batting left-handed was just what I needed to beat the throw.

While I was learning all this, we were playing at home and I continued to hit from the right side in games. We finished the homestand and went on the road to play the Sacramento Solons.

"You're a switch-hitter now, kid," Bobby told me before the game.

A right-hander was pitching for Sacramento, and I went up left-handed for the first time in my career. I held the bat up on my shoulder. The ball came in. I took my first left-handed swing and made contact. The ball hit home plate, went 50 feet in the air and I was on first base with a single.

"Wow!" I'm thinking. "I got a base hit the first time up." I was so excited I stole second and third.

I got up again in the third inning, hit one to deep shortstop and beat it out by a step and a half. I stole second and third again. I was beginning to feel like a baseball player after 7½ years of taking that bat back to the rack after striking out.

Bobby had a way of making you not want to strike out, and you definitely did not want to strike out looking. He used to say that if you swung at the third strike and missed, you looked like a turd coming back to the dugout. But if you stood there and watched the third strike, you looked like a turd with a cherry on it.

So I got two or three hits that first game. The next day I got a couple more hits. I started coming out even earlier to practice switch-hitting and bunting.

The bizarre thing about the minor leagues is that when I went up and hit left-handed for the first time, nobody said anything. If I had done it in the major leagues, I would have heard about it from the opposition. "Spin him around!" someone would have yelled. But in the minor leagues, everyone is so aloof. It's not tightly knit like the majors. I don't even remember most of my own teammates on the Spokane Indians.

I remember the guys who went on to the Dodgers. Larry Sherry and Art Fowler came through Spokane. And Roger Craig, who's done pretty well for himself as a pitching coach and a manager, played with me there in 1959.

Roger Craig was a good guy then and he's a good guy today. He joined the Dodger system as a pitcher in 1950, a year before I did. He had pitched for the Dodgers from 1955–57, but early in the 1958 season he was sent down to St. Paul. In 1959, he started the year with me in Spokane, and finished it with me in the World Series in Los Angeles.

Roger and I used to talk baseball and plan things between his starts. We worked on pickoff plays, just the two of us. We worked out plays on the bus going from the hotel to the ballpark. We talked about them in the dugout and clubhouse. He helped himself be a winning pitcher with the things he could do other than pitching to the batter. I have great admiration for him.

Roger Craig was also the only pitcher I ever saw in baseball who could go into his stretch with the full intention of going home and then give you his best pickoff move.

You see, by the time a pitcher takes his stretch and comes to his set position, he knows whether he's going to go home or attempt a pickoff throw to first. If he's set to go home and sees that the runner on first has a big lead, he has to step off or just lob the ball over.

Pitchers simply cannot change their minds and give you their best pickoff move when they're set to throw home. I spent a lot of time studying pitchers and I learned that none of them can do it.

Except Roger Craig. He could be on the mound on Sept. 29 pitching against the team we're tied for first place with and have the bases loaded in the ninth inning, a 3–2 count on the hitter, and a one-run lead and be in the set position concentrating 100 percent on going to home plate. And he could look back at me and see me give him the pickoff sign and give me his best move.

He was the only pitcher I've ever seen who could do that.

That winter, I played for a team called Pastora in Maracaibo, Venezuela. It was the first time I played winter ball for anything other than the extra money. I went down to work on my switch-hitting. I also stole a few bases.

I stole 42 in a row, in fact. They started calling me El Fantasmo—the Phantom. The 42nd was a steal of second. I tried to steal third, too, and got thrown out for the first time all season. It was a close play, but they called me out. I didn't know it, but they had been betting on me in the stands, and when I got thrown out, they had to round up about five policemen with guns to escort me back to the hotel. Everybody who lost money on me wanted to kill me.

## Chapter 17: Laying it down

While he was teaching me to be a switch-hitter, Bobby Bragan also taught me how to be an expert bunter. It shows that you can teach something you aren't an expert at. Bobby wasn't a fast runner and I don't know if he ever tried to bunt for a base hit, but he could teach bunting.

Not everybody's going to hit .300. Not everybody's going to hit even .250. But anybody can be an expert bunter. It's like baserunning. Not everybody's going to steal 50 bases, but anybody can be an outstanding baserunner. By that, I mean that you can get the most out of what you have to work with.

Few do, of course. I would have thought that after 7½ years in the Dodger system—the best minor league system around—I would have learned to be a good bunter. It wasn't that way. I was spinning my wheels when Bobby Bragan showed me what I believe is the best way to bunt. I've taught that way to nine major league teams. I'm teaching it today.

In 1976, I trained the San Diego Padres. One of my pupils was Tito Fuentes. Tito worked on his bunting that year and stayed with it. The following year he was traded to Detroit and he applied it. He got something like 28 hits on bunts, more than he had got in five previous seasons put together. And his average went from .263 to a career-high .309.

Think about it. I had a .281 lifetime batting average and I got about 20 bunt base hits a year. Take away those 20 bunt hits and instead of hitting .281, I'm hitting maybe .260. I'm not stealing as many bases because I'm not getting on base as much. And maybe the Dodgers don't win as much.

The Dodgers moved to Los Angeles in 1958. They were a losing team and were in the process of replacing all the old stars from Brooklyn. I joined them in the middle of the 1959 season and was one of the players who helped establish the Dodgers in Los Angeles. We won the World Series in 1959, so I had a lot to do with helping to capture the fans. Being able to bunt was a big part of that.

I considered myself an expert bunter. I had six different bunts and every time the opposition defensed one bunt, they made themselves vulnerable to another.

I had a little soft bunt down the third base line I'd hit for a base hit. The third baseman started playing me several feet in front of the bag to take that bunt away. He also crowded the line, because if he played toward the pitcher and I bunted down the line, he had to run towards the line and throw back and across his body. You can throw a lot of balls away like that.

So when the third baseman was playing close, I'd go into my bunting position early and make him charge. Then, instead of softening the ball, I would hold the bat tight and push the ball past him towards shortstop. That worked well against right-handed pitchers, who fell off the mound toward first. I used that bunt to beat Marichal once. That's two bunts. But they could take it away by playing the shortstop in close.

If the pitcher held his position, I had a third bunt I pushed to the second baseman. To field it, he had to charge and throw back and across his body—a difficult throw. The defense for that bunt was moving the second baseman in.

A fourth bunt was a hard one to the first baseman. If I hit it a little off the line toward second, it would pull the second baseman in and also make the first baseman come in. Then all I had to do was beat the pitcher to the bag, and I could do that against everyone except guys like Marichal, Bob Gibson and Jim Bunning, who were falling off towards first.

When they took away those four, I practiced until I could drop a little soft bunt about five feet down the first base line, too far for the catcher to get to, and too close for the pitcher or first baseman to be able to make a play. That's five bunts.

But sometimes I'd look out there and see the third baseman coming down my throat. The shortstop and second baseman are playing in on a line between first and second bases. The first baseman is in as far as the third baseman. I'd look at that and say, "Jeezus! These guys are really working on me, aren't they? I really got them sweating. They're doing their homework."

And I'd bunt anyway and get on base. I'd put a little soft bunt right in the middle of the diamond just about where the cutout of the dirt is around the plate. The only person who can get that is the catcher, and he has to be on his toes, coming forward with the pitch. Most catchers like to sit back on their haunches and can't make that play. And if one did bolt forward, I could pull the bat back to swing, which would make him run into the bat and give me first base on catcher's interference. I did that once against the Giants. It was the incident that set the stage for the famous fight when Marichal hit Roseboro over the head with a bat.

More on that later. The point is anybody can learn to bunt by working at it, but most people don't. So be it.

I refuse to get upset with modern ballplayers who can't bunt or run the bases. They said the same things when I was playing.

So it doesn't drive me nuts to go to a game and see players who can't execute the fundamentals. There were only a handful of players when I played who could do the little things like bunting properly. The game hasn't really changed that way. Managers get mad because someone didn't sacrifice a man over, but very few managers insist that their players learn to bunt. Nobody wants to make waves. And how are you going to tell a $2-million player with a no-cut, no-trade contract he has to learn how to bunt. I tried that when I managed Seattle and I was gone in three weeks.

They don't have a column in the papers to tell who's leading the league in sacrifice bunts. You don't see guys demand that their salaries be doubled because they lead the league in sacrifice bunts. There's no glory for bunters. All bunting does is win baseball games. And nobody appreciates it—other than the manager, a really good fan, your teammates, and, once it's done, the guy who did it.

Learning to bunt takes a lot of time. The manager ends up assuming that some guys can do it and others can't and he leaves it at that. You have to have time for infield practice. You have to have time for batting practice, the great priority. You have time for all that other stuff, but you don't have time for bunting.

My last year in the big leagues was 1972. I had been major league shortstop of the year in 1971, but in 1972, I was 39 years old and the Dodgers decided they wanted to start rebuilding so they put Bill Russell at shortstop and me on the bench.

Every now and then, though, Walter Alston would call on me to bunt. By the time the season was half over, I was out of shape from not playing and I couldn't hit a lick—not even in batting practice. But I could still bunt.

I remember one game when we were playing the Phillies and Steve Carlton was just shoving the bats up our asses. Somehow, we got a man on first base late in the game and Walter Alston called me off the bench to bunt. I laid it right out in front of home plate and our runner got to second easily. I went back to the bench and sat down for another month.

As I went to the dugout, though, I got an ovation in Dodger Stadium. The fans weren't cheering because they were thinking: "Here's somebody who can bunt!" It was because we couldn't do anything against this guy and now somebody walks and somebody else bunted the ball and all of a sudden we had something going. I came back with the greatest satisfaction and feeling of achievement simply because I had bunted the ball.

If I were sitting on the beach today and the Dodgers called me to come to the park and lay down a bunt, I think I could do it.

## Chapter 18: "On your marks . . ."

In the spring of 1959, the Dodgers sold me on an option basis to the Detroit Tigers. The Tigers paid the Dodgers $10,000 to bring me to Tigertown for a look-see in spring training. If they liked what they saw, they could buy my contract outright for another $25,000. If they didn't want to keep me, the Dodgers got me back and kept the $10,000.

Every spring, the Topps bubblegum people came through the camps to sign contracts with every player on each club's 40-man roster and take their pictures for the new crop of bubblegum cards. They also signed everybody on the minor league affiliates who they thought had a shot at the big leagues. They gave the players something like $5 for the rights to their picture for that year.

The Topps man came to Tigertown and was signing everyone on the roster. When he came to me, he asked someone with the team, "That guy over there—Wills? Is he gonna make it?" And the guy he asked said, "Naw. No way."

So they passed me up. That same year I was in the World Series but I wasn't on a Topps card. The next year, Fleer bubblegum came around trying to break into the card market and I signed with them. Fleer didn't care if I signed with Topps, but Topps wanted exclusive rights, so I didn't appear on their cards. Not until 1967, in fact, when I was with Pittsburgh and had played in four World Series did I get on a Topps card.

I had a great spring with the Tigers. I played mostly in "B" games—that's like the second team—but I was 11-for-23 and stole eight straight bases. One of the Tigers' coaches really liked me and wanted the club to keep me. But the Tigers had traded for Rocky Bridges that year. They got him from Washington, where he had hit .263 in 1958. Both of us were in camp. On the last day before the Tigers broke camp, they decided to keep Bridges and returned me to the Dodgers.

Damn. I had felt sure I was going to make it to the big leagues, but now I was back with the Dodgers and headed for another year in Spokane.

But I didn't feel despondent. Being in spring training with the Tigers and having a chance to make the big leagues was the greatest experience I had had in my career. I had been in a major league camp. So I didn't despair over not making the Tigers. If my career had ended right there, I'd have said it was a success.

Besides, going back to Spokane, where my home and Bobby Bragan were, wasn't all bad.

I went back to Dodgertown, and got there the day after the Tigers let me go. I arrived just in time for a big race the Dodgers were having to close out training camp.

The Dodgers had a track that they used to time their people in the 60-yard dash. They used—and still use—60 yards because that's the distance from home to second, first to third, and second to home—the critical distances in baserunning.

We had a guy in camp that year named Earl Robinson who everybody thought was going to be the next Jackie Robinson. Earl was from Berkeley, Calif. He looked like Jackie Robinson. He, Willie Davis and Tommy Davis were in the race. Tommy Davis went to Boys High in Brooklyn and he and Willie ran track in school. Willie was probably the fastest man in baseball at the time.

Nobody knew me at all. I was an obscure journeyman minor leaguer. They didn't know how good a spring I had with Detroit. They just knew I was back. But I had stolen a lot of bases in the minors and was supposed to be fast, so they put me in the race, too.

Thousands of dollars were going on this race. Don Zimmer, who was the Dodgers starting shortstop, Johnny Podres, and Buzzy Bavasi, the team's general manager, loved to go to the racetracks and loved to bet. So everybody was getting their money down. Most of them liked Earl Robinson. A lot of them liked Willie Davis. A few picked Tommy, and maybe one picked me. Maybe that was myself.

Tommy and Willie and Earl were over there on the side making a big show of loosening up and stretching. These guys had all run in school and had had formal training in sprinting. I just ran on the playground.

So they were all strutting and shaking their legs out and looking cute and everybody was going, "Ooh. Give me $500 more on Tommy Davis." Or Willie. Or Earl.

I had loosened up beforehand, and, while they were doing their thing for the crowd, I was over with John Curry. He was the scout who came to my house with Rex Bowen when I signed with the Dodgers nine years earlier. Curry was also the starter for the race.

"Mr. Curry," I said as if I didn't want to bother him. "How are you going to start us?"

"Take your marks. Set. Go!" he said in a quick cadence.

"Would you do that again for me?" I asked as sweetly and naively as I could.

"Sure, Maury. Take your marks. Set. Go!" The "Go!" came right after "Set," just the way he said it the first time.

"Just like that?" I asked. "You're not going to change it?"

"No, no. That's just the way I'm going to do it," he assured me.

"Thank you, Mr. Curry," I said politely and walked away. Ten seconds later, I was back.

"Will you do it for me one more time?" I was so sweet and innocent he couldn't say no.

"Okay, Maury. It's going to be just like this . . ."

"Just the way you're going to do it. Please, sir . . ."

"Just the way I'm going to do it," he promised. "Take your marks. Set. Go!" The cadence was exactly as before.

"You're not going to change it?"

"No."

"Thank you, Mr. Curry. Sir."

I went to get ready for the start. You would have thought it was the Olympics. There were no starting blocks, but Willie, Tommy, and Earl were digging holes in the track and getting down as if they were Jesse Owens in the Berlin Olympics. And then they were down, and then they were humping up like real sprinters. While they were doing that, I was standing there in my baseball stance as if I were getting ready to steal second. I figured that's the thing that I'd been practicing for eight years. I had no experience with track, so why should I get down like a track man?

John got us ready, and somebody called time out. He had to kick a little more. Then they all had to get up and go around some more, shaking out the kinks. And all around everybody was getting another hundred down on Tommy and five hundred on Willie and a couple hundred on Earl.

I'm just standing there. So while I'm waiting, I went to John. "Mr. Curry?" I asked as if I'm the dumbest guy in the world. "Could you do it one more time?"

"Take your marks. Set. Go!" he repeated. The cadence was identical to what he had said before.

Finally we got in our stances.

"Take your marks," John ordered and everybody settled in.

"Set," he ordered, and the three of them hunched up.

WHAM! They went on "o." I went on "G." They were just coming out of their track stances and I was gone. And once I got a smidgeon in front of them on the takeoff, they just pushed me. They pushed me into running as fast as I ever ran. I think I did a 6.1. I could hear Willie Davis coming right behind me, panting like a freight train. You could have thrown a blanket over all four of us at the finish line, but I was right there. At the tape, Willie put his chest out like a real track man, which I knew nothing about. But I beat him. It was amazing how the times were all different on the stopwatches, yet if you had taken a picture of the finish, it looked as if we all got there at the same time. But it was Wills, Willie Davis, Earl Robinson and Tommy Davis.

All the guys who had their money on Earl Robinson started hollering that it was a false start and we should run the race over again. You know how it is when you have money bet and it hasn't left your pocket yet. You haven't given it up.

Buzzy Bavasi and Don Zimmer were on the losing end, too, so they made us run it again. I had given everything I had. These guys were 100-yard dash men. They didn't get started until they got to 60 yards. So they had a lot left and I had used all of mine.

*"What!?"* I said in disbelief. But who was I to argue? What was I going to say? I said, "Okay, if I have to."

I beat them again. Yes, I did.

I don't know who collected, but I never lost a race.

When I played in the minor leagues, everywhere I played, they had some burning speedster and they always had a pregame race to draw the track fans to the ballpark. Wills against so-and-so. I beat every one of them. I beat them on the start, because there was no way I could outrun these guys.

In the big leagues, I challenged Lou Brock many times, but he didn't want to race me. I even went to the public relations director for the Dodgers, Red Patterson, and told him to set it up. We could have filled the park up with people coming to see that. But Lou didn't want to race.

Winning that race in camp in 1959 didn't make me a star, though. In fact, I think my stock went down because I beat those guys who were prospects. You don't want some obscure guy to come out of nowhere and beat the champion.

I never liked seeing a championship team upset in the postseason by some team that's not even half as good but just happened to put it together on a day when the championship team didn't have it. The champion is supposed to win.

I've always been a firm believer in heroes and role models.

## Chapter 19: "This is the big leagues, kid"

About 40 games into the 1959 season, Bobby Bragan told me there was a rumor that the Dodgers were looking for a shortstop. Don Zimmer, who had started the season, had broken his toe, and they couldn't find a replacement. Bobby told me he recommended me and the Dodgers might be calling.

"Huh?" I said. "Me?"

Goddam. What a feeling. I couldn't believe it. I'd spent 8½ years in the minor leagues. Except for Detroit, I'd never been in a major league camp. And they might be calling me!

A week went by. I thought, "Shucks, that must be a rumor." Today, I might think they were playing with my head, but we weren't even sophisticated enough to know if somebody was manipulating us. Things were too tough. Everybody was just trying to get by.

After hearing the rumor, we went to Phoenix. Bragan told me to keep working hard. I played the first game in Phoenix and picked up the paper the next day to read that Ty Cobb had been sitting in the stands. I stole a base and Cobb said, "I like the way that kid slides."

Ty Cobb said that about me? Goddam! I didn't know him at all. I just knew who he was. After 8½ years in the minors I had time to be out of the projects and learn about all the great players. That was really something to have him say that.

We had another game that day and Bragan told me in the clubhouse that the Dodgers had called me up. I was leaving tomorrow.

I thought it was a joke. But it was true. I was to join the Dodgers in Milwaukee.

After the game, I took my glove, spikes and underwear and actually put them in a cardboard box and tied the box up with baling twine. I put it under my arm and carried it all the way to County Stadium in Milwaukee. I went there straight from the airport. The Dodgers were there when I arrived.

Joe Pignatano, the backup catcher, looked at me and said, "What are you doing, kid, bringing your lunch?"

I looked around for my name on the locker. I'm looking at all the names—Gil Hodges. Duke Snider. Pee Wee Reese. All those guys. And over there was Maurice Wills. I went over to the locker, put my little cardboard box down and took my clothes off. They brought a uniform for me. It was number 30.

I had never had a favorite number. I never took myself that seriously in the minor leagues to want the same number. But I kept number 30 throughout my career. When I was traded to Pittsburgh, there was a ballplayer by the name of Andre Rodgers who had number 30. He voluntarily gave up that number before I got there. It was in my locker. Nobody even had to ask him for it.

Walter Alston, the manager, came over and asked me if I was ready.

"Yes, sir."

"You want to play tonight?"

"Yes, sir!"

"Maybe you shouldn't play tonight," he said.

"That's all right," I said. "I'm ready. I'd like to play."

"Sit with me and just take a look first. See what's going on," Alston said.

That's what I did. I sat on the bench next to the skipper, watching everything going on. He kept his eye on me and the next day I was in there, playing short and batting eighth.

After the first inning, I came off the field. I hadn't had a ground ball. "You all right?" Alston said.

"Yes, sir," I answered. "It was fun."

The next inning, again, I didn't get a ball.

"You all right?"

"Yes, sir!"

The next inning, they hit a ball to me. Jeezus Christ! I picked it up and fired it down the right field line. Players were running all over the place. Damn. I went 0-for-3 or something. Finally he took me out.

I think I played two games in Milwaukee. We went to Philadelphia and by then I was 0-for-11. We went back to Los Angeles and Pee Wee, who had retired after the 1958 season and was a coach, said, "Nah. He's not going to make it. He won't make it."

He wasn't saying that to me, but I overheard it. For some reason, I had the presence to be offended. The great Pee Wee Reese, making a statement like that—and he was fully qualified to make it—and I was offended.

Things like that made me work harder. They didn't dampen my spirits. But they hurt.

I can walk a mile with blisters, stand in the rain all day or do whatever it takes. Chop wood. Cut lawns. But to hear somebody criticize me is a pain that really goes down deep and stays there. I remembered what Pee Wee said my whole career. I never held it against him, but whenever I saw him—it was always when he was with the NBC game of the week or at old-timers games—he would often shake my hand. That was nice. I felt the same towards him, but it always rang in my ear: *"Aw, he won't make it."*

I guess out of that came my resolve never to say that somebody's either going to make it or not going to make it. Even if the guy looks like a sure Hall of Famer, I'm not going to say he'll make it. If he looks as if he has two left feet, I'm not going to say he's not going to make it. I know how it felt to be evaluated that way.

A lot of people have written that I got cheated out of all those years I spent in the minor leagues and that I should have come up sooner. But when I got to the big leagues, I realized I had no business being there until I got there. It's like in life, you don't realize how dumb you are until you start learning.

I was scared, but in the sense of being in these big cities with these tall buildings. I was scared of getting lost and not being able to get back to the hotel. I was scared of missing the team bus.

Nobody helped me except John Roseboro, my roommate. I wasn't that impressive on the field and nobody thought I was going to stay. I was just there for a cup of coffee.

Roseboro broke me in to the big leagues. The first day, in Milwaukee, he called room service.

"They bring food up to us?" I said. This was new to me.

He ordered the whole menu. All this food. "You gonna order?" he said.

"I don't know how," I said. "Will you order for me?"

"Okay," Roseboro said. Then he spoke into the phone: "Make it two."

After a while, this guy came up with three tables of food. At the time, the Dodgers didn't give us meal money. We just signed for whatever we wanted. They didn't worry about us spending too much on food, because that was to keep us healthy. If they didn't give us meal money, we couldn't drink it instead of eating.

So the guy rolled in the three tables of food. He pulled back the table cloth, and under the table were more trays. He was taking out these containers forever.

"Are we going to eat all this?" I asked Roseboro.

"Yeah," he said.

I grabbed a dollar. There had to be $60 worth of food there. And I'm going to give the waiter a dollar.

"Put that away," Roseboro said. "This is the big leagues, kid." He put the tip on the check. "You got to give these guys a good tip," he advised me, "or we'll never get served."

After the last game in Milwaukee, we were leaving for Philadelphia. I packed my bags and picked them up.

"What are you doing?" Roseboro wanted to know.

"I'm going to the lobby," I said. "Aren't we going to leave now?"

"You can't carry that bag," he said. "Get on the phone and call the bellboy."

"Why can't I carry it?"

"This is the big leagues, kid."

So this older guy came up and got the bags. I was walking right beside him and this poor man was struggling with our two bags. When he got downstairs, I whipped out a dollar.

"It's a dollar each bag," Roseboro said, stopping me. And he gave the guy two dollars.

We took the Dodger plane to Philadelphia, and when we got to the hotel, the bags had beaten us in from the airport and were stacked in the lobby. I got my key from the desk and went over to the bags, looked them over, and found mine.

"What are you doing?" Roseboro said.

"I'm getting my bag."

"Put the bag down," Roseboro ordered. "You're in the big leagues, kid. Let the bellboy bring it up."

"I'm going upstairs," I protested. "I want to take my stuff out of the bag."

"You can't touch your bag," Roseboro said sternly.

So here's another poor guy, and Roseboro told him to bring both our bags up. He struggled with them and I wanted to help. Roseboro growled at me: "You can't do that. Don't touch those bags."

When we got to the room, I asked Roseboro, "How much do I give the man?"

"I told you, son. It's a dollar each."

I gave the man two dollars.

So John Roseboro broke me in right.

After the series in Philadelphia, we flew home and got to Los Angeles at about one in the morning. All the guys' wives were there, loading them into their cars with the kids and everything and pulling out.

I was standing on the curb with my bags. Roseboro was with his wife and ready to drive off when he came around, pulled up to the curb and said, "What are you doing?"

"I don't know," I answered honestly. "Nobody said anything. Is there someplace I can go?"

"Get in the car," he said.

He took me home with him and put me up for the night. In the

morning, he fed me breakfast. As I was eating, he said, "Okay, you're on your own now, kid."

"Wait! Wait!" I said. "If I had a car . . . oh, hell."

Roseboro made a phone call to the Dodgers. He took me downtown and helped me rent a car. Then he took me to the Adams Hotel, where the black players stayed, on Western and Adams Boulevard. I stayed one night. They had a bar downstairs. It was jumping. Nancy Wilson was performing there.

Damn! I was way over my head. I got out of that hotel and asked the Dodgers where they put the players who just came up. They said the Mayflower, a dive in downtown Los Angeles. So I went there.

To this day, I'm grateful to John Roseboro for all he did for me. I still consider him and Sandy Koufax my best friends on the Dodgers.

A few years back, John wrote a book. It came out around Old-Timers Day. John broke the story about me and Doris Day in his book. He also told about me playing the banjo in our hotel rooms and how he stopped rooming with me because I was getting so popular and had all these girls calling and he couldn't stand it. When I saw John at the old-timers game, I kind of got the feeling he was expecting some ill feeling on my part. But I felt no such thing. I'll never forget what John Roseboro did for me when I came up. He can say anything about me. It's all right with me. To this day I love him.

The Dodgers had their own airplane, a Convair, and everyone had their own seat on it. I didn't know anything about that. The next trip we took, I got on the plane and saw a seat empty in the front next to Pee Wee Reese. It was Duke Snider's seat, but I didn't know anything about that. I sat in it. Duke got on, looked hard at me and stalked off to the back of the plane. I didn't know what was going on.

Pee Wee explained to me in a nice way what I had done. I got up and went back and begged Duke to take his seat. But he didn't want anything to do with it. I sat up there for that trip, but I never sat there again on that plane. I didn't care if it was the only seat left.

I took to sitting in the jump seat in the cockpit with the crew. I never got an assigned seat, and I was too embarrassed to ask for

one. When the Dodgers got rid of the Convair and got a new plane, I finally got a seat.

Duke Snider wouldn't say shit if he had a mouthful. He was very, very aloof. I don't know what he was like in his younger years, but he never talked much while we were on the team together. He was at the end of his career as a regular in 1959, although he did stay with the team through the 1962 season. He ended up playing one year each with the Mets and the Giants. He was bitter at the end. It was the kind of bitterness that stays with you for a lifetime. It's resentment and it's a killer. I know.

I started so badly with the Dodgers I knew I was going back to the minor leagues. They were taking me out for a pinch hitter every game in the sixth or seventh inning.

I was scared. Other than Roseboro, I didn't have any friends. It wasn't as if I'd been to spring training or had been on the 40-man roster. I was an outcast—a journeyman minor leaguer.

One day that year Jim Gilliam invited me to go golfing with him. I had just started learning to play a year or two before. I had moved from the hotel and lived by the golf course and had to go all the way into Los Angeles to pick Jim up. It took me about 35 minutes to drive there and I got to his house at 6:30 in the morning. This was after a night game. I knocked at the door and he opened the little peephole in the door. "I'm not going," he said, and closed the peephole.

What was I going to do? I guess I felt good just getting that close to playing golf with Jim Gilliam. But that was ridiculous.

The press was picking on me. One writer ripped me to pieces. They were picking on Buzzy Bavasi, the general manager, who was saying that we had a chance at the pennant this year. We just needed one more man. And, Buzzy had said, Maury Wills was just the guy to put us over the top.

"Maury Who?" I heard this driving home from the game one night on a talk show. They were ripping me apart. It was brutal. "This is the savior? This is the guy who's going to win the pennant for the Dodgers this year? He can't hit his way out of a paper bag. He can't do this. He can't do that."

They ran down my record: a journeyman minor leaguer, years and years of doing nothing. And now I'm going to be a big guy for the Dodgers.

To make it worse, I was taking Don Zimmer's job. Zimmer had a broken toe. He was one of the original Dodgers from Brooklyn. He was friends with Gil Hodges, Carl Furillo, Clem Labine and he sat with them looking at me intimidatingly. I wasn't even a Los Angeles Dodger in their eyes. I was just a minor leaguer who came up.

One day in St. Louis, I was waiting to get on the elevator in the hotel. The elevator was crowded, but there was room for me to get on. I started in and there was Don Zimmer with a couple of the old Dodgers. He said something disparaging about me loud enough for me to hear. He didn't give a damn if I heard it. Who was I?

When I heard it, I stepped off the elevator and waited for another one. I've never forgotten that.

I thought I was pretty strong on fundamentals after 8½ years in the Dodger organization. It was, after all, an organization known for teaching. But I had only a foundation, and a weak one at that. I found I had to learn how to play the game all over again.

Charlie Neal was our second baseman. He used to stay on me something criminal. He and Jim Gilliam would yell at me in front of the sportswriters and the other players about how I wouldn't give them the proper feed on the double play.

I was giving them the ball where they taught me to in the minors. Where I fed the second baseman the ball—in front of the base, on the base, or behind the base—was supposed to depend on where the ball was hit. I was doing that. I thought everything was all right.

But one day Neal yelled at me: "Give me the goddam ball right over the bag. Give me some good throws."

"What do you mean, give you some good throws?" I didn't know what he meant. "Isn't everything all right?"

"Hell, no! The ball's all over the place!" he barked.

"But I'm doing it the way they taught me and you're making the pivot."

"We don't play that way in the big leagues," Neal informed me. "This guy from first base is trying to take me into the outfield. I want the ball right over the base."

"All the time?" I said.

"All the time!" he insisted. "Let me decide how I want to make the pivot. I got enough to do getting out of the guy's way without worrying about where you're going to throw the ball."

He chewed my ass out, loud-talking me in front of the press, the manager and the coaches. He told everybody he wasn't going to play with me at shortstop if I didn't throw it over the bag.

I had to go out and practice, practice and practice until I could take that ball blindfolded and throw it right over the bag.

In the minors, they had taught me from the book. They're still teaching it that way today. But the second baseman wants the ball right over the bag. Then he can make the pivot any way he wants to.

As for myself, coming across the bag to make the relay on the double play, I wanted the ball right over the bag, too.

Once I got the ball, I learned after a while that the way they teach you to throw in the minor leagues doesn't always work, either. I got that lesson in the spring of 1960, my first full year, when we wrapped up spring training by going up to Yankee Stadium and playing an exhibition against the Yankees.

Bob Cerv, a six-foot, 200-pounder, was on first base and somebody hit a ground ball to second. Charlie Neal gave me the ball on the double play. I came across the bag, looked up, and saw nothing but muscle and spikes and Yankee uniform right in my face. I mean Cerv was airborne and his spikes were coming right at my shoulders. I dropped the ball and ran into right field and everyone laughed at me.

"What in the hell is this!" I asked. "What's this guy doing? He's trying to kill me!"

"Yeah," Neal laughed. "You're playing in the big leagues, kid."

"What are you talking about?"

"You got to learn to throw down here," Neal told me. I was throwing overhand. He meant I should come sidearm, or even submarine on my relay throw.

So I learned to throw from down under. I hit Orlando Cepeda right between the eyes and knocked his helmet into the stands throwing that way. Another time, I broke Cepeda's wrist with a relay. But they stopped coming in high on me when I got the ball before they got to the bag. And if they got there before the ball, I was gone. That's when I learned not to be on the bag when you catch the ball on a double play—the so-called phantom tag. Guys coming in like Cerv is why they do that.

My teammates were on me all the time about everything. I guess I dressed like a minor leaguer because those were the only clothes I had. I had slacks from J.C. Penney's, shirts and socks from Woolworth's, and Thom McCann shoes. I thought I looked pretty good, but they got on me about my clothes, too.

What could I do? I was just a rookie. But I was a very proud rookie and a little volatile—okay, a lot volatile—and a little sore inside because I just got to the big leagues. I had worked my butt off and here I was catching hell not only about my not playing the game well enough for them, but also for the way I dressed.

It got so bad, I asked Walter Alston to send me back to the minors.

"No," he said, "just hang in there, kid."

I went to Pete Reiser, who had been a heck of a player and was now a coach. I told Pete I was going back to the minors if I didn't do something. It was going so bad. Pete started going out with me early to practice.

That was my way of answering all the snide remarks—to go out and practice and practice some more. I went down on the floor of the Los Angeles Coliseum with Pete Reiser when it was over 100 degrees and practiced for two hours before the other guys got there. It made me so mad that I practiced until I surpassed them all in salary, popularity, fame and everything. Many times during my career I was quoted as saying that I worked hard because I had had a taste of what major league baseball was all about and I didn't want to go back to the minors. But the real reason was that those guys were on my ass so much I wanted to show them I could play and I could be better than they were.

They did me a favor in a dubious way. I don't know if I would have been so driven if they hadn't done that to me.

I owe a lot to Pete Reiser. He stayed on me and made me keep going when it was so hot in the Coliseum I could barely breathe. He threw balls to me to hit and hit balls for me to field. He kept me from becoming complacent. A year or two later, we were in Cincinnati and I got three or four hits in a game. That night I went downtown and bought a pipe. I got the man in the pipe shop to mix me one of those sweet aromas. I remembered as a kid smelling pipe tobacco like that and it smelled so good I wanted to smoke a pipe, too. I got on the team bus in front of the hotel in Cincinnati the next day puffing away with my pipe in the side of my mouth. I was looking the part and playing the part.

We got to the ballpark and I went to my locker and changed into my uniform still puffing away on that pipe. Oh, that was cool!

Pete Reiser saw me. Without saying a word, he came over, ripped the pipe out of my mouth, walked to the other side of the clubhouse and—WHAM!—slammed that pipe into the trash can. Then he went back to his locker.

I sat there looking at him. I didn't say a word. On the bus back to the hotel after the game, I sat down with Pete and asked him, "Pete, why did you do that to my pipe?"

"A pipe is a sign of a contented man," Pete told me. "I don't ever want you to be contented."

I never smoked a pipe again.

## Chapter 20: Back to the barracks

We won the 1959 pennant by two games over the Giants and went on to beat the White Sox four games to two in the World Series. I started every game, got five hits, stole a base, and had one more run and one fewer error than Luis Aparicio, Chicago's all-star shortstop.

I had finally got going in late August when I stopped platooning with Don Zimmer and became the starting shortstop and started getting three and four hits a game. We went to Seals Stadium late in the year to play the Giants with the pennant on the line. I got 11 hits in the three-game series and we wrapped up the championship. The Giants series was played during San Francisco's Pacific Festival week. The most valuable player of the three games was supposed to win a trip to Japan, and I won it. That was a big thrill for me. I never took the trip, though. I'd been in the minors 8½ years and all of a sudden I'm going to take a trip to Japan? I didn't even know where Japan was.

In the World Series, I started to get a lot of publicity. Besides my hitting, I made some defensive plays that don't show in the boxscore. One big one was in the second game when I threw out Sherm Lollar, the White Sox catcher, trying to score from first on a long double. Ironically, Charlie Dressen, a Dodger coach, had worked with me on that play just before the game.

On that play, it was my job to go out for the relay from the left fielder, who was Wally Moon. The second baseman backs me up and the first baseman trails the runner. In the minors, we were taught to rely on the man behind us to tell us where to throw. Charlie told me you can't do that in the big leagues because the crowds make too much noise. He told me you have to take a peek at the runner while the left fielder is making his throw. The runner's body motion tells you if he's going home or holding at third.

I did exactly that. While Wally Moon was throwing, I peeked at Lollar and saw him approaching third at full speed and the third base coach waving him around. I looked back at Wally to pick up the ball and I didn't have to rely on Charlie Neal to tell me where to throw. I couldn't have heard him anyhow. I just got the ball and in one motion turned and fired home to John Roseboro. Lollar was out by 10 feet. That play helped turn that game and the Series around.

The winner's share from the Series came to $11,000. That was about twice what I was making and more money than I had ever seen at one time in my whole life. I figured not only would I have some money in the bank for a change, I could buy some good clothes and get everybody off my back about the way I dressed.

When money's involved, good news sure does travel fast. Every creditor in the world came out of the woodwork to collect on bills I had left all over the country when I was in the minor leagues. One guy even came with a marshal to collect on a bill for $400 that I had forgotten about from years ago. They threatened me, saying they were going to take my car.

It wasn't until after the 1962 season when I broke the stolen base record and became a star that I was able to buy some nice clothes. Heck, after that, every men's store in town wanted to give me clothes.

I had become the starting shortstop in late August or early September and had had a good Series. Now, my dream was to go to spring training and stay in the major league barracks instead of in the minor league quarters, where I had spent my entire professional career.

I went to Florida in the spring of 1960 feeling good. And they put me back in the minor league barracks.

I cried. I asked them why. They told me to change clothes in the minor league clubhouse then come over and join the team in the major league clubhouse for practice.

They brought in five guys I had to beat out for the starting shortstop job. The one who intimidated me the most was Charley Smith, who was a very promising shortstop. He played most of the games in spring training and I was sure he was their guy. But they were just letting him play his way off the team. They ended up trading him after the season to Philadelphia, and, in 1964, Charley Smith became one of the never-ending stream of New York Mets third basemen.

That 1960 season, I stole 50 bases for a team record, and hit .295, which was better than Hank Aaron that year. I thought I was established.

The following spring, 1961, I got into the major league barracks at last, but they brought in four or five new guys to compete for the shortstop job. I wasn't sure I had the job until a couple days before we broke camp.

I led the league in steals again in 1961. When I got to spring training in 1962, it was the same thing again. I had to beat out another bunch of challengers. Not until I stole 104 bases did I go to spring training knowing I had the job and could take my time getting in shape.

It took that long to prove that speed and base-stealing and defense were important and that what I brought to the club was worth more than raw power. They had to ask whether those qualities were enough to offset somebody who might be able to pop 25–30 home runs but couldn't do the other things.

That's the reason I spent so many years in the minor leagues. I didn't fit into the long-ball style of play. They weren't even scouting speed at that time. They were looking for big guys who hit the long ball. I do believe that after I stole 104 bases, they started scouting for speed.

Willie Davis had the speed. During his time, he was the fastest player in baseball. If he had wanted to incorporate base-stealing into his game, he could have stolen 200 a year. And when I stole 104, he did finish second in the league—with 32 steals.

## Chapter 21: Martin Luther King

When I first joined the Dodgers from Spokane in 1959, I lived in the team hotel downtown. After the games, I didn't know where to go, so somebody on the team took me one night to a black nightclub on Crenshaw Boulevard called the Sportsman's Lounge. Athletes from all the sports went there, including a lot of the veterans from visiting teams. Charlie Neal and Jim Gilliam stopped there regularly.

The owner of the place took a liking to me. After a while, he found out I was staying at the hotel. He had a buddy who was a baker on a ship. The nightclub owner introduced me to him. It turned out that the baker would be gone for a month to six weeks at a time on voyages and while he was gone his house was empty. He said he'd love to have somebody stay there while he was gone, so I moved in.

Somebody else I met took me to the Mt. Sinai Memorial Baptist Church one Sunday. The pastor of the church was the Rev. H.B. Charles, a prominent black Baptist. Everybody was excited about having Maury Wills, the Dodger rookie, come to their church and I ended up getting introduced to the Rev. Charles.

The reverend asked me where I was staying and how I was getting on. I told him how I came to stay with the baker. Within a week, the Rev. Charles sent somebody over to the baker's house with a car to pick me up and get my belongings. He said he didn't think I should be staying there by myself, so he took me into his home. Living with the reverend cut down on my night life and kept me out of trouble. It also kept me from being lonely. I ended up living with the Rev. Charles during the season for five years—until my wife threw me out of the house in Spokane in the spring of 1965. Then I got an apartment.

It was through the Rev. Charles that I met Dr. Martin Luther King Jr. Dr. King was already well known at that time. He had come to prominence during the Montgomery, Ala., bus boycott. Ralph Abernathy traveled with Dr. King.

You could feel the aura throughout the house when Dr. King was there. Everyone was quiet and didn't move around much. Family members tended to stay in their rooms and show him respect. The Rev. Charles would bring me into the kitchen to talk to Dr. King.

I knew I was sitting with a great man. He didn't talk much and there was always a man with him. I never saw him alone. It was almost as if he was kind of staying apart from the public. I don't want to say he was hiding, but it was almost as if there was some fear in him even then.

It didn't seem he was a baseball fan. It seemed he was driven and single-minded. He didn't seem to have time for sports.

The Watts race riots had taken place Aug. 11–16, 1965. Thirty-four people were killed, more than 1,000 were injured, and more than 4,000 arrested. The rioters did $175 million worth of damage. But, somehow, things didn't get bitter in other areas of Los Angeles. The Watts riots were confined to Watts. The Rev. Charles didn't live in that area. His house was in a section of town called View Park. It was a racially mixed middle-class section on its way to becoming predominantly black.

The Watts riots disrupted the city, but the ballgames went on as usual. Reporters didn't talk to the black players about it. Today, there's more sophistication among the media and the players. Back then, not one reporter asked me what I thought of the riots.

My only connection with the riots was through a business partner I had in a dry-cleaning business. My partner was Jewish and he was very afraid. In Watts, the people were burning all the Jewish establishments. They thought they were being taken advantage of and they took it out on the Jewish merchants. When they got done burning just about everything in Watts, they started moving out towards other areas. My partner, being Jewish, became concerned that they might come to his shop. So I sat outside the establishment so people would know I was involved in the business and that would keep them from harming it. That's the only direct involvement I had with the riots. Otherwise, the games went on as ever. Only you could see the smoke and flames from Dodger Stadium.

As far as we were concerned, though, Connie Mack Stadium in Philadelphia was rougher on an average night than the Watts riots. The stadium was in a bad section of town and the writers had to stay there after the game filing their stories. Many times, I stayed with my brothers and their friends, who used to drive up in a couple cars from Washington, D.C., to see me play. I'd have them wait with a car or two and take the writers back to the hotel. The writers appreciated that because they were really afraid to come out in that darkness around Connie Mack Stadium.

While I stayed with the Rev. Charles, I went to church services three times on Sundays. I'd go once early in the morning, then take in the six and eight o'clock services at night after the game. Every Tuesday that I could I went to the Baptist Ministers Congress meetings with the reverend.

Rev. Charles frequently called on me to speak to the congregation. I was comfortable talking about how my spiritual strength helped me on the baseball field.

I excelled in baseball through my spiritual strength. That's how I stayed alive when I was killing myself with drugs and alcohol. I never let go of that spirituality. It was like an umbilical cord holding on to me, keeping me barely above water through the years of my addiction.

It was the same spiritual faith and strength that I had as a player, when, after every base I stole and every hit I got, I said, "Thank you, God." I said it audibly, but not loudly enough for the umpire or the baseman to hear. If they had, they would have thought I was crazy. But they didn't think the Catholics were crazy when they made the sign of the cross before they stepped in to hit. I thought that was amusing.

There's a story about a rabbi and a priest who were watching a prizefight. The referee called the fighters to the middle of the ring to give them their instructions. They touched gloves, stepped back, and, just as the bell rang, one of the fighters made the sign of the cross.

"Father," the rabbi said, "will that help him?"

"If he can fight it will," the priest responded.

I never thought that God was a fan of any team, but I always believed God will give an athlete the strength and courage to do his best. God will do that for anybody. God can't give everyone four hits. God can't give a pitcher a shutout or a no-hitter. That wouldn't be fair to the other team. And God can't give both pitchers a no-hitter and a shutout because that would ruin the game. God knows that.

## Chapter 22: Perfect practice

Praying for strength is fine, but any time you start praying the ball isn't hit to you, you're in trouble. It's a horrible feeling not to want the ball. Many times I've been on teams where nobody wanted the ball. There were times I didn't want it myself.

That's when I decided that just practice wasn't good enough because I found that practice doesn't make perfect. I decided I had to have perfect practice.

Perfect practice is for when the pennant race is tied and there are runners at first and third. You're playing on the road and it's the bottom of the ninth, one out, and you have to have the double play. Or maybe they try to pull the double steal.

You have to have the defense for it. You have to want the ball. That's when perfect practice comes into play.

It's not for April, May and June. It's easy to play in a major league game—I don't care what part of the season it is or what inning it is—when the score is 8–0. It's easy to play if you're seven games up with a week to go. Everything is beautiful out there. It seems the hop is always good and there's no play you don't make.

Perfect practice is for August and September, when the dog days come and the pennant race and the games get close.

Early in my career we played at the Los Angeles Coliseum,

where you could plant potatoes in the infield. That's when I didn't want the ball. There wasn't any such thing as a good hop.

I didn't start perfect practice until after the 1962 season when I stole 104 bases. All of a sudden I was a personality in baseball. I was a star. I was the team captain. The Dodgers were depending on me. I wasn't a home-run hitter. It was all the little things I did that made the difference, and the better I got, the better it seems the defense got against me. There never was an element of surprise when I stole a base. Everybody in the park knew when I was going. So I started putting in perfect practice in order to keep stealing the bases. I had to figure out when a pitchout was coming.

I got attuned to catchers' and pitchers' signs playing shortstop. If a right-handed hitter was up and the pitcher was going to throw a curveball, I had to anticipate that the batter was going to pull the ball to the left side of the diamond. That's how an infielder gets a good jump. When people say a fielder has a lot of range, it's because he's working with the pitcher and the catcher. If the pitcher gets the ball in the right location, the infielder is always ready to move where the ball is likely to be hit.

It helped as a baserunner, too. By taking my lead early, I could see whether the catcher was putting down one finger for a fastball, two for a curve, a wiggle for a change-up, or a fist for a pitchout. I would steal on the change-up or curve.

When I got to second as a baserunner, I had to see the catcher give the pitcher the signs only two or three times and I knew what they were. Then, if I wanted to steal third, I could wait for a good pitch to run. For example, if a left-handed hitter was up, I looked for a sign indicating a breaking ball low and in. That's a good pitch to steal third on.

That's perfect practice. When I teach baserunning and base-stealing, I try to teach the form and technique that will enable the good base-stealer to steal in the World Series when the whole world is watching. When the game is on the line, you can't have guesswork.

Bunting is the same way. You can't go out there and put in a whole hour on bunting and say, "Hey, we just put in an hour on bunting." If everybody's doing it wrong, you're just making bad habits permanent. If that's the case, practice isn't making you perfect. It's not even making you better.

In the last few minutes of batting practice, I used to play a game called "bunt one." You got one pitch, and if you laid down a good enough bunt you got an extra swing.

I was the first man in the cage, and the first guy is the one who calls the game. Whenever I called bunt one, Willie Davis and Tommy Davis wanted to punch my lights out. They'd try it a couple of times, but they'd foul off the bunt and have to get out of there. They wouldn't get a base-hit swing. They'd get pissed off and call the game off.

"Screw that game," one of them would say. "I don't care if you are the captain, we're not playing it."

That's the attitude most ballplayers take. They're not going to waste time trying to learn to bunt when they can be using the time to do something they like to do. They like to do it because they're already good at it. Practicing the things they're not good at is no fun, so they don't want to do it.

You have to continue to practice the things you do well or they'll get away from you. But you have to take part of the time to practice the things you can't do well. That's what practice is all about.

## Chapter 23: Playing like Cobb

I read Ty Cobb's autobiography after I stole 104 bases. Al Stump, the writer who collaborated with Cobb, interviewed me and gave me a copy of the book. Some of the things we had in common were amazing. Some of the things I said were almost the same things he had said. And if the words weren't the same, the meaning was identical. I even slid like Cobb, feet first and late, throwing my body to the outfield side of the bag. I'd just catch the corner of the bag with my left toe.

Anybody who got spiked had it coming—the base paths belong to the runner. Some guys who are knocked down or spiked will go for the first player on the other team they can get instead of going after the guy who got them. Cobb wouldn't do that.

One time Cobb was trying to beat out a hit and the pitcher went over to cover first. The pitcher had wronged Cobb in some way and Cobb came after him. The pitcher got to the base first and kept running towards the grandstand. Cobb chased him twenty or thirty feet on the other side of the foul line. When he caught him, Cobb jumped at his back and cut the bejeebers out of him with his spikes.

I'm with him on that. And I didn't care how long it took me to get back at a guy. You can ask Clay Carroll about that.

The incident started in 1966 when we were playing Atlanta and Billy O'Dell—a left-hander who was the easiest guy for me to steal off—had gone to three balls and no strikes on me. I got the take sign on the next pitch. So just as he was getting ready to release the ball, I crouched and made a little feint.

"Ball four."

"Goddammit!" O'Dell yelled at me. "You better keep your ass still! Next time I'm going to hit you in the freakin' head!"

"Whaddya want me to do?" I yelled back as I trotted down to first. "Just get the ball over the plate!"

I didn't like to mouth off at pitchers too much. I was too little to be getting into fights and I didn't want them to get mad and start gunning for me. I had them under control already. They couldn't pick me off and I was going to steal no matter what they did.

The one thing they didn't want to do was walk me. On some teams, it was an automatic fine for a pitcher to walk me. So they tried so hard to throw the ball over the middle of the plate that they couldn't do it, like O'Dell. Or maybe they would get it over and I'd tap a little single somewhere or bunt it. So I didn't yell at them much.

But this time, I got to first and O'Dell was still looking at me. So I said something to him and got him really mad. He took one step toward me but the umpire got in front of him and stopped that.

The next time I got up, O'Dell was out of the game, and Clay Carroll was pitching. Now, it wasn't easy to hit me with the ball. As Willie Mays once said, to hit me, you have to hit a moving target. But I didn't expect Carroll to throw at me, and he caught me off guard and hit me in the ribs. Okay. I wasn't going after him right then. He was too big and I didn't want to get hurt.

Several years later, Carroll was pitching for Cincinnati in a game at Dodger Stadium. By then, he was one of the top relief pitchers in the National League. I got up against him in a sacrifice situation and laid a bunt down the first base line that the first baseman had to field.

Carroll ran over to cover first. And, as I was running toward him—BAM!—it came back to me. I saw it as plain as day, as if it had happened the inning before: *Clay Carroll hit me in the ribs!*

I was sacrificing and I didn't care about the out. I just wanted to get him. In fact, I had to slow down a bit and wait for him to get to the base.

He stepped on the inside corner of the bag, giving me plenty of room to hit the bag without hitting him. But I took direct aim and came down right on his ankle. I even twisted my spikes a little bit.

I ran halfway to the right field foul pole before turning around and coming back. I was out. It didn't matter. When I turned to walk back, Clay Carroll was lying by first base. The trainer was putting tape and gauze and everything else on him, trying to stop the bleeding.

I walked over and poked my head in this huddle of five or six Cincinnati Reds who were all gathered around him.

"Hey! You all right?" I said, my voice full of concern.

"Yeah, Maury, I'm all right," he said. "I know you didn't mean to do it."

"Okay, old buddy," I said.

I walked back to the dugout and scratched him off the list.

I didn't want to do anything to ruin his career, but I did want to sting him. I'm sure he might have thought about it later that he had hit me in the ribs. I never said anything to him about it, though, and he never said anything to me.

Cobb said you can't steal bases only when you have to. You have to keep running. It's like anything else. Say I've gone two games without a hit. I haven't been on base and I haven't stolen a base. Now all of a sudden we get hot and have a blowout going. Even though we don't need it, I have to steal a base in this game to get my rhythm back because I've gone two games without a steal. If I don't I can lose my edge.

Or maybe a guy threw me out trying to steal. I have to get right back on first base and I have to go right away. I don't care what the score is. By catching me stealing, that guy has increased his confidence and lost some of the intimidation I had created in him. So I have to get back out there and steal the base right now just to condition his ass.

Sometimes, I stole a base when I didn't need to just to make them hate me more; just to rub it in. I wanted them to hate me more so they'd want to get me worse than ever. And the harder they tried the more likely they were to throw it away.

I read all this stuff in Cobb's book after I'd already done it. Our reasoning was the same. There wasn't any sense in laying off and being a nice guy because they had already taken offense to what we did. You may as well keep making them hate you more and more. That's why when the players came to vote for the all-star team—the fans didn't vote in those days—they didn't vote for me.

All that mattered to me was that the general manager who signed my paychecks liked me and that the fans cheered when the public address announcer said:

"And now hitting for the Dodgers, Captain Maury Wills."

I carried Cobb's book with me and read it year after year. It was a great inspiration to me.

## Chapter 24: Flashing spikes

I think I spiked more guys than Ty Cobb. I could go into the base and make my little hook slide and just bring that spike across and cut them and stay on the base. Sliding late put me in a position to spike the guy more than the guy who slid early. It didn't make any of the basemen back off because I did it in a way that appeared accidental.

It wasn't, though.

Teams were always trying to figure out ways to keep me from getting my good lead at first base. The Giants came up with a play where, instead of holding me on, the first baseman played directly between me and second base so when I took off, I'd run into him. That didn't work. I just took one step back towards right field and ran past him.

Then the first baseman got directly behind me. That almost worked because I couldn't see him and didn't know where he was. I beat that move by eliminating any fear of failing, taking my normal lead and ignoring the guy behind me.

Then Joe Torre, who was playing first and catching for the Milwaukee Braves at the time, came up with an excellent ploy one night in Milwaukee. When I got my maximum lead, I had to dive head first back to first to beat the pitcher's pickoff throw. What Torre did was go down on his right knee so that his knee, thigh and lower leg were between me and the bag as he caught the ball from the pitcher. When I dove, I hit his leg with my shoulder and couldn't get to the bag. He picked me off.

I bitched to Stan Landers, the umpire. I told him that the rule states that the baseman can't block the base until he has possession of the ball. The only ones who get away with that are catchers on plays at the plate, and they're not supposed to, either. But Landers always had a problem with me and he called me out. He let Torre block me off.

It's like the so-called phantom tag at second base when you're turning the double play. Out of all the double plays I made in the big leagues, I guarantee you that maybe one per cent of the time I was actually on second base when I caught the ball. I would touch the base and then catch the ball as I was crossing it. I was off the base, but with the smoothness and rhythm of the play, it looked good. Sometimes, the umpire would walk by after the play and say, "Hey, Maury, give it a little better shot next time."

"Okay," I'd say, "but not with that guy sliding at me."

One year the umpires started calling that play and messing the game up. They ended up going back to the old way of letting the fielders hit the bag before they caught the ball.

I felt the same way about Torre's move and I really got in Landers' face about it. The fans in Milwaukee were booing me, which made me feel uncomfortable. For the most part fans on the road cheered me because they appreciated my ability and liked the idea of a little guy like me outthinking all those big guys. But now they were booing me and I wasn't only mad, I was embarrassed.

I got on the team bus after the game carrying a paper bag. Nobody knew what was in it—my spikes. I asked the bus driver to let me off a couple blocks from the team hotel. My teammates were razzing me, figuring I was going to mess around on the town a little bit. Hell, there wasn't anything to do in Milwaukee but have room service. I said I just wanted to walk around a little.

I walked to a hardware store, went in and bought a file. I put the file in the bag with my spikes and walked back to the hotel. I went straight to my room, sat on the edge of the bed, took everything out of the bag and started filing my spikes.

My roommate at that time was Willie Crawford, a big, strapping guy with a high-pitched voice. "Whatchya doin?" he asked.

"Can't you see? I'm filing my spikes."

"Whatchya doin' that for?" Willie asked.

"You saw what happened today, didn't you?" I replied and kept on filing.

Recognition hit him: "Oooooooh. Yeah."

I filed those spikes down, first the front ones then all of them. I looked at those damned things. They were glittering.

I always had five or six pairs of spikes because every shoe company in the country gave me shoes to try out. The next night, I put one of the other pairs on to start the game and left my sharpened spikes in the clubhouse. Early in the game, I got on first again and took my lead. The pitcher threw over, Torre went down on his knee and blocked the base, I slid into his leg, and I was out again.

I went straight to the clubhouse and put on my special spikes. I got on base again and took my lead. This time, when the pitcher threw over and Joe went down on his knee, I came back in the air, feet first. Not sliding on the ground, but in mid-air—WHAM!—I went right over his leg and hit the bag.

Joe jumped up and I pulled my spikes out of the bag as if I were pulling a cork out of a bottle. When I got them out, the base was gashed and stuffing was coming out of it. Joe looked at the bag and looked at me. Jeezus Christ! But he didn't say a word.

Now I'm kind of scared because Torre is a big guy and I'm afraid he's going to pinch my ear off. We got into a cat-and-mouse game. Sometimes I'd dive back head first and sometimes I'd go feet first and he's trying to guess which way I'm coming. If I come in feet first, he wants to stay up because he saw what happened to the bag. But if I come in head first, he wants to block the bag and pick me off again. The pitcher is throwing over and I'm going in head first and he's guessing wrong and not going down, then I'm going feet first and he's jumping out of the way.

This went on for seven, eight throws. All on one play, as if the ballgame didn't matter anymore. It was just Joe and me with the pitcher throwing over.

And, man, he guessed wrong. I went back as hard as I could in mid-air just like I hit the bag the first time when I pulled the stuffing out. He put his knee down there, and my spikes went right into his leg. I pull them out like the cork out of the bottle and blood starts running all over the place. Joe is hobbling around bleeding. I'm standing on first base figuring: "This guy is going to kill me!"

Joe refused to go out of the game to get sewn up, so they took him in the dugout and wrapped him up with tape and gauze.

I looked at the first base coach, Greg Mulleavy, who was about 60 years old, to see if he was going to help me. He just stood there. I looked at the Dodger dugout, which seemed like a hundred miles away on the other side of the field, to see if my teammates were on the top step ready to come out to defend me. And they're all sitting back on the bench with their legs crossed, having a cigarette, looking up in the stands. La-de-da-de-da.

Torre came back out of the dugout to a big round of applause. He walked right towards me and I stood there with my head down and my back towards the dugout facing center field with my hands over my face.

But Joe just ran out there beside me, patted me on the leg and took his position. All he said was, "Let's go." He realized he was blocking the bag and the runner was entitled to do anything to get to the base.

I took off for second on the next pitch. I figured to hell with staying there. I was going and I didn't care if I was safe or out. I don't even remember what happened. I just got out of there.

The next night, in the last game of the series, Joe Torre was catching and I was trying to score from first on a long double. The ball got there before I did and now Joe Torre is standing there with the ball in his mitt and all his equipment on. He didn't try to tag me. He wanted to make me eat the ball.

He came right at my face with the glove on one hand and the ball in the other. Luckily, I was still quick and agile. That's what made a lot of guys mad. Like in my football days, they couldn't get a good blow in at me. He came down with the mitt and the ball and I just pulled my head aside at the last second and he hit the ground. I think he made a hole there. He got me out, though, and the collision alone shook me up enough.

But he did it all in the course of the game, the same way I did. That's the way we played. We didn't grab a bat and punch somebody's lights out. It was just, I got him with the spikes. Okay, he got me at the plate.

I've always had the greatest respect for Joe Torre. But he never put his knee down to block first base again.

Ron Hunt, a second baseman who came up with the Mets and later played one year for the Dodgers before going on to the Giants and the Expos, had a different trick. When he was covering second on an attempted steal, he could catch the ball and, with perfect timing, come down with his knee right on the thigh of the runner. He got Ron Fairly that way once and Fairly came back to the dugout cursing and moaning. He was limping 10 days from that bruise. If you slid head first, Hunt would come down on your collarbone the same way.

One day we were playing the Mets at Shea Stadium and I went into second on an attempted steal. Hunt dropped right down on my quadriceps muscle—the big muscle on the front of the thigh. It was the worst pain I ever had. I was dying but I couldn't let him know that he hurt me. That's a hell of a trick.

I wanted to get even. I tried to come in high on him a few times, but he was alert. He could take care of himself. I never could settle that score.

Sometimes a pitcher would spin me around. To spin someone around, you throw at his head. You can get away from that pitch, but you have to spin to get out of the way. If a pitcher wants to hit someone, he has to throw at the body a little higher than the waist and just behind the hitter. You can get him every time that way in the ribs or the small of the back. If a pitcher wanted to try to put some fear in me, he was better off spinning me around than hitting me. If he hit me, that just put me on base.

Getting hit—especially in the head—is the only fear in baseball. One or two guys with a knack for doing something crazy would actually try to get hit. In my day, John Roseboro and Ron Hunt were like that. More recently, Don Baylor was good at getting hit. Out of hundreds of players, though, you have maybe three only who are macho enough to stand there and let the ball hit them—but not in the head.

Roseboro got to the point where he would barely move even if there was a 90-mile-per-hour fastball coming right at his head. He'd let the ball skim right by his nose. I asked why he didn't try to get out of the way.

"I'd rather get hit than let the pitcher make me look silly skipping rope or spinning me around trying to get out of the way. I'd rather get hit and get it over with," he said.

"SPIN HIM AROUND!" That was Gene Mauch's favorite saying. When he was managing, Mauch would stand on the top step of the dugout yelling that. I always thought it was chickenshit for a manager to stand up there and say that. I thought it was really bush.

Three of our pitchers—Stan Williams, Larry Sherry and Don Drysdale—just loved to go after batters. If I got spun around and one of them was pitching, they would come up to me in the dugout and say, "Do you think he meant to do that?"

"Hell, yes, he meant it," I'd yell.

"I'll get him for you," they'd say eagerly.

"No," I protested. "Leave him alone. The score's only 1–0 in our favor. Don't mess the game up."

They'd argue with me, begging for a chance to hit the guy: "It'll be all right. Let me get him for you."

Usually, they already had someone on the other team they wanted to knock down and they were just looking for an excuse to do it.

# Chapter 25: All's fair . . .

Jimmy Lefebvre and Wes Parker came up to the Dodgers in 1965. Lefebvre was a rookie, Parker was a second-year man, and they were both scared to death. Walter Alston put their lockers on each side of mine in the clubhouse. I was there to settle them down so they wouldn't be too nervous. Both turned out to be outstanding ballplayers.

One day we were getting ready for a game and I asked Parker a question.

"Hey, Wes," I said. "The Giants are outside. We got to go! Right?"

"Right, Captain!" Parker said. So far so good.

"Okay, Wes," I went on. "If you're playing first base and some Giant hits a double and he's rounding first and everybody's eyes —including the umpires'—are on the ball and you have a chance to put your foot out there and trip that guy, nobody would see it. If that would save the game for us, would you do it?"

"No," West said.

"Huh?" That wasn't the right answer. I ran it past him again.

"No," he repeated.

"Look, Wes," I said, getting a little worked up. "Suppose there was a guy who you knew would trip you if you were the runner. Would you trip him then, Wes?"

"NO!" He was very firm about that.

"Wes," I ordered, "you gotta trip that guy. All right? You gotta trip him!"

But he never said he would do it.

That's the difference between him and me. I would trip somebody to win a ballgame. Both feet. Definitely. The situation never came up, but I did things that were the equivalent to tripping the runner.

We were playing Montreal in 1969 or '70. A kid named Don

Hahn was on first when Rusty Staub hit a double in the gap. Hahn was running on the pitch and he didn't know where the ball was hit. So I looked up and yelled, "I got it!" as if it were a pop fly.

Hahn got about five feet from second when he realized that I was going to catch this ball on the fly. He turned around and charged back to first base.

Meanwhile, Rusty Staub was headed for second, running wide open because this was a sure double and maybe a triple. And he ran right past Hahn, who was charging back to first. Staub was automatically out for passing the runner ahead of him.

When Hahn got back to first base, he finally realized that the ball was in the gap. So he turned around and charged back toward second. Only by this time somebody had chased the ball down. He threw it in, and I tagged Hahn out at second.

Double play.

To me, that's like tripping.

Vin Scully, the Dodger announcer, thought that trick was dirty pool. He said on the air it shouldn't be allowed; that Maury Wills was making a farce of the game because if that had been a pop fly, the infield fly rule would have been in effect and the batter would have been automatically out. In that case, the runner can advance at his own risk.

I had another trick I used when there really was an infield fly. I'd go up as if I were going to catch the ball, and suddenly the ball would hit the heel of my glove and drop out as if I had missed it. I did miss it—on purpose. The runners, not knowing the rule book, would take off for the next base. When they did that, I threw over and made the double play on them because the batter was already out automatically.

Scully didn't like that and neither did the umpires. They all said that play shouldn't be allowed. After a while, the umpires were practically holding the runners on the bases. They'd be yelling at the runners: "You don't have to run! The batter's out! YOU CAN STAY THERE!"

"Why don't you write the guy a letter?" I complained. "Send him to school. Let him read the rule book."

"Maury," they'd tell me, "you can't keep pulling tricks like that."

They were legal, though. I started carrying a rule book with me in 1962 and kept carrying it until 1972 when I retired. I wanted to learn things about the rules that maybe I could use. It was part of perfect practice.

I don't know how many pitchers know whether the 60-feet, 6-inches from the mound to the plate is from the front of the plate to the back of the rubber, the back of the plate to the front of the rubber, or what. It's from the back of the plate to the front of the rubber. Likewise, I don't know how many base stealers know that the bases are 15 inches on each side, so if you run from the back inside edge of first to the back inside edge of second, it's 22½ inches shorter than the 90 feet from the first base line to the middle of second base.

I read the rules to get better, because everybody else was getting better, too. Guys were studying me all the time. Bill White, when he was playing for the Phillies and I was with the Pirates, told me once, "You know, Maury, when you first came up, we'd go over the Dodger line up before the first game of a series and when your name came up, they said, 'Who's next?'

"Now, we spend 40 minutes on you. We spend the whole goddamned meeting figuring out how we're going to get you out."

Bob Friend and Vern Law, two outstanding pitchers for the Pirates, used to beat the Dodgers regularly. Friend didn't throw hard. In fact, we used to run up to home plate to hit against him. And he'd send us back talking to ourselves. He gave you a lot of movement. When you don't get any hits in a game, we call that taking the collar. Well, Friend wasn't overpowering like Bob Gibson, who gave you a collar that's choking you to death. Friend gave you what we called a comfortable collar. You hit a couple good but right at someone, you just miss one and hit a pop a mile high and then you squeak one through the infield but the shortstop makes a hell of a play on it and just gets you at first. You're 0-for-4 but it seems like just bad luck.

One day, Friend had just beaten us decisively. After the game, I realized how when I was interviewed by Vin Scully as the star of the game, Scully really dug into all my techniques and thoughts. I gave away some of my secrets that way, and if anybody from the other team was listening, they could use that information to combat me.

I turned on the radio and Vin Scully was saying that Bob

Friend would be his guest on the post-game show. I had to listen to this.

Friend came on and said, "There's an unwritten rule in baseball that when you got two strikes on a guy you have to waste a pitch. Before you know it, you're 2–2 and the batter's even with you and then you're 3–2 and you're in a hole." He said he and Vern Law didn't believe in that. "A lot of times," he said, "when we get two strikes and no balls on a guy, we just throw a fastball right down the middle or on the corner. The guy is looking for an off-speed pitch outside the strike zone, so his bat isn't as quick. So we throw the fastball and he either hits it on his fists, breaks the bat or just looks at it go by."

"And you do that consistently?" Scully asked.

"All the time," Friend said. "That's the way we pitch."

"I'll be a sonuvabitch," I thought. From then on, I must have hit .350 against those guys. When Vern Law or Bob Friend got two strikes on me, my bat was ready to move. Sometimes, I'd invite an 0–2 count. I was getting two, three and four hits a game off Pittsburgh all the time just on the strength of listening to the post-game interview.

I told my teammates, but they were busy having a beer or being disgusted over the loss or talking about where they were going after the game. I don't know if anybody ever paid attention to me. I don't think so—at least not until after I stole 104 bases. After that, my status on the ballclub changed tremendously. Players started listening more to what I had to say.

Another thing we used to do against Pittsburgh was steal their signs. From second base, we could steal every sign Smoky Burgess, their catcher, gave. Smoky was short and squat. He went 5-foot-8, 190 pounds. He was an outstanding hitter, but he couldn't get his knees together when he gave the sign. He'd put the sign right out in front where it was easy to see. And he didn't like to use sophisticated signs. His whole career with the Pirates he used the third sign he gave with men on base.

When I was on second, he'd show the sign and I'd read it. The batter is standing there looking at the pitcher, and right over the pitcher's shoulder the batter can see me taking my lead off second. If it was a fastball, I'd take my first step toward third with my right leg. If it was a breaking ball, I'd step across with my left leg. The batter knew exactly what was coming.

Some of the guys complained because they knew what was coming but they didn't know the location. If they couldn't know if it was going to be inside or outside, they didn't want to know the pitch.

So I put my hands on my hips. If it's an inside fastball to a right-handed hitter, I'd drop my right hand off my hip and step with my right foot. Outside fastball, I'd drop my left hand and step right. Inside curve: drop my right hand and cross over with the left leg.

I'd do that and Tommy Davis' eyes would get as big as teacups. He'd hit the ball over the scoreboard in Pittsburgh, against the scoreboard, up in the vines, off the light towers. We killed them, just wore them out. And they couldn't understand how we were doing it.

I was traded to the Pirates after the 1966 season, and I tried to give them the signs. Nobody wanted them. Not even Bill Mazeroski, their great second baseman. He said, "I can't hit if I know what's coming."

I can't understand that. If you can't hit knowing what's coming, how can you hit when you don't know?

The one reason some guys can't hit when they know what's coming is that they hate to get crossed up. If you're looking for a curve and the pitcher throws an inside fastball, you stand in there waiting for it to break and you get creamed.

Rather than have that happen, some guys don't want to know. But that only happens if the guy on second has promised to give the signs and then misses one. So he guesses. That happened with us, too.

To fix that, I told the guys if I missed the sign, I would just stand there and not do anything. That way the batter had confidence that I wasn't going to cross him up.

The hardest thing to hit is the knuckleball. You just don't hit a knuckleball on a good day. But I had no problem hitting Phil Niekro because I learned to read him. I noticed that when he brought his hands over his head at the top of his motion, he would squeeze the glove closed if it was a fastball and he would leave it open if it was a knuckleball.

Knowing the knuckleball is coming is no help. You know it's coming 90 percent of the time. Here it is. Now hit it.

But the knuckleball pitcher is not always on. He has to find the exact point of release that will make the ball break in the strike zone. When Niekro was on, he threw shutouts. Otherwise, he didn't know where it was going, either.

With most guys, Niekro would throw the knuckleball when the count was 2–2 or even 3–2. But when I was up, he didn't want to mess around and walk me. When the count got to 2–2 on me, I'd watch that glove. He'd squeeze it and my eyes would get big as teacups. So I did all right against Niekro.

## Chapter 26: Diamond doctor

Today, pitchers who scuff the ball or throw a spitter are frowned upon. We had guys who did all that stuff. We figured if you could get away with it, more power to you.

I used to cut the ball for one of our pitchers. This guy used to sharpen his belt buckle and he'd been cutting the ball on that. But people got wise to that, so we got a different idea.

I started cutting the ball for him. I put a little piece of emery board in the stitches on the heel of my glove. The emery board was never in the way when I caught the ball. When I got the ball when we were throwing it around at the beginning of an inning, or after an out, I'd just rub the ball across the emery board as I took it out of my glove. I'd throw it to the pitcher, he'd take a look at it, find the spot he wanted, and make the pitch.

You can guess all you want about who that was, and if you guessed Don Sutton, what can I say?

Another thing I'd do is, when we were playing on a hard infield, I'd tell the outfielders to throw the ball in to me low and on one hop after an out or a hit. That way, the ball would skid on the hard infield and get a scuff mark.

That worked at Dodger Stadium where the infield was made of crushed red brick mixed with Georgia clay. The Giants called that infield the brick yard. Candlestick Park, where they used to water the base paths to make it hard for me to steal, we called the swamp.

The Dodger infield was like artificial turf it was so hard. It was hard to run on, hard to slide on, hard to field on. That red brick looked pretty against the green grass, but it would bake hard in the sun and was always cracking. That infield didn't help our pitching staff at all, although with our speed it helped us offensively.

We also did a few things to the field to help us. I made sure that the ground crew had the base lines sloping in on both sides of the infield. I'd roll a ball down each line and if it wasn't sloped enough, I told them to slope it more. That was to keep my bunts from rolling foul.

Then there was the pitcher's mound. With Don Drysdale, Sandy Koufax, Johnny Podres and those guys, they changed the mound every day. Sandy threw overhand so he wanted the mound to be extra high to give him more leverage. Drysdale threw sidearm, so he wanted the mound low. Other guys wanted it sloped one way or another.

The ground crew would be out there at eight in the morning before anyone was in the stadium. They knew who was going to pitch so they fixed the mound the way he liked it. The relief pitchers had to be ready to deal with whatever way the mound was that day.

When I was managing the Seattle Mariners at the beginning of 1981, I had Tom Paciorek, an outfielder, who liked to stand way forward in the batter's box. That's supposed to be to the batter's disadvantage because it gives him a fraction less time to react to the pitch. That's why most batters try to stand as far back in the box as possible. They're always rubbing out the back line and you'll see the umpire measure off the box with a bat and draw a new line in the dirt. But Paciorek liked to stand forward and it worked for him.

One day Paciorek hit a home run and the umpire called him out for stepping over the front line of the batter's box. Before the next game, I went to my grounds crew. Normally, the grounds crew uses a wooden frame to outline the batter's box, which is six feet long from the outside of the front chalk line to the outside of the back line. The chalk line itself is about three inches wide.

"Look," I told the crew, "when you make the batter's box tonight, don't use that frame. Do the box free hand. And when you do, I want you to make it six feet long from the inside of the lines instead of from the outside. Push it forward."

I figured that way I'd get an extra six inches for Paciorek.

We were playing Oakland that night and one of the damned kids on the crew went over and told Billy Martin, the A's manager, what I had asked them to do.

When the game started, Martin came out and protested. The umpire measured the box with a bat and threw me out of the game. I got suspended three games for that and that was one of the incidents that helped get me fired.

My own ground crew! It never would have happened with the Dodgers.

## Chapter 27: Don't let up

I always figured you have to break their backs. You get a team down five, six, seven runs in the second inning, they're not dead yet. You have to bury them. After you get the lead, if they come back and get the bases loaded with nobody out and you can hold them to one run, that's breaking their backs. That demoralizes them. Then you go out and get a couple of more runs by stealing some bases, bunting, sacrificing, using the squeeze play. Any time a team can tie the game with a grand slam, they're not dead.

Put a squeeze play on with a five-run lead in the seventh inning and they go crazy. People think you're not supposed to do that, that you're rubbing it in. You're not supposed to steal bases when you're ahead and you're not supposed to squeeze or sacrifice. You just play the game out and don't embarrass anybody. Pete Reiser called that honeymoon baseball.

When a team's six runs ahead and a guy hits a 500-foot home

run, the only thing the opposition says is, "Boy, that guy can hit!" But let me come out and steal a base when we're six runs ahead and it's, "We'll get you!"

We might be leading 7–2 in the eighth inning and as I was going to the bat rack to get my bat, I'd ask Walter Alston and whoever was pitching: "Do we need any more runs?" If the pitcher said: "I'm fine. I got them from here," I wouldn't steal. But if they said, "Hell, yes," I went out and stole a base. Everybody thought I was being a hot dog, but it wasn't that at all. We were down 8–0 in the second game of the three-game playoff with the Giants in 1962 and we came back and won. And in the minors once, I was in a game where we had a seven-run lead with two outs and nobody on in the ninth inning and we lost. Keeping that in mind, I figured we never had enough.

I used the daily grind as a way to succeed because I knew the other players hated the grind. They especially hated the first game of a series after a long trip across the country, or a game when it was raining and you didn't have any pregame workout.

I made it a point to be pumped up for those days. Certain players would have good games against good opposition because they would be all pumped up. But they would be lousy in a game against the Padres, which was an expansion team when I was playing, with nobody watching. Some racky-tack pitcher would be getting them out. There was no challenge for them because there wasn't a name pitcher out there for them to get up for.

Those were the pitchers I just wore out. The pitchers who were throwing slop and couldn't even break a pane of glass were the pitchers the other guys tried to send over the roof and they ended up popping out. Those were the pitchers I bunted on. Those were the pitchers I just stood there against and peppered the ball instead of trying to cream one just because I'm 3-for-3 off him. If I went up and tried to show that I could cream one, too, because two of my teammates just did, I was going to pop it up. So I'd just go up and hit it between the shortstop and third baseman and I'm 4-for-4. Do it again and I'm 5-for-5.

Now the next day when we go to St. Louis or San Francisco and we're facing a top pitcher like Bob Gibson or Juan Marichal, I might just scratch out one hit in five at-bats. But I went 5-for-5 the night before, so I'm 6-for-10, which is .600, for the two games. If I had been happy with two hits my first two times up and then screwed around against the racky-tack pitcher and tried to show I can pull the ball or hit it out of the park, I'd be only 3-for-10. Now all I have to do is come up one more time and not get a hit and I'm 3-for-11 and then 3-for-12 and the average goes whoomp. I'm batting .250.

Some players who have everything going for them get complacent or start goofing off or trying to do something unnatural. They mess up their chance to improve their average. I never messed around like that. I didn't give away at-bats. If you get to the plate 600 times a year, six hits—that's one hit a month—is 10 points on your average. Four hits a month—one more hit a week—is the difference between .250 and .290, or .275 and .315.

But guys give at-bats away. They get two hits the first two times up and they know they're going to have a good day so it doesn't matter what they do the next two or three times up. Going 2-for-4 or 2-for-5 isn't bad.

Not for me. If I were 2-for-2, I'd say, "Shoot, I'm starting the game all over again now." When I went up the third time, I treated it just like the first time up. Everybody wants a base hit the first time up. That's the way it works. You get that hit the first time up and you can't take the collar. You can relax a little.

But if I got 2-for-2, I wanted 3-for-3. I'm up there and, goddammit, I can remember those lean times. Now I want 4-for-4. And now I have it and we're winning 14–0. The fourth or fifth relief pitcher is in there and everybody just wants to get the game over. Your own teammates might get pissed at you for getting another hit and prolonging the game.

I don't care. I want 5-for-5. I'm going to really bear down. If the pitcher throws one over my head or makes me skip rope because I've already stolen four bases, too, I might even bunt that sonuvabitch. Hell, Frank Howard just hit two completely out of the ballpark and the pitcher didn't throw over Frank's head. But just because I stole four bases already, he's going to pick on me. So I bunt.

That happened in Philadelphia once. I bunted and, damn, if the ball didn't roll foul. I got back in the box and—WHOOM—the ball came right behind my head. When a pitcher throws there, he's trying to hit you in the head, because your natural reaction is to throw your head back. You got to throw your feet out and go down so fast your cap stays in the air.

I picked myself up, dusted myself off, and bunted that sucker again. For a hit.

## Chapter 28: It takes a thief

I got my rest. I came to the park early. A half hour before the game, I wouldn't sign any more autographs. They teach you in the minor leagues to sit on the bench and watch the other team take infield and outfield practice. When guys get to the major leagues, they just drop that.

I continued to watch.

A guy who's got a gun for an arm suddenly may not be throwing well. Or maybe a player who always took two or three steps before he threw the ball may have improved. I needed to keep up with those things on an everyday basis. So I watched.

I didn't always have company. On the Dodgers, I often had to ask Walter Alston to break up the card games the guys used to have in the clubhouse until half way through the national anthem.

I always watched the opposing pitcher warm up. As sure as I need air to breathe, I needed to be out there watching that pitcher warm up. I wanted to see him breaking off his curveball. The bullpen was usually in foul territory down the left field or right field foul line. Even from a couple of hundred feet away, I could see the ball breaking. I hated those new parks like Philadelphia where they put the bullpens under the stands and you couldn't see the pitchers warm up.

The main thing I wanted to see was the last five minutes of his warmup. That was when the pitcher threw from his stretch position. And what he did in the bullpen before the game was the same thing he was going to do on the mound during the game.

He wasn't going to warm up using a quick delivery and then get in the game and kick high.

I looked for my keys—the sign that told me the pitcher was going home and I could break for second. The keys haven't changed since I played. They will stay the same as long as baseball is played.

For 80 percent of right-handed pitchers, the key is the left shoulder—the shoulder pointed toward the plate. Those pitchers open the shoulder—rotate it toward first a little—to look at you. A pitcher wants to get a good look, and he has to open his shoulder to do that. Once he closes his shoulder, he has decided to go home. If he closes it and then opens up and goes to first, that's a balk. So it doesn't matter what else he does. He can be like Luis Tiant and have that herky-jerky motion down to his set position. I don't even look at that. It's the shoulder that tells me when to go.

The next class of right-handers—about 15 percent—have taught themselves to keep the shoulder closed when they look at first. A lot of guys say you look at the left heel. When he lifts the heel, he's going home. By the time they started talking about that, I had already gone to the back of the left knee. He's got to bend his knee to pitch. As soon as he bends it, I break for second.

The final class of right-handers are the five percent I called leaners. This pitcher's entire body leans toward the plate when he's going home. Don Drysdale was a leaner, but he picked a lot of guys off because he could start to lean without picking his foot up. If you went on the lean, he had you.

A few guys had no pickoff move. Those were the power pitchers like Sandy Koufax, Tom Seaver and Nolan Ryan. They had to kick high to push off and generate their power. They weren't going to worry about shortening their release just to stop a few baserunners. They let the guy run. So he stole a base. So what? They'd just concentrate on striking out the batter.

Everybody thinks that because left-handers face first base when they get in their set position, they're harder to steal off. That's not true. That's because there's something different about left-handers. They think left-handed. I like to say they're weird.

We're all creatures of habit, but left-handers are creatures of left-handed habits. It's something totally different.

I realized this one day when I was studying Billy O'Dell, who pitched for the Orioles, Giants, Braves and Pirates during a 13-year career. I was watching his head and I noticed that if he was looking at home when he made his first move he threw to first. He figured that if he was looking at home, you'd think he was going to throw there. If he wanted to go home, he'd look at first when he made his move to make you think he was going to throw to first. This is how the left-hander thinks.

It didn't matter what he did in the stretch position before he came set. Billy O'Dell would take his stretch position and look home, look to first and check home again. That didn't mean anything. I was looking for his first move after he came set. If he's looking at me, then he's going home.

O'Dell would get set then look home, and when he threw to first I'd be back standing up. I could take another step off the bag and already I was 10 feet off. He'd get the ball again, get set, look at the plate, and I'd be back again standing up. Hell, I can take another step off. I'm like 12 feet off the bag now. It's getting ridiculous.

Finally, O'Dell figures it out: "He's going back to the base on the first move I make. That's why I can't pick him off. I may as well just throw home. But before I do, I'll take a look at him."

So he looks at me—which means he's going home—and I start running and there's nothing he can do. The catcher didn't even fake a throw to second. That's how big a jump I had. That's the kind of lead I'd get off left-handers.

If a pitcher tried to change his key and go home with a little balk move, the umpires didn't call it. They felt I'm the champion base stealer, they didn't have to go out of their way to help me. They let me hold my own.

You'll notice that when you watch major league baseball games and see when the balks are called. It's when a slower runner is on. They don't call balks so much when Rickey Henderson is on, but they do when Dave Henderson is. They let the base-stealing champion take care of himself.

That was fine with me. I didn't want them to call balks. If the pitcher was changing his key to hold me on, that changed his rhythm to the plate and then it's ball one, ball two, ball three, ball four. He can't change his rhythm and keep his control. And if the umpires start calling balks on something the pitcher is doing as a rule and make him do something different, they're changing the pitcher's key on me. That makes it tougher on me. So I'd tell the umpires, "Don't call a balk on him. Leave him alone. He's all right."

You have to study the pitchers and see what you think is the key and then you have to believe it. If it works in practice, it works in the game. But a lot of players I've worked with in practice get out there in a game and say, "I don't know if this stuff works now." You got people in the stands. You got umpires. The records count now, and all of a sudden they get psyched out. They get to thinking about safety first and start hugging the base.

I can teach someone how to steal a base in 15 minutes, but it's going to take me a long time before I can drill into them that it works and they shouldn't be afraid.

In order to be an outstanding base stealer, you have to eliminate fear of failure. It's like being a safecracker. You can't be down there on your knees turning around every second to see if somebody's looking. You have to get down there and if the man comes and taps you on the shoulder, that's the way it goes.

You have to have the confidence that if you get picked off in the first inning of a World Series game, you can still steal in the ninth inning when it means the game. It's like falling off a horse. You have to get right back on.

It's better to get picked off first base being aggressive than to be thrown out at second for being too conservative at first. The rule is this: You only pick off the good base-runners, because they're the only ones who get off far enough to be picked off.

I was signed as a pitcher and I took an interest in the position. That's how I got the ability to read pitchers. I was in tune with them. You might say I was a pitcher historian.

In the same way, Roger Craig was a base stealer historian. He had a knack for reading the energy and intensity of the runner on first, looking to see if he was going to go. That's how Craig knew to call so many pitchouts for the Tigers and the Giants.

That's why one of the secrets of stealing bases is being a good actor.

Say we were down a run in the ninth inning and I walked leading off. I'd take my time getting to first. When I got there, I'd stay on the bag while Jim Gilliam got ready to hit and the third base coach made like he was giving the bunt sign.

I'd give no sign of being eager and intense. That's a dead giveaway. I'd just take a lazy lead as if Gilliam's going to bunt me over. The pitcher gets into his stretch and looks over at me before he gets his sign from the catcher. He's not looking to see how far off I am, because I'm not going to take a big lead yet. He's looking to get a reading. So I give him all kinds of vibes and body language that say: "I'M NOT GOING ANYWHERE. Goddammit. He's gotta bunt me over. I wish he didn't have to. Shucks."

He takes his stretch and gets set. He looks over again, and now I have my maximum lead. But he doesn't even see me. He got his reading when he looked the first time. Now he just looks and throws home. He's more concerned with throwing a high fastball and fielding his position for the bunt. That's why he's not giving me his best shot at first.

I know this because I've been out there at shortstop when the pitcher from the opposing team is on second base. The guy can't run. He isn't going to run. He's three feet off the base. But my pitcher gets in the set position, he looks at second, he steps off, he feints a throw. Finally he throws home: "Ball one." He does the same thing again, stepping off, faking a throw: "Ball two."

I walk to the mound and have a talk with my pitcher. "This guy's not going anywhere," I tell him. "If he was, I'd hold him on. If you want, I'll hold him on. But just look at the catcher. Don't even look back here."

"Okay, Maury," he says.

And what does he do? He gets on the mound, takes his stretch position, and starts checking the runner and stepping off and faking throws again.

He can't help it. He's mechanical like a robot. As soon as he gets his sign from the catcher, he's decided he's going home. And I've stolen second.

So I don't want to jump around off first base with a big lead. Like Rickey Henderson. Rickey is way out there early. He's putting on a show. He knows he's going to get the attention and that's why he takes a big early lead. Otherwise, it makes no sense for him to be that intense and ready to go before the pitcher even gets the sign from the catcher. When the pitcher looks over to first base to see if Rickey Henderson is off, everybody in the ballpark looks at first, too. They're not looking at the pitcher looking at first. They're looking at first because that's what the pitcher is looking at. They're looking at Rickey Henderson, the base stealer.

But I don't call Rickey Henderson a hot dog. I say he's got charisma.

## Chapter 29: "Eat a steak!"

I never had the feeling I did anything extraordinary. Even after winning the World Series, my teammates would be celebrating, but I'd be thinking that I'd just done my job. It just meant that there was no more baseball until spring.

I'd sit down with the writers after the regular-season games and say, "Thanks, gentlemen, but I didn't do anything other than what I get paid to do or what you'd expect Maury Wills to do. Yes, I had a good day, but I didn't think it was *fabulous.*"

Out of 13 years as a major leaguer, there were maybe four days when I thought I was great. They usually took place coming down the pennant stretch when we were playing Cincinnati when Frank Robinson was with them or when we were playing the Giants. It was when Maury Wills needed to be at his peak. I always looked forward to playing a series that was crucial at the end of the season against guys like Robinson, Vada Pinson, Willie Mays, Willie McCovey, Orlando Cepeda, Juan Marichal, and Gaylord Perry. Whoever was going to win the game depended on how the top player from each team did.

There is no guarantee that each guy is going to be on. But I always felt there was no such thing as my not having it at such a time. The object wasn't to be hot against San Diego or Atlanta, but to be hot against the team that's right on your neck coming down the pennant stretch.

Those were the days I'd come in the clubhouse and say to the writers: "Yup. I was really hot stuff. Yes, you're right, gentlemen. Yes, I was. Goddammit, but I put it together. I was hell on wheels out there. I impressed myself."

I had one game when I had two home runs at the Polo Grounds against the Mets, one of them inside the park. But that didn't mean I put it all together. It just means they played me shallow and I hit a line drive in the gap and the ball rolled forever. The Polo Grounds was short down the lines, but from left center to right center it was enormous. By the time they chased the ball down and threw it in, I was back in the dugout.

Hitting a home run was a fluke for me. In 14 years I hit only 20, and six of those were in 1962—the year I hit two in one game. It just meant I was guessing fastball and had the bat moving while the pitcher was in his wind up. Only one time in my career did I hit a home run when I was trying to.

That happened against Elroy Face, the great Pirate relief pitcher. We were killing them and Face was throwing sliders in on my fists. He was a right-hander, so I was batting left-handed and the ball was breaking in on me. I knew he would pitch me that way, and I opened up. I turned on it, as they say today, and got the fat of the bat on it and hit it into the upper deck down the right-field line in Forbes Field.

It felt great when it went out. When I got to the dugout, the first person to greet me was Walter Alston. "Don't let that spoil you," he said, meaning don't start swinging for extra-base hits. He wanted me to just get those little singles and keep stealing bases.

The Pirates didn't razz me or say anything. When I started hitting it out, they knew it wasn't their day. They just wanted to get it over with.

I was a self-made hitter, and I was a good hitter. I had 2,134 hits in my career and I didn't play 20 years like a lot of the guys with big numbers. I was always second on the club in hits and average behind Wally Moon or Tommy Davis. I got every kind of hit conceivable from home runs to choppers off the plate to 10-foot bunts. I've had four hits in a ballgame and the ball didn't go 100 feet on all of them put together. On paper, they look like line drives.

Mostly, though, I hit singles. In 1962, the year I broke the stolen base record and was the National League Most Valuable

Player, I had 208 hits and 179 of them were singles. That's not hitting the ball very far. If I was hitting any in the gaps with any kind of sting on them, I would have been on second base with doubles. But if you add the bases I stole to the bases I got on hits, I led the team in total bases that year.

A lot of times guys would look at me in batting practice and say, "Hey, Maury, that looked great! You're really stinging the ball."

"No," I'd correct them. "I'm hitting the ball too hard. That's right at the outfielder. I want to hit it a little softer so it falls in front of him."

There was one time I got a new batch of bats and began hitting the ball sharply and the outfielders would just stand there and catch it. I didn't want those bats. The wood was too good. I wanted the bats that no matter how well I hit the ball it would just go over the infield. I wanted bats made out of balsa wood.

Frank Robinson would just go nuts when I got hits like that. He'd hit the ball 500 feet for a home run and then I'd get up and hit one off the plate and I'd have a single. I'd steal second and third and score on a groundout. And that run was just as big as his line-drive homer.

"EAT A STEAK!!! SWING THE BAT!!!" he'd scream at me. It just drove him crazy.

Most ballplayers don't like to hear that. In the 1989 National League playoffs, Shawon Dunston of the Cubs got jammed and hit a little blooper over Will Clark's head at first base. Kelly Downs, the Giants' pitcher, told Dunston to swing the bat and Dunston ended up going after Clark. "Swing the bat!"—that's like calling him a nigger. That's how degrading it is to a hitter. It's calling him a pussy.

The idea is to hit the ball like Will Clark or Kevin Mitchell—a screaming line drive somewhere. That Clark is some kind of hitter. His ground balls don't squeak through the infield or bounce over the pitcher's head and barely get past the shortstop and second baseman closing in on it. His shots are hits from the moment they leave the bat. They're either up against the wall or over it. That's a *hit.*

When you hit one off the fists and it barely drops over the first baseman's head, that's not legit. That's why Frank Robinson used to yell at me. He was my nemesis. I'm flattering myself when I say that, because I'm putting myself in a category with him.

But you have to be good to get hits like that. For one thing, you at least have to make contact. A lot of guys miss that high, inside fastball altogether. If you hit that pitch you hit the pitcher's very best pitch. That's why he yells, "Why don't you swing the bat!"

I laughed. They were just showing their frustration. They'd give their left testicle to do that. When a guy hits a line drive and the center fielder takes one step and catches it while it's still rising, and then I go out and bloop one and I get a base hit, they're going to be mad.

"SWING THE BAT!!!"

"Hey!" I'd yell back. "You're hitting the ball too hard."

I was just a little guy and pitchers always tried to overpower me, even if it meant deviating from their strength. If I hit an off-speed pitch and knocked it off home plate or dribbled it through the infield, the manager would chew that pitcher out.

"Knock the bat out of his hands!" managers were always telling their pitchers. Players from other teams told me this. "Why are you giving that little sonuvabitch garbage up there? Bust him in on the fists. KNOCK THE BAT OUT OF HIS HANDS!!!"

I was willing to live with those remarks because I made the pitchers get out of character pitching to me. They didn't want to walk me. And it's easier throwing a fastball for a strike than a breaking ball. So they'd try to bust me inside and deviate from their strength. My base stealing did that. It's like what having Bo Jackson in the backfield did for the Los Angeles Raiders. Even if they didn't give him the ball, the other team couldn't be as aggressive on defense because if they were charging, he might go right past them.

Everybody figured that because I was a little guy who hit to the opposite field, they should throw inside to keep me from going the other way. If only they knew that's exactly the pitch I wanted. If they were smart enough, they'd have figured out that since I was a late swinger, they should pitch me on the outside of the plate. That pitch I'd just foul off into the dugout on the opposite side of the field.

Instead of trying to turn on the ball, I kept my hips locked. I'd get my hands through between the ball and my body and drag the barrel of the bat through the strike zone. I'd hit drives right down the third base line. If the third baseman moved over to guard the line, all I did was open my stance a little so my hands would go through with a little more freedom and I'd hit line drives between the third baseman and shortstop. Dixie Walker helped me learn to hit that way.

Gene Mauch stayed up nights trying to figure out how to get me out. If you could keep me off base, you had a pretty good chance of keeping the Dodgers from getting a one-run rally. Mauch came up with high fastballs, figuring I couldn't get on top of the ball. I laid off of that pitch, but when I did try to hit it, he was right. I popped it up. So if I had to hit it I bunted it. It was a good pitch to bunt. It was right in my eyes.

I understood what they mean in baseball when they say, "Stay within yourself." It means don't try to be what you're not. Realize your limitations and be the best that you can be in terms of what you are all about. Do that and you can be a star.

I didn't have to get out there like Frank Robinson and hit homers and knock in runs in order to be in the same category with him.

That's why those guys didn't like my style of play. They wanted to kill me, to chew me up with their spikes on the double play because here I was getting all this attention and being a star doing my little old shitty shit.

## Chapter 30: The All-Star Game

In the early Sixties the players, not the fans, voted for the All-Star teams. And it seemed they almost always voted for someone else to play shortstop. Players voted for guys they liked, and I wasn't the most popular player around.

From 1961–66, though, I was always picked for the team. If I wasn't voted on, I was picked by the All-Star manager. The one time I didn't go was 1964. Walter Alston managed the National

League All-Stars that year and asked me to come. I figured if they don't want to vote for me, screw 'em.

In 1962, I had 50-some stolen bases by the All-Star break. I was hitting .300-something. And they voted me second behind Dick Groat, who apologized to me. I liked Dick Groat and had a lot of respect for him. He was a nice guy and a good player—the captain of the Pirates.

They were still playing two All-Star games that year, and I went as the back-up shortstop. The first game was in Washington, D.C., and it was special. It was the first time I got to play in my hometown in front of my family. I ended up being named the Most Valuable Player.

I got my chance in the top of the sixth inning of a scoreless game. Stan Musial was sent up to pinch-hit. Before he went up, I told him, "Get a hit, and I'll come in and pinch run for you and we'll score." It worked out just that way. Musial singled and they called me in to run.

The next guy up singled between short and third, and Rocky Colavito of the Indians came in to field it. Colavito had one of the best arms in the game. Because of that, I was able to pull one of those little plays of mine that won ballgames but kept everyone from voting for me for All-Star teams.

In the All-Star game, everybody wants to do whatever their specialty is. They want to show off. I want to show off my legs. Willie Mays and Mickey Mantle and the other sluggers want to show off their power. They don't want singles or doubles or even triples. Reggie Jackson doesn't want to hit a home run in the first row of the bleachers. He wants to hit that sucker over the bleachers. He's not satisfied with a wind-blown fly ball that just makes it into the seats at Wrigley Field. He wants to hit it over the buildings on the other side of Waveland Avenue. Johnny Bench wants to gun down Rickey Henderson.

The fans don't want to see Sandy Koufax throw three scoreless innings with no hits and all fly-ball outs. They want to see him strike everybody out.

And what does Rocky Colavito want to show off?

His arm. He wanted more than anything else to throw out this fast baserunner.

One thing I had read about Jackie Robinson was that he was known for making a wide turn at second and then hesitating just long enough for the outfielder to think he was going to go back to the bag. An outfielder with a good arm might try to throw behind him and catch him coming back. That's when Robinson would break for third and make it easily. I visualized that happening all the time.

All of a sudden, in the sixth inning of the All-Star game, I found myself in that same position. I took off from first on the hit and went around second wide, then feinted as if I were going back, hoping I could lure Colavito into throwing to second base.

A lesser player would have followed the book and thrown the ball to third. He wasn't going to take a chance. But Colavito wasn't a lesser player. He fired into second and I threw it into high gear and continued to third base.

I ended up scoring from there and then scored an insurance run in the eighth. We won 3–1 and I was the MVP.

Colavito ended up with a bum rap. People thought he wasn't a heads-up player for trying to catch me off second. But I learned that it's only the good players you can pull plays like that on because the average player doesn't think. He doesn't have the common sense to fall prey to a trick. As somebody said: Don't waste subtlety on people who are too dumb to perceive it.

My last All-Star game was in 1966 at Busch Stadium. The players had picked Chico Cardenas of the Reds over me and I didn't want to go. Walter Alston kept telling me to go, though, and finally I said I would.

It was a brutal day, 105 degrees on the field, and everybody was popping the ball up. I'm watching them and harassing Walter Alston.

"C'mon, skipper, get me in there," I'm begging.

"No, no. I'm waiting for the right spot for you," he keeps telling me.

The American League had scored in the second inning when Hank Aaron lost Brooks Robinson's fly ball in the background of white shirts and let it fall for a triple. Sandy Koufax wild-pitched Robinson home. We got the run back in the fourth off Jim Kaat and that's how it stayed until the bottom of the 10th when Tim McCarver got a hit and Ron Hunt bunted him over.

"All right, Maury," Alston said. "Here's your spot. Go get 'em."

Sonny Siebert, a hard-throwing right-hander, was pitching. During infield practice before the game, I had leaped trying to catch a line drive and pulled a muscle in my side. I got in the on-deck circle and started taking some swings and realized I couldn't swing left-handed.

Now I'm reaming myself out: "Why am I acting like such a fool? Why don't I tell somebody I can't swing the goddam bat. I'm begging to get in the game and I can't even swing the bat."

While these thoughts are going through my head, the American League manager, Sam Mele, took out Siebert and brought in Pete Richert, a left-hander. And I have no problem swinging right-handed.

Richert and I had been teammates from 1962–64 and before that we had been through the minors together. The Dodgers didn't have room for him on the staff so they traded him to Washington in 1965. And now he's on the American League All-Star team as a relief pitcher.

He and I had gone out the night before to Gaslight Square in St. Louis. We listened to the Dixieland music and I played my banjo with the band and we had a good time. When we went back to the hotel and were saying goodnight, he said, "I'm going to whip your ass tomorrow. I'm going to stick the bats right up your ass. I'll show that sumbitch Walter Alston up for trading me."

So I went up right-handed and Richert threw two pitches. The second one I lined into right center to drive in McCarver and win the ballgame.

I was so full of joy and Richert probably had his head down. I had nothing against him. I wished the poor guy could have got me out and made a good showing. At the same time I felt good because I wanted that hit. I wanted it because the National League players wouldn't vote for me and I had to wait so long to get a chance to play.

I felt I should have been the MVP, but they didn't give me that, either. I really wanted that for all the wrong reasons—to show them up. I walked back to the hotel alone, a two-hour walk. And I laughed all the way thinking about how the guys who didn't vote for me were probably wishing I had struck out.

## Chapter 31: Family feuds

The only time I got into fights was with my teammates.

There were a lot of fights on the Dodgers. Back in the Seventies, the Oakland players fought a lot among themselves and it was a big thing in the papers. We fought a lot more than they did. We were protected, though, and the fighting never became public. It was all part of the tradition. People didn't fight in other clubhouses because nobody cared enough. We did, and the fights we had were usually over something relating to the game.

There were even times when we got a little flat and guys would get together and stage a fight just to wake everybody up.

I went after Tommy Davis once over a sweater. When I first came up, the guys were all over me because of my clothes, which they didn't think were up to big league standards. So one day, it must have been 1960 or '61, I went out and bought a beautiful, Dodger-blue sweater. We were in Milwaukee when I first wore it, and I thought I was so cute when I got on the team bus at the hotel to go to the ballpark.

Tommy Davis saw the sweater and started laughing. "Where'd you get it?" he said sarcastically. "At a fire sale?" He was pointing out all the flaws in it. Before long, he had everybody on the bus laughing at my sweater.

I was at a disadvantage. I couldn't come up with verbal zingers like Tommy could. He was a kid from Brooklyn who grew up with that stuff, and he was gifted with an ability to rag people.

I got mad. I had bought myself a nice sweater and finally felt like a major leaguer, and now he was picking me apart. When we got off the bus and went into the clubhouse, I told him I wanted to talk to him—outside.

We left the clubhouse and I told him to follow me. We walked out under the grandstand, where nobody could see us. When we got there I pushed him in the chest. Here I am, 160 pounds soaking wet, pushing Tommy Davis, who's 190 and strong as a bull, and yelling at him, "C'mon and fight!"

"I don't want to fight you," Tommy said.

"Yeah, you do!" I yelled. "I'm tired of this crap!"

"Aw, I didn't mean to make you mad," he said calmly. "I was just talking about your sweater."

"You knew what you were doing!" I shouted. "C'mon and fight!"

"Maury," he said, "you're too little. If I beat you up, people are going to say I should be ashamed of myself. And if you beat me up, I'm really in trouble. I don't want to fight."

We were down there a long time. I kept shoving him in the chest. I had tears in my eyes. My pride and my ego were hurt. And he wouldn't fight.

Finally we went back to the clubhouse. Everybody else was all dressed in their uniforms and getting ready for the pregame meeting. They knew we'd come on the bus, but they had no idea where we were. They just saw us walk in together in our civvies.

"Where you been?" they wanted to know.

"Outside," I said.

I had another fight early in my career with Norm Larker, another big, strong guy who played first base and the outfield. In 1960, Norm was going for the batting title—he wound up hitting .323 in 440 at-bats. Naturally, he wanted to play every day, but he was sharing first base with Gil Hodges.

So one day Norm wasn't in the lineup and he was really unhappy. To get some of his frustration out, he was hitting fungoes to the outfield during pregame practice. He was standing on the right side of the diamond hitting fly balls to left field. Normally, the guy hitting fungoes to that side is supposed to wait until the shortstop gets out of the way before he hits the ball because he can't always be sure he's not going to hit a line drive and hit the shortstop.

But Norm didn't care about that. He was mad and he was trying to hit the ball over the big screen down the left field line in the Coliseum. He was trying to hit the ball so hard he was topping it and line drives were whizzing right past my head.

After one went a little too close, I yelled over to him: "Hey, Norm! Watch it with those things!"

"I know what I'm doing," he yelled back.

WHOOM! Here comes another one right by my head.

"Hey, Norm. I asked you to be careful!" I yelled. "Can't you wait until I move over?"

"Don't worry about it," he hollered. "If I hit you, come and get me."

He hit the next one in the air but the one after that came so close it nicked the bill of my cap. With that, I quit infield practice.

I grabbed a baseball and went to within 20 feet of him. I wanted to hit him right in the ribs with it, but I threw the ball so hard, it flew off like when I was a cockeyed, little seven-year-old kid in Washington, D.C., throwing sticks in the river. I was so wild I hit my brother in the head with a stick and he was standing next to me. That's the way I was throwing at Larker. I was crazy with rage, throwing the ball as hard as I could at his ribs from 20 feet away. And I hit him in the kneecap. I missed by that much.

Then I ran inside to the clubhouse. I knew he'd be coming after me. He had to. When I left, he was out there writhing on the ground in pain, holding his knee.

We had double lockers—stalls, really—in the Coliseum, and each cubicle had a set of swinging doors in front of it like the doors in a public restroom. The floors in the clubhouse were polished concrete. Walking on them in cleats was like ice skating. I went to my stall, sat down, took off my spikes and started putting on my crepe-soled shoes.

John Roseboro, who shared the stall with me, looked at me curiously. "What are you putting those shoes on for?"

"I think I got a problem," I said.

"What?"

"Norm Larker's coming in here after me," I said. I told him the story of what had happened.

"That's pretty sneaky," he said, pointing at my crepe-soled shoes. "You're going to have traction and he's going to be sliding all over in his cleats."

I closed the swinging doors and waited. Way down the hallway I could hear Norm Larker's cleats chattering on the cement. They got closer and closer and finally stopped in front of my locker. I could see his feet under the door as he was standing there before bursting in, just like in the old cowboy movies when the guy busts through the swinging doors of a saloon.

WHAM! The doors flew open inwards.

"YOU THREW THE GODDAM BALL AT ME!" Norm screamed in a voice trembling with rage.

"I told you to be careful," I said, standing up. "You could have hit me in the head."

Norm just stood there sputtering until someone shoved him from behind and he fell on me. I thought he was coming after me and I shoved him back. Norm slid backwards on his cleats, and hit a big equipment trunk with the back of his knees, and ended up sitting on the trunk. I came after him, ready to start hitting him. But before I could throw a punch, Frank Howard came up behind me, grabbed hold of my collar, and lifted me up with one hand.

"What's going on?" Howard demanded.

"Let me at him, Frank!" I yelled.

Somebody else grabbed Larker before he could get back at me and broke up the fight. I think he would have chewed me up if they hadn't stopped it.

Even today, when I see Norm Larker at old-timers games, he brings up that incident. "I still remember, you hit me with that ball," he said the last time I saw him. "Yeah," I said, "that was a long time ago. I'm sorry."

It's amazing how individuals can carry things so long. Bobby Thomson hit the shot heard 'round the world in 1951 to beat Ralph Branca and the Dodgers in the playoffs and when they both come to an old-timers game, Ralph knocks Bobby down every time he pitches to him. I saw him do it at least three times. Some things people don't forget.

Walter Alston challenged the whole team once. We had just dropped a doubleheader in Pittsburgh and were on the team bus heading for the airport, which is quite a ways outside of town. It was a hot day and it was a school-type bus with no air conditioning and barely enough power to creep up the big hills outside of town. We had all our bags with us, so we had to sit sideways. To top things off, the Pirates, who were leaving town for a road trip, went zooming past us on one of the hills in their big, air-conditioned, Greyhound-type bus and they were all pointing and laughing at us through the windows.

Everybody was bitching and moaning at Lee Scott, the traveling secretary, about the bus. Walter Alston was sitting in the front listening to it, and nobody knew it, but he was fuming. Suddenly, halfway to the airport, he told the driver to pull over and stop the bus. He stood up, turned around and said a few well-chosen words.

"If anybody has anything to say about this goddamned bus, say it now," he roared. "I'm going outside, and if you want to say anything, step off the bus and tell me. You can come one at a time, two at a time, or you can all come at once."

He stepped off the bus, lit a cigarette, and stood on the side of the road for a few minutes. When nobody accepted his invitation, he came back in.

"Nobody?" he said, looking straight at Frank Howard, the biggest guy on the club. "Okay. Now sit!"

You could hear a pin drop the rest of the way to the airport.

That was Walter 100 percent. You only saw him explode maybe once or twice a season because once he did he didn't have any more problems with us for a long time. He wouldn't harp on petty things or collect fines for little things. He'd just take so much until he couldn't handle it anymore and then he'd get it all out.

Walter Alston named me captain in spring training of 1962. Pee Wee Reese and Duke Snider had been captains, but they were gone. We had only had three or four captains in the history of the club, so that was quite an honor. I got to take the lineup card to home plate before the game and when we played the Giants, I'd be standing there with *Willie Mays.* Willie was a year older than me, but by 1962 he was in his 12th year and was a superstar.

There wasn't a lot of hoopla about it. Walter Alston just told the team one day I was the captain. I remember how I felt, though. I was honored, but I didn't like being given that role. I guessed that they made me captain because they felt that I could light a fire under Tommy Davis and Willie Davis because we were all black.

They had a different makeup than the others. Tommy was from Brooklyn and Willie was from Mineral Springs, Ark. Tommy didn't really wake up until after his first time or two at bat. The first time up, they'd get him out and maybe the second time, too. Then the third time—it could be Bob Gibson out there, it didn't matter—boy, Tommy was ready. He hit .320 and .330 as it was. I wondered what he would have hit if he woke up before the game started.

Tommy and I lived four houses from one another. He would come over and have coffee with me. Our kids would play together. We were good buddies. Then we'd get to the ballpark and be at one another's throats. It was amazing. And the next morning, we'd be right back sitting down together having coffee.

I took my position as team captain too seriously. One day the coaches were trying to get Tommy's attention from the bench. Tommy played left field and they wanted him to move but they couldn't get his attention. So they caught my eye and asked me to tell Tommy to move over. When I did, Tommy turned his back. He didn't want me telling him where to play. Finally he gave me some hand signals that said: "I'll play my position. You play yours."

When the inning was over, I went in the dugout and waited for him to get in.

"Let me tell you something, Tommy Davis," I began, and before I could get any further, he came after me.

"Let me at that little sonuvabitch!" he yelled as five guys jumped on him and held him back. Meanwhile, I'm yelling, "Let him go! Let him go!" Good thing they didn't. He would have pinched my ear off.

While they were holding him, somebody reminded me that I was supposed to be hitting. I went down and got a bat, and as I stepped out of the dugout to go hit, I turned around and told Tommy, "If you want more of me, I'll be inside after the game."

After the game, I let him go into the clubhouse first. I wanted to see where he was when I came in so I could avoid him. When I walked in, he reached out from behind the door and picked me up and somebody—probably Frank Howard—saved me again.

Tommy and I are like brothers. We fought a lot but we get along great to this day. He still laughs at me. We did all right on the field, too. When I stole bases, more often than not, Tommy Davis drove me in. I wouldn't have scored 130 runs in 1962 without him and he wouldn't have driven in 153 without me. No one in the big leagues has driven in 150 runs since.

Tommy and I became closer after my playing days. Of all the people I played with, he has shown the most compassion for me over my addiction. Tommy seems to take it harder than anyone, even my good friend Johnny Roseboro. It seems when I was hurting so badly I didn't even know I was hurting, Tommy would go on a crusade to find me. He'd track me down and give me hell. When he saw me looking bad, he told me I looked like crap. He told me when everyone else kept quiet.

Tommy's been calling me ever since we've been out of the game, getting me to make appearances and helping me make a couple of bucks. Tommy finds me. Tommy really loves me.

Willie Davis had great talent. He could be as good as he wanted to be on any particular day. He was the premier center fielder in the National League. But he was so quick and and so good that he was nonchalant about everything. He was so talented that he committed the cardinal sin of drifting under fly balls instead of charging over, getting under the ball, and waiting for the ball to come down. In the second game of the 1966 World Series against Baltimore, he did that and when he had finally drifted over to where the ball was going to come down, he looked up and the sun hit him at the same time. He didn't have a chance to put his glasses down and the ball dropped for an error. Later in the inning, he was going to show that the error was a fluke and he drifted under another fly ball and the same thing happened. He ended up with three errors in the fifth inning—a record.

We lost the Series in four straight, but Willie's mistakes weren't the cause. Baltimore's pitching just shut us down.

Anyway, the Dodgers thought that by naming me captain they could get more consistency out of Willie, but it just alienated him.

Being captain of the team, I had a little kangaroo court. John Roseboro and Dick Tracewski were the judges. If somebody did something like not running out a ground ball or not putting his sunglasses down and losing a fly ball, we'd fine him.

One day Willie Davis hit a ground ball in a double play situation. Willie was so fast he didn't get doubled up even when he hit a shot and this was a slow bouncer. But he was so disgusted with the way he hit the ball he just "Cadillac-ed" it to first base and got doubled up. After the game, I called my court together. The judges fined him something like $50 and I let him know about it.

That made Willie so mad he told Walter Alston. The skipper didn't say anything right away but a couple of days later he got mad about something and when he was done lecturing us, he added: "And furthermore, what's this kangaroo court crap? I don't want anyone fining my players. If somebody needs to be fined, I'll do the fining."

Then he turned to me: "Who told you you could have that sort of thing on my club anyhow, Wills?"

Here goes my little ego. "You said I was the captain and I could do things like that. I fined him. Yeah. I fined him and he should be fined."

"There'll be no more fines and no more of this kangaroo court," Alston ordered.

"If that's the way you feel about it, I don't want to be captain of this team anymore," I shot back in front of the whole team. "I resign!"

Alston didn't say anything. About three days later, I walked into his office as humbly as I could. "Skip?" I pleaded. "It's about my captain's position. Can I have it back?"

"You never lost it," he said.

He never said another word about it. I walked out of his office shaking my head. What a man.

I had a lot of feeling for Walter Alston. He never had more than a one-year contract and the Dodgers always seemed to have either Charlie Dressen or Leo Durocher—both former Dodger managers—there as a third base coach just to remind him that a replacement was ready. Dressen had managed the team from 1951–53 and was fired simply because he asked for a two-year contract. Alston replaced him in 1954.

It had to be uncomfortable for Alston to have Dressen and then Durocher there. Dressen and Durocher were demonstrative, flamboyant men and Alston was quiet and low-key.

I hurt for Walter Alston. I was happy just to be there, but I'd been through enough hardship to relate to someone having something hanging over him like that.

Every time the club started losing a few games, the papers would be full of columns about what a bad job Walter Alston was doing. Then the next day, the guys who wrote the columns would be in his office and he would be nice to them.

I walked into Alston's office one day after that had happened and said, "Didn't you see what that guy wrote about you?"

"Yeah, I read it," he said.

"How the hell can you treat him so nice?" I asked.

"Maury," Alston said, "that's just life. It's no big deal." He managed the team for 23 years.

Walter didn't carry grudges, so the team didn't, either. That's why conflicts didn't hurt us.

We were in St. Louis one time when Tommy Davis said he couldn't play because of a pulled hamstring. Then Walter Alston found out that Tommy was out dancing all night at a local disco. Walter called him on it during the team meeting and Tommy had some smart-ass reply. Alston told him to take his uniform off right there because he was suspended for the rest of the season. We really felt bad about that because we needed Tommy in the lineup.

We got him back, of course. I don't even know if Alston collected a fine from him. With Walter, when it was over, it was forgotten.

I learned a lot from Walter Alston. A lot of things happened between Tommy Davis, Willie Davis and me. If I held on to them, I could really dislike those guys. But I would always think back and say, "Hey, we were all young and trying to play major league baseball. We were all intense. That was life. That's all."

I never stopped loving them—Tommy and Willie.

## Chapter 32: Dodger Blue

We didn't have cliques on the Dodgers, and we didn't have any real animosities among the players. Some guys hung out together, but there was no resentment between those who did and those who didn't.

The wives did have cliques, though. I don't know what it's like today, but when I played, wives caused as many problems among the players as anything else. They caused more trouble than the media ever could.

The wives would bitch because one wife was sitting in the front row and her husband was a pitcher who only played once every four days while another wife whose husband played every day was sitting in the second row. Both seats were right behind home plate, the best seats in the house, but they'd cry about it anyway.

So the wife who was in the second row would tell her husband about it. And heaven forbid that somebody make an error behind a pitcher whose wife was at the game. The pitcher's wife would turn and glare at the wife of the guy who made the error. If she was mad enough, she might start telling the other wife she ought to find out what her husband was doing on road trips. Then the second wife goes home and tells her husband what so-and-so's wife said about him, and what does he do on road trips, anyway?

Maybe one or two pretty girls are sitting in the family section and nobody knows who they are. It doesn't matter whether there's any hanky-panky going on or not. She's not a wife and the wives have to find out who she is because she's too pretty to be sitting there alone. So the wives watch her to see when she applauds and when she gets excited. They check her out until they've figured out who left her the tickets.

As far as I know, the wives didn't split up into groups along racial lines. I think prejudice is usually harbored by men more than women. As far as I know, race wasn't an issue among the women.

Coming to the games was a social event for the wives. There was competition over who had the best clothes or the most luxurious fur coat. What was an issue was who was the queen leader. That's another thing the wives would struggle for. Among the Dodger wives, the queen was Virginia Drysdale—Ginger.

It was never Don and Mrs. Drysdale. It was Don and Ginger. That first-name identity was the ultimate status. The wives didn't want to be known as Mrs. So-and-so. They wanted their own first-name identity and it was quite an achievement when they got it. On the Mets it was Tom and Nancy Seaver. On the Dodgers, after Drysdale retired, it was Steve and Cyndy Garvey.

Ginger was a lovely woman, as sweet as could be. She was the wife who would sashay in with her fur hanging just as the national anthem ended and everybody was settling down. It was quiet then. The pitcher was taking his last few warmup pitches, and everybody was sitting down in anticipation of the game. That's when Ginger would come in.

As she made her entrance, one voice would ring out: "Here comes Ginger!" That was Jeri Roseboro, John's wife. She was the freest spirit of all the wives.

Gil Hodges was probably the nicest of all the established Dodger heroes who moved west with the team from Brooklyn. Clem Labine was a nice man, too, and Carl Erskine, who never had much to say, prays for me and writes to me to this day.

But there was a warmth about Gil Hodges. He looked you in the eye when he spoke to you. He was that way with me from the beginning. And he was indirectly responsible for my nickname—"Mousey" or "Mouse."

Charlie Dressen, the former manager who was a coach when I came up, gave me the nickname. I'd go 0-for-1, then 0-for-2, and every time I made an out I'd come back and put my bat quietly in the bat rack and sit down. Other guys came back after making an out cursing, throwing things and raising a general ruckus. Dressen liked that.

One day he called me over and chewed me out for being so passive. "Goddammit," he said, "you made an out! I want to see you come back and throw that bat around. I want to see some spitting and kicking. I want to hear some swearing."

"That's not me, Charlie," I tried to explain.

"Whaddya mean, it's not you!" he bellowed. "Are you a man or a mouse?"

"I'm a man!" I declared.

"Well, show it, then!" he ordered.

The next time I made an out—which was probably the next time I batted—I came back to the dugout and swung the goddam bat all over. I cursed like a longshoreman. I kicked and screamed. Then I threw the bat so hard it caromed off the dugout wall and went careening past Gil Hodges.

Gil sat there calmly and said, "Com'ere, kid."

I went over to where he was sitting.

"You gotta be careful throwing those bats," he said quietly. "Because if you hit somebody—especially me—you might get your butt kicked."

Meanwhile, Charlie Dressen is as pleased as he can be. "Thatta way, tiger!" he's telling me.

The next time I made an out, I came back to the dugout, laid the bat quietly in the rack and sat down. Dressen looked at me and roared, "You're a mouse!" The name stuck.

Duke Snider wasn't playing much toward the end of his Dodger career and he was bitter. I'm not sure why. It was none of my business then and it's none of my business now.

I went into a slump in the middle of the 1962 season and went to Duke for advice. "I can't understand it," I said. "I know I can hit in the big leagues. I hit good for two years but now I can't do a thing."

I remember him saying, "Kid, if you're a good hitter, don't worry about it. If you aren't hitting in April, it'll come in May. If not May, June. If not June, July. Or August or September. It'll be there before the season's over."

That was all the advice he was in the mood to give me. Coming from Duke, I accepted it. It turned out he was right. It did work out. I finished the year with 208 hits and was the National League MVP.

Johnny Podres and Don Zimmer had also been Brooklyn Dodgers. They were like two peas in a pod. They both liked to go to the racetracks. They'd bet on the clouds moving overhead. But they didn't bet on baseball games. All their gambling was legal.

Podres was as good as any pitcher we had. He wasn't as prolific as Sandy Koufax, but he was as outstanding as any pitcher I played with or against. He was a money pitcher, and yet it seemed he didn't want to go any further than the seventh inning. He could be in the seventh inning of a big game with a no-hitter and a shutout going and he'd start looking to the bullpen. You'd think maybe he was running out of gas, but he just didn't want to finish the game.

Johnny could go nine and sometimes did. He just didn't want to. I guess he didn't have the confidence, the self-assurance to go those last two innings. The players said he was tighter than a frog's ass—that's when your ass gets so tight it's watertight. That's not to be confused with a red ass, which refers to a guy who's really ticked off. Ron Fairly was the biggest red ass in the game. When you have the red ass you're mad. When you have the tight ass like Johnny, it means you get tight in a pressure situation. Podres knew they said that about him and he didn't care. I remember going out to the mound late in a game and Johnny was so wound up his teeth were chattering.

The Dodgers were fortunate to always have a relief king—Clem Labine, Ed Roebuck, Ron Perranoski, Phil Regan, Jim Brewer—so Podres got away with being a seven-inning pitcher. And Walter Alston figured if we got that from him, we'd be all right.

Johnny did like to drink. He got drunk a lot after games. I believe sometimes he got drunk the night before he was scheduled to pitch, too. A couple of times, Walter Alston had to go and bail him out of some jail when he got in trouble.

One time in Chicago, the police department called Alston and said, "You got to come down here and get your pitcher, Johnny Podres. We're holding him for disturbing the peace in a bar." So Alston had to get out of bed and go downtown.

A day or two later, we're still in Chicago, and Alston gets another call in the middle of the night. The police had Johnny again. "I'm not losing any more sleep over him," Alston said. "Let him sleep it off down there. I'll get him in the morning."

Sandy Koufax and Don Drysdale were complete-game pitchers. Claude Osteen was a finisher, too.

Osteen, who pitched for the Dodgers from 1965–73, was a surgeon on the mound. When he got to the late innings, he lost his velocity, which wasn't great to start with, but he had pinpoint control. If the ball wasn't moving as much because he'd lost some zip, he could still put it anywhere he wanted. I liked playing behind Osteen. I could see from shortstop the pitch and location the catcher was calling for, and, because I could depend on Claude to get the ball in that location, I could always anticipate and get a great jump on the ball.

There were times when we had a new third baseman I would go to the mound in a tight situation and tell Claude to give a right-handed pull hitter a fastball on the outside of the plate. If he threw that pitch inside, a pull hitter would hit it down the third base line. If he put it outside, though, he would pull it right to me at shortstop practically every time. I wanted that ball in the late innings of a close game when everybody was tense.

One time we were playing the Giants in late September in a

pennant race. The rafters at Dodger Stadium were bending from the noise. I think Jim Ray Hart was the hitter, and I remember going to the mound and telling Claude to put it on the outside of the plate.

"I got to have the ball," I told him. "Make him hit it to me."

Osteen put the ball right where he wanted it. Hart swung and hit it right to me, and that sucker went right through my legs. I think we lost the game. I told Claude after the game I owed him three for that error. I know I personally won him two games, but I don't think I ever got the third for him.

An error like that didn't bother me though, any more than getting thrown out bothered me as a base stealer. I wanted the ball in tight situations. Not all of my teammates did. And nobody wanted to take a high pop-up in a Dodger Stadium day game under a high blue sky. The ball seems to hang in the sky and doesn't look as if it's ever going to come down. That's when guys start yelling, "TAKE IT!" "I NEED SOME HELP OVER HERE!" They'll say they're having trouble with the sun, but it's not the sun. It's the ball.

Somebody hit one of those one day right between home plate and the pitcher and slightly to the first base side of the infield. Bill Sudakis, the catcher, took his mask off, tried to find the ball, and looked around for volunteers. Wes Parker was playing first and he didn't want any part of it. Whoever was pitching was delighted that pitchers aren't supposed to field pop flies, and Bill Grabarkewitz, the third baseman, was fudging on it, too. It was one of those "I got it, you-take-it" situations. I ended up running in all the way from deep shortstop as hard as I could. I dashed through the whole convention of infielders and caught the ball. I was going so fast my momentum took me almost to the backstop. And as I stopped and turned around to trot back across the diamond, a fan yelled at me: "Hey, Wills! Stay at your position!"

That happened late in my career when Jim Gilliam was gone. There were times when Jim was playing second, though, when I'd hear him yelling to me, "Come over and help me. I got the sun over here." I'd yell back, "I got the sun over here, too." But I had to run over sometimes and get the ball.

Jim Gilliam didn't hang out with anybody. The Dodgers gave us four tickets to give away to each game, and I always seemed to need a minimum of seven or eight tickets to take care of all the people I promised tickets to. I was always running around trying to borrow tickets from other players. Jim Gilliam left tickets for his family, but never for anybody else. I always admired him for managing to stay free of that kind of stress. At the same time I wondered how it was possible. It was good for me, though. Most days I'd borrow his extra tickets to put on my guest list.

Charlie Neal, who was the second baseman when I came up, was traded—sold, really—to the Mets after the 1961 season when he was still in the prime of his career. He had a conflict with the Dodgers about something and they decided he had an attitude problem. His attitude was that if he didn't like something he said so. He'd call them all the MF word if he had to. That didn't work. Nobody's bigger than the establishment, especially the Dodger establishment. I found that out.

Charlie became an original Met and just withered away. By 1963, he was just 32 and out of baseball. It shows how the mind affects your ability to play. Charlie Neal became ill psychologically and emotionally. Before you knew it, he was through.

There was no question that being a Dodger brought out the best in a player in my day, just as being a Yankee did in the American League. The tradition and spirit of those franchises made players come closer to their potential. I saw average players who became winners when they were traded to the Dodgers.

Jim Brewer and Daryl Spencer came over as role players and played well for us. Ron Perranoski and Phil Regan became outstanding relief pitchers when they joined the Dodgers. Wes Covington came from Milwaukee and got some big pinch hits. Guys like Andy Carey and Lee Walls were leaders from the bench. Claude Osteen blossomed as a Dodger. There's a mystique about wearing Dodger blue. No question about it.

A lot of players played for other organizations before joining the Dodgers, but when they come to old-timers games, they think of themselves as Dodgers first. Frank Howard had his glory days with the Senators, but he's a Dodger.

Tommy Davis played eight years with the Dodgers. That's less than half of his 18-year career. From 1959–66, he was a Dodger. Then he played for the Mets, White Sox, Seattle Pilots, Astros, the A's, Cubs, the A's again, the Cubs again, Orioles, Angels and Royals.

But Tommy will always be a Dodger.

# Chapter 33: Sandy and Don

At old-timers games at Dodger Stadium, Don Drysdale is always the next-to-last player introduced. Sandy Koufax is last. Drysdale gets a nice round of applause, but modest. So do I. The guys who get the biggest receptions are the guys from the Seventies—Steve Garvey, Ron Cey, and Bill Russell. Those are the players today's fans remember best.

But Sandy Koufax still gets the whole stadium. The reception he gets is dramatic.

I often wonder how Don feels about that. Because during their playing days, Sandy was always second to Drysdale in terms of being the image of the ballclub. Drysdale was put in that position. He was made to be the role model just as Garvey was.

You couldn't make a better choice than Drysdale as the image of the Dodgers. He was more outgoing, more of an extrovert, than Sandy. He was young, tall, blue-eyed, handsome and, being from Van Nuys, Calif., he was a hometown hero. He was always presented as the image of the club, the glamour boy. When people talked about the Dodgers, it was always Drysdale, Koufax and then Wills.

Sandy didn't want that role, but he felt that he at least could have been offered the spotlight. They could have let it be his choice. I don't think Sandy ever appreciated that it was Drysdale and then Koufax and Wills. The connotation was that you're going on talent, and if that were the case, you had to say it was Koufax, Drysdale and then Wills.

A friend of mine once told me that it really should have been Wills, Drysdale and Koufax. I entertained that thought for a long time. I played every day, after all. But as much as I tried, I could never make myself believe that it should be Wills ahead of Koufax and Drysdale.

Don was a presence in the clubhouse. He was more rah-rah

than Sandy. Don was more sociable than Sandy. Don had more fun. He would participate in the little antics that are a part of baseball—pillow fights, water fights, hot feet, card games. Sandy didn't do any of that stuff. He was a no-nonsense person who led by example. Sandy never said a word.

Sandy pitched four no-hitters including one perfect game. Some of those games, the opposing hitters couldn't get the ball out of the infield. Maybe they hit one easy fly to center in the ninth inning, and the only time anyone got halfway decent wood on the ball it was an easy roller to the infield.

After a game like that, I would overhear Sandy telling the writers, "I was just lucky."

Once I got behind the mob of writers around him and yelled right over them: "Sandy, do you mean to say that you didn't want to strike out those last two guys and get the no-hitter? If you didn't feel that way, at least tell them that."

It's only human to feel that way, but what did Sandy say? He said, "No. Winning the game is what's important." Then he'd say he was just lucky to strike out the last 17 batters or whatever.

"No way," I said with the writers listening in. "Tell the people you're that good, Sandy. Tell them you wanted that no-hitter."

He wouldn't change his answers.

We talked about that privately. He said he didn't want to go into what he was feeling. He felt that his thoughts were his personal property. He didn't feel he had to share them with everybody.

Sandy kept to himself. There was no telling what he did or didn't do. He was a secretive guy. He'd never leave tickets for anybody. If a friend of his came to the game to watch him pitch, the friend had to buy her own ticket. If the friend wanted to see Sandy after the game, she had to go to Sandy's home. Sandy wouldn't see anybody at the ballpark.

I don't know if Sandy ate in his room all the time or not. He seldom went out with the guys. He didn't drink. Once in a while he might go to dinner with Johnny Podres or Ron Perranoski and Don Drysdale, but he never went out the night before he was going to pitch. Never. Nobody knows whether Sandy and Don were friends but them. I know they didn't pal around.

Drysdale and Perranoski had the closest camaraderie of any

two players I ever saw. On road trips, if you saw one, you saw the other.

But Sandy was always alone. One time, during the period when we won three pennants in four seasons from 1963–66, the Dodgers had a victory party at the Dodger Stadium Club. Everybody was there but no one had seen Sandy. Finally, he walked in with Jill St. John. We all almost fell down.

Sandy had something in his childhood that he carried resentment about. I don't know enough about it to speak with authority, but I know he had some deep-rooted grievances. He hasn't changed much. I think he still carries them.

He was a bonus baby from Brooklyn. When the Dodgers signed him before the 1955 season, the rules were that if a team paid a player a certain amount to sign, the player had to stay on the major league roster. His first year was 1955 when he was 19. By 1959, when I came up, his record was 20-21 after four years in the big leagues. I watched him develop. He hurt his arm that year, but he also set the first of his records when on Aug. 31 he struck out 18 Giants in one game.

He couldn't have set that record without me. I was hitting eighth that day and he was hitting ninth. Late in the game, we had a man on first and one out. Walter Alston told me to bunt him over. If I bunted him over, Alston was going to pinch-hit for Sandy and Sandy wouldn't have had a shot at the record. But I failed to bunt the man over and Alston left Sandy in to make history. I always reminded Sandy of that.

He had an inner pride that drove him. He had a lot of hurt in him, too, probably from the way the Dodgers treated him early in his career. It took him a long time to come into his own. I don't know that he felt the team showed him the patience early in his career that he wanted.

When he retired prematurely after going 27–9 in 1966, he said his arm was bad, and it was. But he could have continued to pitch. He could pitch with the pain. He just decided he didn't want to go through the pain for Walter O'Malley, the Dodgers owner. He would have done it for the Dodgers, but not for O'Malley. He and Don Drysdale had gone through a bitter hold out that spring. I'm sure the holdout and the negative publicity he got soured Sandy.

As far as I know, I was closer to Sandy than anyone on the

team. He used to stay long after the games in the trainer's room to ice his arm and I'd stay to ice my legs. The trainer would leave us with bags of ice and tell us how long to stay there and then he'd leave. So Sandy and I got to talk a lot. He opened up to me.

I'd do things for Sandy I wouldn't do for Don Drysdale. There were times when Sandy had a shutout going in the ninth inning with a man on third and less than two outs. If we had a big lead and the batter hit a ground ball to shortstop, the runner on third might just Cadillac home, figuring I'm going to go for the sure out at first because his run doesn't mean anything. But I'd fire it home and nail him to keep the shutout alive. I could have let him score, but I wanted Sandy to have the shutout. He deserved it. He'd strike out the last guy or pop him up and the game would be over.

Sometimes, he had a shutout going with a man on second and the batter would hit a ground ball up the middle or toward the hole between short and third. I'd dive and knock that ball down so the man on second couldn't score and ruin Sandy's shutout.

At first, Sandy would get in the dugout and thank me for helping him out. After a while, he didn't say anything. He'd just look at me—"Hey, Mouse!"—and nod his head.

We had a close camaraderie that way. He'd do the same sort of thing for me. If I made an error behind him, he'd turn to me and give me a sign to not worry about it. Then he'd strike the next two guys out and get me off the hook. When we got to the dugout, I'd say, "Thanks, Sandy." He'd say, "Don't worry about it. I owe you four or five."

After an inning, he used to come down to the end of the dugout where I was sitting smoking a cigarette. He'd be breathing hard and he'd say, "Gimme a puff off your cigarette, Maury." And I'd give him a puff or a whole cigarette if he wanted it.

After two or three years of that, I finally asked him, "Where are your cigarettes?"

"I don't buy cigarettes," he said. "I don't smoke that much."

"You mean you left yours in the machine," I corrected him.

That was one of his little idiosyncrasies. He didn't want to buy a pack of cigarettes because he didn't consider himself a smoker. He just had a couple of puffs now and then, maybe three times a game.

Sandy didn't like to throw to first to hold the runner. To show

Steve Sax is a pretty good bunter, but, then, he had a good teacher.

Los Angeles Dodgers, Inc. Copyright © 1990 Los Angeles Dodgers, Inc.

When the Dodgers held Maury Wills Day in 1971, I thought I had a lot of baseball left, but I guess they were trying to tell me something. It was my last year as a starter.

Los Angeles Dodgers, Inc. Copyright © 1990 Los Angeles Dodgers, Inc.

When I had to dive back to first on an attempted pick-off, and the play was so close even I couldn't bear to look, I knew I had my maximum lead.

In spring training at Vero Beach, while the big guys practiced hitting, I practiced bunting from both sides of the plate.

Sandy Koufax (center), Willie Davis (right) and I were the stars of Game Five of the 1965 World Series. Sandy shut the Twins out on four hits while Willie and I traded roles: He stole three bases and I whacked two singles and two doubles in the 4–0 win.

Associated Press Photo.

Sandy and I renewing acquaintances before Sandy Koufax Day, Sept. 29, 1969.

UPI/Bettmann

The 1962 Hickock Belt winner arriving in Buffalo to pick up the hardware, Jan. 22, 1963. Gannett Rochester Newspapers

In 1962, it seemed that every night I broke another stolen base record and got another base. This one broke Bob Bescher's National League of 81 set in 1911. UPI/Bettmann

One of my jobs as captain of the Dodgers was taking the line-up card to the umpires before the game.

Los Angeles Dodgers, Inc. Copyright © 1990 Los Angeles Dodgers, Inc.

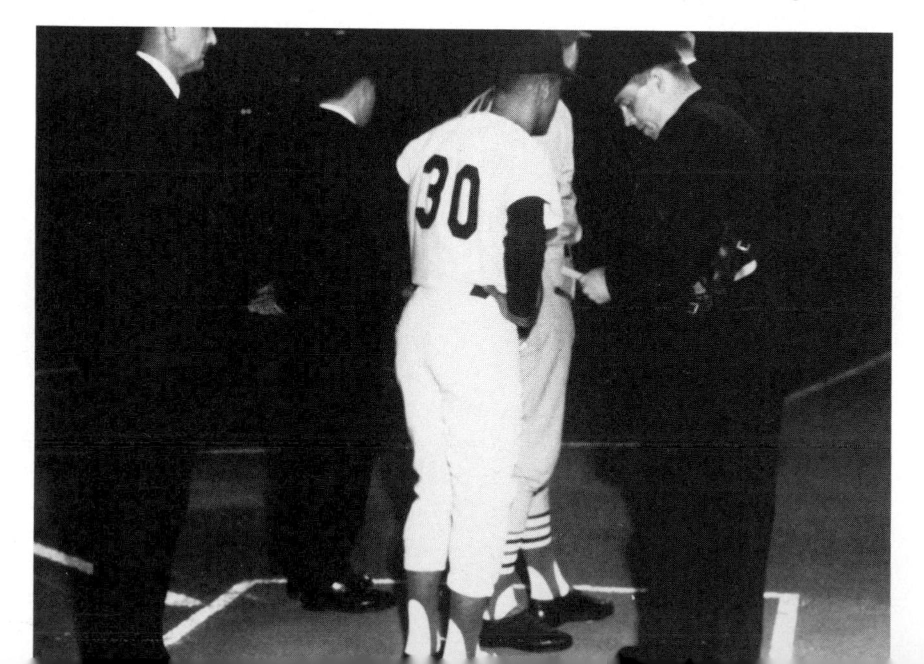

This is how you throw from down under on the double play. That's Hal Smith of the Cardinals hitting the dirt.

UPI/Bettmann

It took me more than two years and 1,100 at bats to collect my first home run in 1961, and when I did, the telegrams came rolling in.

Associated Press Photo.

When the Rangers came in to play Seattle late in 1980, it was the first time a father had managed against his son's team in the big leagues. It was a proud moment, even if Bump and I weren't on the best of terms at the time.

National Baseball Library/Cooperstown, N.Y.

When I got to spring training in 1966 after a short holdout, I was making $85,000 a year—a lot of money in those days—and dressing the part.

UPI/Bettmann

Three generations of Dodgers: That's Roy Campanella from the Fifties in front; me, Sandy Koufax and Willie Davis (left to right) from the Sixties, and Steve Garvey from the Seventies.

Los Angeles Dodgers, Inc. Copyright © 1990 Los Angeles Dodgers, Inc.

When Seattle named me to manage the Mariners late in the 1980 season, I was just the third black to manage in the major leagues.

National Baseball Library/Cooperstown, N.Y.

Stolen base 104 came in the 165th and final game of the 1962 season. I played in every one of those games. The stolen base record was broken, but 165 games played in a season is a record that still stands. That's Jim Davenport covering third for the Giants.

When VOX came out with a new line of electric guitars and amplifiers in 1967, they hired me to help introduce them at the Waldorf in New York. The dancers are Carin Kahgan (left) and Judy Eirlisch. Associated Press Photo.

At bistros like Your Father's Mustache in New York, they used to keep a banjo for me to play when I came into town. This was in 1966. I found, though, that when I wasn't a star anymore, my banjo playing wasn't as good.

National Baseball Library/Cooperstown, N.Y.

I've instructed a lot of teams, not all of them from North America. Here I am at Vero Beach showing a Korean team and the Dodgers how to get a jump. Los Angeles Dodgers, Inc. Copyright © 1990 Los Angeles Dodgers, Inc.

One thing that hasn't changed in baseball—getting in shape in spring training.



Maury Wills, Dodger.

Unlike the runners of today, I almost always went in feet first. In this steal of second against the Giants, I'm very close to the base (23A) and just starting my slide. As Chuck Hiller gets the ball and turns, (23B) I'm sliding away from the play and just catching the bag with my toe—safe. Los Angeles Dodgers, Inc. Copyright © 1990 Los Angeles Dodgers, Inc.

Father and son at peace at last: Bump and I at a 1990 fantasy baseball camp.

Jonathan Gallen

It's always a thrill to do a curtain call in Dodger Stadium. This one was July 1, 1990. The occasion was Maury Wills Night during the Dodgers' year-long centennial celebration.

you how great a pitcher he was, he didn't even have a pickoff move, he wasn't exactly a good fielder and he wasn't a good hitter like Gibson and Drysdale. The only thing he could do was strike you out, not give you any hits—and win. He didn't need a pickoff move because he kept men off first base. If somebody did get on and the situation called for a sacrifice, he'd tell us, "Don't get fancy and try to get the lead man and end up not getting anybody. Just make sure you get me one."

We'd get him the one and he'd get the rest.

The Dodgers pitted Drysdale and Koufax against one another salary-wise. They favored Drysdale over Koufax. Don always pitched the season openers. I remember one day there was a doubleheader and Sandy and Don were scheduled to pitch. Sandy preceded Don in the pitching order. That meant he was supposed to pitch the first game of doubleheaders. But this day, they switched them around. Don was going to pitch the first game. To a pitcher, that's the same as switching days. No pitcher wants to sit around the clubhouse waiting for three or four hours to pitch the second game of a doubleheader.

I don't know if Don requested the switch, but when Walter Alston came out to the clubhouse to tell Sandy that Don was going to pitch the first game, Sandy really got vocal. That was the only time I ever heard him get that way.

In 1965, we played the Twins in the World Series. Don pitched the first game of the Series, Sandy pitched the second, and Claude Osteen pitched the third. Don came back in the fourth game, Sandy in the fifth, and Claude in the sixth. The rotation was set up so that Don would pitch the seventh game on three days' rest. But when it got down to the last game, Walter Alston asked the team who they wanted to pitch. We picked Sandy on two days' rest over Don on three. Sandy shut out the Twins and we won the Series.

Sometimes teams let the guy who's starting the next day go home early. One day Don Drysdale wasn't at the ballpark during one of Sandy's no-hitters. When someone got to Drysdale to tell him what Koufax had done, Drysdale's comment was, "Did we win?"

That's being snide in a horseshit way. It's a bad reflection on the other eight guys out there to suggest that our pitcher could hurl a no-hitter and we could lose because our team was so poor. Those are the kinds of things Don would say.

My dad passed away during spring training in the early Sixties and I went to Washington, D.C., for the funeral. I didn't even see him before he died. I just caught the funeral procession and flew back to spring training. I hardly knew him.

That spring, all the writers had been doing stories about how the Dodgers were going to bounce back that year and how Maury Wills was going to lead them. While I was at my father's funeral, the papers hit the stands in Florida quoting Drysdale as saying: "If Maury Wills is supposed to be the big man who's going to win it for us, we're in big trouble."

I saw that headline when I got back to camp. I called Drysdale outside the clubhouse.

"Did you say this?" I said, looking up at him.

"I didn't say that," he said.

I left it at that.

If you made a mistake behind Don, he would kick the dirt on the mound in disgust. After the game, Don would explain to the writers that he didn't kick the dirt to show up the person who made the error, and maybe he didn't. Maybe he was just disgusted that the opposition got a break and he had to shut them down. But who has time to interpret it that way? We were only human, and the poor guy who made the error—I was one of them sometimes—was dying out there. If it was me, I felt like every eye in the stadium was on me. Then he'd kick the dirt and I'd mutter, "Fucker!" I felt bad enough already. But that's the way he was.

So if Don had an 8–0 shutout going in the ninth with a man on third and the ball was hit to me, I didn't throw home to nail the runner and preserve his shutout like I did for Sandy. I threw to first and got the sure out. And if there was a man on second and someone hit that grounder in the hole or up the middle, I didn't dive for it to keep the man from scoring for Don like I did for Sandy.

I would never purposely make an error or not give it my level best as a defensive player behind Don. But I didn't have to dive and scar myself all up on that hard Dodger infield for him when the score already was 8–0. Maybe I had stolen four bases and my legs were all bruised up and I didn't want to bruise them any more. I really didn't have to dive. If the runner scores, it's still 8–1. So I didn't do it for Don. But I did it for Sandy.

I was with Pittsburgh in 1968 when Drysdale was setting the record by pitching 58 consecutive scoreless innings. That record stood until 1988 when Orel Hershiser went 59 straight innings. Drysdale was beating us badly when I singled off him late in the game. He kept firing the ball over to first base, trying to pick me off. Finally, I told Ron Fairly, the Dodger first baseman, to run to the mound and tell Drysdale I wasn't going to steal the base. We were losing by something like 7–0 in the eighth inning. For me to steal that base, I would have to have been on a mission to break his scoreless inning string. But down seven runs, there was no reason to try to steal. Stealing second wasn't going to win the ballgame. The best I could do was break his string, and I didn't want to do that.

Drysdale didn't believe me, though. He kept throwing to first. He must have thrown over 10 times. He didn't pick me off because I wasn't far enough off the bag.

If he had thrown at my head while I was batting and then I got on first, I might have stolen second and third out of spite. But he didn't. So I didn't, and he kept his string going.

Not that Drysdale had anything against throwing at hitters. When we were still playing in the Coliseum and I was new to the big leagues, I saw Frank Robinson, who was with Cincinnati, come up to the plate once in a situation that called for an intentional walk. John Roseboro, our catcher, looked over at Walter Alston, and Alston came up to the top step of the dugout and held up four fingers, the sign for an intentional walk.

Roseboro stood up, held his hand outside the plate, and put up four fingers to Drysdale: Put him on.

Drysdale called Roseboro out halfway to the mound. Roseboro shook his head in agreement with whatever Don said. When Roseboro got back to home plate, he got down into his crouch as if they had decided to pitch to Robinson.

Alston jumped up to see what was going on. Frank Robinson took his stance next to the plate, leaning over it. Before Alston could do anything, Drysdale threw the first pitch—right at Robinson's head. Frank left his cap hanging in mid-air and went down hard. Ball one.

Roseboro threw the ball back to Don and got back in his

crouch. Robinson got back up again. Here's the same pitch, right at Frank's ear. Frank goes down. The cap stays in the air. Ball two.

By now, Alston knows what's going on. He sits back in the dugout and calmly crosses his legs. Frank Robinson is glaring at Drysdale. The next pitch—WHOOM! The same spot. Ball three.

With each pitch, Robinson got closer and closer to home plate and leaned over even more in defiance of Drysdale. After the third knockdown, Robinson got up and started out toward Drysdale and Don started toward him. The umpires got between them before anything could happen.

Roseboro got back in his crouch. WHAM! The cap stays in the air. The body goes down. Frank Robinson gets up, dusts himself off and goes to first base. Drysdale put him on just like Walter Alston wanted.

On the first pitch to the next batter, Frank Robinson takes off for second base. I sure didn't go over to cover and I don't think Charlie Neal went over, either. Robinson came in with his spikes glittering up in the air. He hit the bag and slid halfway out into left field trying to get somebody. We let him have the base.

On the next pitch, Robinson took off for third, looking for somebody to cover the base so he could cut him up. I think Jim Gilliam took one look at him, stepped back, and said, "Go ahead. Take it."

"Wow!" I'm saying to myself. "This is the major leagues. These guys know how to play baseball."

## Chapter 34: The Roseboro-Marichal affair

Unlike Don Drysdale, Sandy Koufax wouldn't throw at anybody, which is part of the story of how Juan Marichal came to hit John Roseboro over the head with a bat. But most of all, it started over me. John Roseboro was nice enough to give me the credit for it.

Marichal and Koufax were pitching against each other on Sunday, Aug. 22, 1965. But the seeds of the incident were planted in Saturday's game, when we were having a tough time. I couldn't get on base, so I resorted to trickery.

I had this little soft bunt I would lay down the first base line. I had had a lot of success against the Giants with that bunt, one, because they had tough pitchers and I had to resort to bunts to get on, and, two, it was much easier for me to bunt in Candlestick Park than to hit away.

Defensively, it's tough playing in Candlestick. When the pitcher, the third baseman, and the first baseman charged in for the bunt, they had to plant themselves, turn and throw off balance to first in a swirling wind. That increased the odds of bunting successfully. But it was even tough to run there. It was tough stealing second base at Candlestick when the wind was blowing in from left field, in my face.

I got the idea of going into my bunt position early. When a batter shows bunt early, the catcher automatically comes up on the balls of his feet and moves forward. That's why a batter should never fake a bunt when the man on first is trying to steal. It gets the catcher up and moving forward, and that makes it easier for him to get off a good throw to second. I always told the man hitting behind me to fake a swing when I was stealing. That made the catcher stay back. Normally, when I was going to bunt, I waited to show it to keep the catcher from getting a good jump out of the box.

Knowing how catchers react, this time I showed bunt early. Tom Haller, the Giants' catcher, started coming forward. At the last instant, I pulled the bat back, but I did it in a sweeping motion and hit Haller in the mask with the bat. That's catchers' interference.

There was a big argument over the play, but I wound up on first base and we got a little rally going. It was an effective play, and it steamed the Giants. We wound up winning the game in 11 innings, 6–4. Podres got the win in relief.

The next day, Juan Marichal was pitching against Sandy Koufax. I led off the game and with two strikes on me, I laid a perfect bunt down the third base line for a hit. Jim Gilliam also bunted for a single and Ron Fairly, who was hitting fourth, doubled in two runs.

The next time through the order, I came up and—WHOOSH! —Marichal left my cap in the air and I went down. Gilliam came up next and—WHOOM!—he goes down. Then Willie Davis gets up and—BAM!—his cap's hanging in the air and he's down, too.

After the inning, we came into the dugout and John Roseboro was talking to Sandy Koufax. "Okay, Sandy," John was saying, "if he wants to play that way, we can play that way. When Marichal comes up, let him have it."

"Oh, no. I can't do that," Sandy replied.

"What do you mean, you can't do it?" Roseboro demanded. "He's doing it to us. Just stick one under his chin. You don't have to hit him. Just stick it under his chin and make him go down."

"No, John. I don't want to do it," Koufax said.

I had moved over and was listening to the conversation. I'm always listening to things I'm not supposed to hear. That's how I got in trouble later in life, too. Finally, I butted in. "Why not, Sandy?" I asked.

"I don't play that way," Sandy said firmly. "I don't want to hurt anybody."

"C'mon, Sandy!" Roseboro pleaded. "What are you talking about?"

I walked off using every kind of body language I knew to show I was disgusted that Sandy wouldn't do it. When I came back, Roseboro had taken another tack.

"Okay, Sandy, I'll tell you what to do," Roseboro instructed. "Give me a low, inside curveball down in the dirt—a bad pitch that he can't hit and one that I have to go down to my left to catch. I'll fall to my knees and catch it down low, and instead of standing up to throw the ball back to you, I'll stay in my crouch. I'll be inside, almost behind him, so when I throw it back, I'll hit him right in the goddam head. I'll cream his ass."

Sandy didn't think that was such a great idea.

I thought it was terrific. "Great plan, Johnny!" I shouted. "I like that. I'm always the one trying to figure out stuff like this. Where did you get that from, Gabby?"—we called him Gabby because he never talked—"That's great!"

Finally, with quite a bit of reluctance, Sandy said he'd do it.

We went out on the field. I knew what was going on. John knew what was going on. Sandy knew. I don't think anyone else had any idea of what we had planned. The guys on the bench were sitting there trying to keep warm, disgusted over having to play in Candlestick where we had such a tough time winning. The crowd was its normal crazy self for a Giants-Dodgers game. Somewhere in the stands, the Dodger Booster Club was marching around with banners and cowbells and Dodger jackets and caps.

Now Marichal comes up and gets ready to hit. He hit right-handed and stood straight up with the bat on his shoulder. He'd raise the bat just when the pitcher was ready to release the ball. After the pitch, he never left the batter's box. He just stood there with the bat on his shoulder looking at the pitcher.

I'm standing at shortstop in great anticipation as Roseboro puts down two fingers for the curve. Sandy shakes him off. Roseboro gives the curve again. Sandy shakes him off. Roseboro gives the curve again. Sandy shakes him off. "C'mon, Sandy," I'm pleading silently at shortstop. "Throw the goddamned curveball. Throw the curve!" Finally, Roseboro put the fastball down and Sandy threw it for strike one.

I don't know what the count got up to, and I don't want to exaggerate. They say no story's a good story unless you enhance it, but this one doesn't need enhancing. I know that Sandy did not want to throw the curve and he kept shaking it off and Roseboro kept putting it down. And I'm still praying for the curve at short.

So Sandy finally accepts the curve. He winds and he kicks. WHAM! Sandy Koufax, with his pinpoint control, threw the curve down and in, just where John wanted it. Some other pitchers might have thrown the curve and hung it up high or outside and that wouldn't have worked. Even high and tight wasn't going to work. It had to be low and in so Roseboro could go down and scoop it out of the dirt. That's just where it was.

After the pitch went by, Marichal relaxed, put the bat back on his shoulder, and stood in the box looking at Koufax. Roseboro is on his knees behind him with a full shot at Marichal. Just as John went to throw the ball, though, he had second thoughts. "No, I might kill him," he said to himself. "I'll just give him a message. I'll just tick his nose."

WHOOSH! The ball flies past, just ticking the end of Marichal's nose. When a hard-thrown ball goes past you that closely, it makes a noise like a bullet.

Marichal turned around, the bat still on his shoulder, and looked at Roseboro. "Don't you hit me with that ball," he said.

"Huh?" Roseboro said. "What you say, fella?" And he started to raise up out of his crouch.

Marichal saw Roseboro getting up and he thought John was coming after him. He got scared, and how many people wouldn't be scared if they saw Roseboro coming for them? Marichal still had the bat on his shoulder, so BAM! He hit Roseboro on the head. Just as hard as he could.

Roseboro went back and down. Anybody else would have said, "Okay, fella. You made your point. Just don't hit me again." But Roseboro, as gutsy as he is, came back after Marichal a second time and Juan hit him again. It happened so fast, nobody really realized he hit John twice until we saw it on film. John went down again, then got back up and came after Marichal a third time.

Marichal is terrified now. He's already hit Roseboro twice over the head with a bat and the guy's still coming after him. Marichal knew he was about to be killed if he didn't get out of there.

Marichal dropped the bat and started running, but he was so scared, he didn't have the presence of mind to run toward his own dugout. Instead, he runs straight out toward the middle of the infield where we all are waiting to get our hands on him. Suddenly, he realized what he was doing and made a right turn toward the Giants dugout on the first base side of the field.

I was still standing at shortstop, in shock at what had just happened. But Lou Johnson, our left fielder, had run all the way in and was after Marichal. Meanwhile, Mike Kekich, a rookie Dodger pitcher, caught up to Marichal and tackled him. Then everybody piled on. The Dodgers are all trying to get to him. Lou Johnson is digging like a gopher trying to get down into the pile of players. The Giants are trying to keep us off the pile. And at the bottom, Kekich is holding Marichal in a bear hug. When everybody found out later he was just holding Marichal, we wanted to kill Mike for not squeezing him to death. When the umpires finally got everyone unpiled, Marichal didn't have a scratch on him.

The funny thing about Roseboro is that when Marichal hit him, he didn't bleed at all at first. It wasn't until Marichal was at the bottom of the pile and Roseboro was trying to get to him that Willie Mays grabbed John to calm him down and saw the blood.

"Jeezus, John!" Mays said. "You got blood all over your face."

I looked back and blood was pouring out of John like oil from a well.

Shag Crawford, the home plate umpire, threw Marichal and Roseboro out of the game. John was in shock anyhow. He might not have known where he was. All he knew was he wanted to get Juan Marichal.

We wound up losing, 4–3. Marichal was suspended a number of days, but it worked out that he only missed one start. Warren Giles, the National League president, fined him something like $1,700 and we knew the Giants would pay that. Having major league ballplayers' mentalities, we bitched about the leniency of the penalties. And, as luck would have it, we went to New York to play the Mets right after that game, and that's where we learned about how easy Giles went on Marichal.

# Chapter 35: Warren Giles

When Warren Giles announced his penalties against Juan Marichal, the New York media were all over our hotel getting comments. Maury Wills, with his ego, had to say: "Warren Giles is a gutless son of a bitch."

The next day, the headlines in big, bold letters on the New York sports pages read: "GILES IS GUTLESS S.O.B. — WILLS."

Warren Giles was fuming. He called the Dodgers and demanded a public apology. "I want it now, or I'm going to suspend that boy for the rest of his life. I'm going to put him out of baseball," Giles warned.

The Dodgers asked me to issue an apology. They called a press conference and brought me in to say I was sorry. I refused to apologize.

Word got back to Giles. "He better do it before the week's over," Giles demanded. Still, I refused. Finally, the ballclub got me to agree to call the league office and apologize privately. But I never apologized publicly.

That was my second run-in with Warren Giles. My first came in 1962 when I was stealing all the bases. We went into Candlestick for a series with the Giants. When we took batting practice and infield practice before the game, the wind was swirling as usual and the infield was dry. It didn't even have a layer of top dressing on it. The wind had blown that away. As usual, they had grown the grass at least four inches high, which they always did for us so we couldn't get our little, squeaky ground-ball singles.

After the teams leave the field and go back to the clubhouse to change into their game uniforms, the grounds crew sprinkles the infield down. That holds the dust down and helps smooth it over. This day, they didn't just sprinkle. They took the nozzles off the hoses and stood in one spot in front of home plate with the water on full force. They figured this was a good way to keep me from bouncing the ball off the dirt in front of home plate for one of those singles that go 50 feet up and 50 feet out. The ball doesn't bounce real well off mud.

Then they went down and started doing the same thing around first base, where I would get my lead to steal second.

They'd been doing this for a while when somebody burst into our clubhouse all excited. "You should see what they're doing to the infield!" he shouted.

"What? What?" everybody wanted to know.

"They're watering the thing down like you wouldn't believe!"

We ran outside to see what they were doing, and these guys are standing out there with the hoses. From first to second you could plant rice it was so muddy. From second to third and in front of the plate it was the same thing. But down the first and third base lines it was dry as a bone.

We came back in the clubhouse and appealed to Walter Alston to go out and do something about it. Alston, in his nice, calm, collected way, said, "Well, I'll see what's going on." He went out and said a few things to the umpires. The umpires told the grounds crew to clean it up as best they could.

There was no such thing as cleaning it up, it was so bad. They put some sand down like they did when it rained, but that made it worse. Now it was slushy. I went out to first base to test it and I actually sunk in the mud up to my ankles.

When the umpires came out to start the game, I started bitching at them. I was leading off, and I told the home plate umpire what I thought of him.

"You didn't do anything about this," I told him. "You ain't got no freaking guts."

"What did you say?" the umpire asked me.

I was more than happy to repeat it for him: "I said, 'If you don't do something about this field, you ain't got no freaking guts!' "

The umpire was only about 18 inches away, but he said one more time, "I didn't hear you."

"I said, 'YOU AIN'T GOT NO FREAKING GUTS!' "

He took his mask off, stepped in front of home plate and said the magic words: "You're outta here!"

When he said that I really got in his face and started woofing at him. Frank Howard finally came out and picked me up, tucked me under his arm like a loaf of bread and carried me back to the visiting team dugout. All the way I was kicking and screaming like a little kid, "Let me go! Let me go! Let me go!"

After the game, I repeated everything I told the ump to the press. When the newspapers and the umpire's report made their way to Warren Giles' desk, he fined me $50 for making such a scene.

They don't give you forever to pay those fines. You have to send them in immediately. As luck would have it, we left San Francisco the next day and flew to our next series in Cincinnati, which is where the National League offices used to be.

When we got to Cincinnati, Lee Scott, the Dodgers traveling secretary, called me in my hotel room. "Maury," he said, "you got to pay the fine."

"I ain't paying no fine," I told him.

"C'mon, Maury," he begged. "You've got to pay the fine."

"No way," I said and hung up.

The next thing I knew, Lee Scott was knocking at my door. "I talked to the ballclub, Maury," he said. "They said to pay them with your check and we'll give you our check for the $50. It won't cost you anything."

"I don't want to pay the fine, and I'm not going to pay the fine," I insisted.

John Roseboro, who was still my roommate, listened to this. Finally, he said, "C'mere, roomie. Take the check. I've got a plan."

"What's the plan?" I asked as I took the check from Lee.

"Take your check," Roseboro explained, "go down to the bank, and get $50 worth of pennies. Pay him in pennies."

"Pay him in pennies?" I said, the light beginning to go on in my head.

"Yeah," Roseboro said with delight. "Can't you see that?"

"That's a lot of pennies," I admitted. "How many pennies is it, John?" We tried to figure it out, but we gave up. We just knew it had to be a big sack.

It was already four o'clock and the bus left for the park at five. I hurried down to the nearest bank. I gave the teller $50 in cash and asked for $50 worth of pennies.

"I'll have to go to the vault to get it," the teller said.

"That's all right, ma'am," I said. "I'll wait." She gave me a cloth bag filled with 100 rolls of pennies—about 80 pounds worth. I dragged the bag back to the hotel room and dumped all the pennies out of the rolls into the bag. Then I dragged the bag down to the league office and went upstairs to Warren Giles' receptionist.

"Is Mr. Giles in?" I asked politely.

"Yes, he is."

"Could you tell him Maury Wills is here to see him?"

She came back and ushered me to Giles' office.

"Mr. Giles," she said, "Mr. Wills is here to see you."

"Come in," Giles said cordially.

I walked into the office struggling with the bag. I hoisted it onto his desk and turned it upside down. Pennies cascaded everywhere.

"Mr. Giles," I said, "here's your fine. Could you count it for me, please? I'd like a receipt."

I hesitated a moment to see his reaction and then walked out to the reception area. I waited about 30 seconds and listened to him sputtering in his office and having apoplexy. I decided to leave.

By the time I got back to the hotel, Lee Scott and Walter

Alston were going crazy. Giles had called them and issued a warning: "I'm tired of this boy's crap. If this gets out to the press, I'm going to suspend him for life."

"What the hell's the matter with you, Maury?" Alston asked me. "Why do you do things like that?"

I said something very insightful. I think my exact reply was, "Uh . . . huh?"

That was 1962. And when I exploded again in 1965, Warren Giles remembered the pennies.

In the meantime, every time I played in the All-Star Game, Giles would come in the clubhouse and give us a two-minute pep talk before the game. Then he'd come over to me and say, "Give 'em hell, Maury! Kick the crap out of them!"

Years later, after I had retired and Warren Giles was no longer National League president, I was an announcer for NBC. Whenever I went to an All-Star game or World Series, Giles would come into the NBC hospitality tent. When he saw me, he always came over with a warm smile and said, "Hi, Maury! You know, even though . . ." And he'd go on from there as friendly as could be.

## Chapter 36: Giant killing

We didn't need pep talks when the Dodgers played the Giants. There was no "I like you—I think you're all right, too." Grudges got carried not only from game to game but from year to year. It was like a war all the time.

Orlando Cepeda, the big Giant first baseman, was one of the real nice guys in baseball. That didn't count for anything when he got up to hit against the Dodgers. Our pitchers liked to try to intimidate him by sticking the ball under his chin. Then they'd come back with curves and sliders low and away.

Cepeda got even when he got on first base. When he was on first, he hoped and prayed for a ground ball in a double play situation so he could come down there and take you out good. They didn't call him the Baby Bull for nothing.

I hadn't been in the big leagues two years when I had my first run-in with Cepeda. We were playing at the Coliseum and Cepeda was on first. I had no roots in the Giant-Dodger rivalry. I hadn't done anything last year that made them want to get me. But somebody hit a ground ball and I went to take the throw at second on the front end of the double play and here comes Cepeda looking to take me into left field.

I had been in the league long enough to learn to throw underhanded on the pivot. That's how I threw when Cepeda came after me, sliding with his hands up high. The ball hit him in the wrist and broke it.

I was new to this. I wanted to apologize when I saw he was hurt. But everybody let me know it wasn't necessary. I wanted to go see him the next day, just to make sure he was all right, but my teammates told me no. "He'll take care of it," they assured me. "He's a Giant."

That gave me some roots in the Dodgers-Giants war. And when Cepeda healed and came back to the lineup, there he was again on first base in a double play situation, there was another ground ball to the right side of the infield, and here he came after me again. I came down again with my underhand throw and this time I hit him right in the helmet—right where it says "SF." The helmet went flying toward the stands. The ball went in the stands. Cepeda just shook his head and ran off the field. He'd done his job. The batter was safe.

Later in my career, I pulled one of my best plays against Cepeda. It happened at Candlestick Park. I was at first base and Juan Marichal caught me leaning toward second. He threw to first and I was hung out and frozen—picked off.

Most players, when they get picked off, just figure they're dead. They give up and they get tagged out. But with my idea of perfect practice, I figured there had to be a way out of it. The obvious way is to get in a rundown and try to get the defense to throw the ball as many times as possible. In a perfectly executed rundown, the defense gets the runner with one throw. If you make two throws, that's okay, too. If you make three throws, which is too many, but you get the guy out, you can live with it.

But if you have to make four throws, the manager has you out there practicing the play.

The more times you throw the ball back and forth, the better the chances are that somebody will throw the ball wild or hit the runner. So the runner tries to duck and dodge, back and forth, back and forth.

That doesn't happen too often in the major leagues, though. That play is just hoping for luck. There had to be a better way.

Through my perfect practice, I came up with a play that would work.

For the idea to work, the first baseman has to be a big guy who's slow and cumbersome. You use his lack of mobility to beat him. You can't pull the play off if you're caught in a rundown between the shortstop and second baseman, who are generally as quick and agile as you are.

The play starts when the pitcher picks you off, and the first baseman has the ball. He holds it up high and starts running you to second. Most guys will take off for the bag, the first baseman throws to the shortstop, and they have you. In this play, though, I didn't break for second. I stayed as close to the first baseman as possible—so close that he figured he could tag me out in one or two more steps. So he kept chasing me with the ball held up high and I just shuffled along toward second, maybe a foot out of his reach. By staying close to him, I limit his options.

The first time I pulled it in the big leagues was in 1963 or 1964 against Dick Stuart of the Pirates. He chased me all the way to second base, and when I got there, I was safe on the bag and he was still standing there holding the ball over his head.

That wasn't exactly the result I was looking for, but I took it. My idea was that I'd stay close to the first baseman so that when he did throw the ball to second, I could put on the brakes and change direction so fast he wouldn't have time to get out of the way. That way I'd run into him and I'd get second base on an interference call.

That's exactly what happened the first time I pulled the play against Cepeda. I stayed just out of his reach, and when he threw to second, I threw it into reverse and ran right into him.

If you think Candlestick Park shook during the World Series earthquake in 1989, you should have been there when they awarded me second base.

The next time I got in that situation against the Giants, I broke for second when the pitcher picked me off. Now, instead of throwing the ball to the man covering second, Cepeda took dead aim and tried to hit me with the ball as hard as he could. The ball whizzed past my ear like a bullet and ended up in deep left field while I ran all the way to third. That's the kind of intensity that ruled every Dodgers-Giants game and that's how upset Cepeda was when I made him look silly.

Another time against the Giants, this time in Dodger Stadium with Don Drysdale pitching, Willie McCovey was up in a double play situation with Jim Ray Hart on first and another runner was on third. McCovey owned Drysdale his entire career. Willie was a left-handed pull hitter, and in this situation, Drysdale had me play directly behind second base.

Sure enough, McCovey swung at one of Drysdale's low, sinking fastballs—some people actually called them spitters—and hit a ball into the dirt that bounced over Drysdale's head and came down right on second base. It was a tailor-made double play. I caught the ball with my right foot on the bag and cocked to throw to first. When I looked up, though, Jim Ray Hart was coming at me like a runaway beer truck.

Now Jim Ray's reflexes were a little questionable. Bob Gibson broke his jaw once with an inside fastball that everybody felt Hart had plenty of time to get out of the way of. But Jim Ray, who was called Old Crow because that's what he drank, was fearless.

I'm ready to throw to first to complete the double play, but I said to myself that if I threw underhanded like I normally did, I'd kill Hart. I figured he'd try to go down at the last instant to get under the throw but he didn't have enough time and he'd get creamed. I also couldn't throw it over him, because that would send the ball over Ron Fairly's head at first. I decided the only thing to do was throw the ball overhand right at his forehead. I figured his reflexes would get him out of the way. It's amazing all these things can go through your mind in a split second.

By now, Jim Ray Hart was 10 feet from me and still running upright, intent on hitting me and taking me into the Dodger Stadium bleachers. So I threw the ball right at his forehead.

And that's just where it hit him. WHOP!

Did you ever see a duck-hunting film where somebody shoots

the bird and it folds up and falls? That's the way Jim Ray Hart went into second base. He was lying there with his eyes rolled up into his head and his mouth open. I thought I'd killed him.

All the Giants rushed around him. I looked around and didn't see one Dodger uniform anywhere. Willie Mays was right next to me. Willie McCovey, Len Gabrielson, who's 6-foot-4, Tom Haller and Orlando Cepeda are all around me saying things like, "What's he trying to do, kill the guy?"

"I threw it right at his head," I tried to explain. "I thought his reflexes would get him out of the way, right?" Then I just tippy-toed over to the Dodger bench where all my teammates were.

They took Hart out of there on a stretcher. I went to the hospital after the game to see him. The nurses told me he was resting quietly and he'd be fine. I called in the morning to check on him again, but they said he had been discharged. He went to Milwaukee with the team that day and hit two home runs. So he was all right.

Those are the kinds of things that went on at Dodgers-Giants games. I'll never forget that while Jim Ray Hart was lying on the ground, some woman in the left field stands was beating another woman over the head with her high-heel shoe because she was rooting for the Giants. It was a battle when the Dodgers played the Giants—on the field and in the stands.

# Chapter 37: Pitchers

Bob Gibson was the toughest pitcher for me to hit. He didn't have a good curveball, but he had a little slider he'd throw in on my fists. It was small but hard, and I just couldn't get around on it. Once in a while, I'd top one off the plate and I'd be on first base by the time it came down. But I can't remember ever hitting him hard.

As a rule, pitchers can't bunt, can't hit, can't field, can't run and can't slide. The only thing they can do is throw the ball longer and harder than anyone else. But Bob Gibson was a good athlete. He was as good a player as there was and he could help himself out at the plate.

There was one thing that Gibson couldn't do, though. Ron Fairly told me about it: "Gibson can't throw to second."

"What do you mean?" I asked.

"He can't throw to second," Fairly repeated. "For some reason, he can't make that pivot and throw to second to hold a runner."

Telling me this is like giving the fox the keys to the henhouse. The next time I got to second base against Gibson—which wasn't often—I took a big lead. I mean I was off at least 15 feet. Gibson got in his stretch position and looked back at me.

"Hey!" he yelled. "You, fella! You're a little far off, aintcha!"

"You talking to me?" I yelled back.

"Yeah, you!" he yelled. "You know you gotta hit again!"

"Oh," I said and hurried back toward the bag. "Excuse me."

Gibson would throw the goddammed ball at your head as soon as look at you. You'd be on the ground trying to get up and you'd say to him, "Hey, brother!"—an appeal to racial solidarity.

"Don't give me that brother crap," he'd snarl back. He never said anything to anybody at All-Star games. He didn't want to give away anything to people he played against, and he didn't want to make friends with opponents—especially hitters. I felt the same way. I didn't talk to pitchers at All-Star games, although I wouldn't have minded making friends with Bob Gibson—just to lighten him up a little bit.

I loved to hit against Juan Marichal. He was a great pitcher, maybe better than Gibson, but he didn't intimidate me. Marichal wasn't a power pitcher. He had about five pitches he could throw at any time and get them over the plate. You knew when Gibson was in the hole he was coming in with his fastball. Marichal could have the bases loaded with the winning run on third, one out, and he would throw the screwball and get it over.

If you were looking for raw speed, Nolan Ryan was as fast as anyone I ever saw. I hit against him when he was with the Mets early in his career. I hit against Tom Seaver, too, and I'd rather hit against Seaver than Ryan. Ryan's ball was straight, but it was heavy. If you didn't hit that sonuvabitch on the fat of the bat, you'd break your hand. You just don't like to hit against guys who throw that hard. Even though you know what's coming, the ball is so heavy it's like hitting a shot put. That, and he was wild. He never knew for sure where the ball was going.

I've had a Ryan fastball go by me up high that hit the catcher's mitt with such a pop it made my ear ring. Ryan and a couple of other pitchers could do that. Dick Selma, when he was a top reliever for the Phillies in 1971, was one of them. Jim Maloney, a starter with the Reds, was another. There were times when I heard their fastballs sizzle like bullets as they went by.

Bob Veale, a left-hander from Pittsburgh who struck out 276 batters in 266 innings in 1965, could throw hard, too. He was wild and he wore thick glasses that he was always wiping off. He was a guy you just didn't want to dig in against. Ryne Duren, who pitched for just about everybody in baseball, was another one like Veale. He was so wild he hit a guy in the on-deck circle once. He may have done that on purpose, but he had me back on my heels a couple of times.

That's a saying among pitchers: "Get him back on his heels." You get on your heels and you're dead. You can't move. That's how I was on curveballs before I learned to be a switch-hitter. Later in my career, I learned from watching Pete Rose that if you stay on the balls of your feet and keep your weight forward, you have balance. He wasn't just being gutsy and defiant standing that way. He was putting himself in a position to protect himself better. That's how fighters stand. You can go all kinds of ways if you stay on the balls of your feet. Human nature tells you to get back on your heels, but if you give in, he's going to get you.

I put that theory to the test against Phil Regan after I was traded to the Pirates. Regan was a relief pitcher for the Dodgers. They called him The Vulture. We had been teammates, and now I was a Pirate and standing in against him with a count of two strikes and no balls. I had always been good to him. I was good to all my pitchers. I dove for ground balls, I cut the ball for them, spit on it for them, whatever. So I didn't expect Phil Regan to throw at me.

But he did. He threw right at my shoulder, and somehow I managed to get out of the way. I got back up, and now I dug in á la Pete Rose, on the balls of my feet, looking defiant. And Regan threw three more balls and I walked. Normally, I didn't say anything to pitchers, but as I was walking down to first, I said,

"You gutless sonuvabitch." He heard me and he put his head down and shied away. I immediately stole second and third.

When I got back to the dugout, Danny Murtaugh, the Pirate manager, came up to me and said one of the nicest things anyone has ever said to me. "Maury," he said, "you're a real pro."

That was in 1967. I saw Phil Regan in 1989 at the Dodgers old-timers game. I went up to him, looked him right in the eye, kind of punched him and shook his hand. I squeezed it real tight and kind of shook him around. He knew what it was all about. Damn right he remembered.

## Chapter 38: The best of the rest

Frank Robinson hated my guts. He didn't care whether the Reds won the game or lost the game. He didn't care whether we completed the double play or not. When he was running from first to second on a ground ball and I was covering second, he would leave the base path to get me. He'd leave the ground 15 feet away. If the ball got there first, I made him eat dirt, and when the ball didn't get there in time, I just took off for right field. I never knew how it started because I never did anything to him. It must have been because I was a little guy.

Frank Robinson would hit the ball out of sight. Then I'd come up and bunt one or tap one off the plate or hit it just over the infield, steal second, steal third, and win the ballgame or tie it up. I was his nemesis.

One time there was a public incident in which he was picked up with a gun on him. It was a big deal in the papers. The next time I saw him I said, "You got your gun?" That was a cheap shot and he came out of the dugout after me. His teammates had to pull him back.

Frank Robinson was the most aggressive baserunner of my day. Tommie Agee was a hard slider. Johnny Roseboro was a hard slider. But that goddammed Robinson was lethal. He wasn't just after me. He was after everyone. He'd trip himself to win a game. If Frank Robinson was playing solitaire, I think he'd cheat himself.

Roseboro was the toughest catcher I ever saw. Tim McCarver, who was nice enough to call me the smartest base stealer ever, was the second toughest. I saw them collide once in St. Louis, when McCarver was trying to score against Roseboro. They were both laid out, and both of them limped off the field.

Daryl Spencer was a 6-foot-3 infielder, who played a couple of years with the Dodgers in the early Sixties, and he was a rock. I was sliding into second head first one time, and he put his knee down in the small of my back and ground it in.

"What are you doing? What are you doing? Let me up," I screamed.

"Slide right, you little sumbitch," he growled.

I saw Daryl Spencer jump into Eddie Mathews, the Braves third baseman, about a mile from third base and sink both sets of cleats into Mathews' thigh right above the kneecap. Mathews got up, looked down at his leg, and saw all the blood. He started to go to the dugout to get stitched up, but he had second thoughts. Instead, he went back to third and leveled Spencer. He punched him out like a light.

Football players are known to go into a bar and just rip it up. Eddie Mathews was like that. He could tear a whole bar apart by himself. He was a bull. You didn't mess with him. He had a lot of anger. It could have been from the constant rivalry between him and Aaron.

I couldn't name a personal all-star team. I had such regard for so many players, it would be unfair. I mean I'm not qualified to pick. It would be guesswork. I would end up picking the Mantles, DiMaggios, Mayses, Robinsons, Kalines, Clementes—my own favorites. Or I'd think of one particular play that impressed me instead of the overall picture. It's almost absurd trying to pick an all-star team when I've seen so many great players.

The most interesting thing to me is to pick the most underrated players. Felipe Alou comes to mind. The guy could hit, throw, run, field. Felipe Alou was feared more when he played for the San Francisco Giants than Willie Mays, Willie McCovey and Orlando Cepeda.

Felipe Alou came up with San Francisco in 1958, then played

for the Braves from 1964 through '69. He was on the same team with Aaron and Cepeda, who also played for the Braves in 1969 after stints with the Giants and the Cardinals. Alou was the guy who killed us, not Hank Aaron or Cepeda. Aaron wouldn't wear us out. He'd get his 2-for-4—a double here and a single there—but we'd get the guys out in front of him so he couldn't do any damage. Alou would do the damage.

It's ironic that Hank Aaron broke Babe Ruth's all-time home run record when he wasn't known as a home run hitter. He really wasn't. Hank Aaron was known as a line-drive hitter and a guy who hit for average. He hit his home runs with such consistency throughout the season that you didn't notice them so much. It wasn't as if Aaron hit three home runs today, or two grand slams, or hit 10 home runs in a week. No, he got his one and two here and there throughout the entire season and before you knew it he had 40 for the year. In the meantime, he was hitting his damned line drives all around the park and you had to keep guys off base in front of him. If he didn't get a hit, it just meant you pitched around him.

Hank Aaron would have got more infield hits if he could run. But he didn't run out ground balls very well. He did, however, get the biggest leads off first base I ever saw. He got a bigger lead than Lou Brock, Rickey Henderson or Vince Coleman. You couldn't pick him off and you couldn't stop him from stealing a base when he really wanted it. He just didn't do it often enough for it to bother you.

You couldn't have a home run hitter like him stealing 50–60 bases a year. It took so much out of a player to steal that many bases and still hit for power and average. Aaron and Willie Mays could not steal 60 or more bases and be able to hit as well as they did.

Athletes are in better condition today and stealing is more important than it was when Mays and Aaron played. You just didn't figure a guy who hits 40 home runs was going to try to steal bases like Jose Canseco does today because they were going to get bruised and tired. If a home run hitter got to first base, he just stood there until the next home run hitter came up and hit the ball.

The mentality of home run hitters was such that they didn't want somebody moving on the bases when they were hitting. It's distracting. And they didn't want the pitcher throwing to first base two, three and four times to hold the runner when they were waiting to hit. Sometimes, batters would tell the manager to make that sonuvabitch keep still on first base so they could hit.

When those big hitters got on first, they kept the same mentality. They didn't want anybody moving on the base so they didn't move themselves. That's why guys like Aaron didn't steal many bases.

It's changed today. Players have a greater appreciation for the stolen base. Stealing a base affects everybody, even the outfielders, who have to cheat a little to get in close in case there's a wild throw to one of the bases. Players also have a greater appreciation for total performance today. They didn't scout speed and arm strength in my day.

Felipe Alou was a total player. He was fast enough to play center and he had a good enough arm to play right. With the Braves, he played center field because they had to hide Rico Carty in left field.

You always try to hide the guy with a big bat who can't field. They used to hide those guys at first base, but players like me ran that guy out of the infield and out into left field.

Ed Bailey was a catcher for the Giants. One day, the Giants tried to put him at first base to get another bat in the lineup. I made them take Ed Bailey off first base in the fourth inning. The first time up, I bunted right down the first base line. He got the ball and was waiting for me holding the ball in his glove at waist level. I ran as hard as I could right up to him. Just when he thought he was going to tag me, I put a hook slide on him, then got up and scrambled to first base safely. Meanwhile, he was still standing there with the ball in his glove and everybody's booing him.

The next time up, I did the same thing and they had to take him out of the game. I used to tell my teammates we had to make the other team pay when they tried to sneak another bat into the lineup like that. They were trying to strengthen their offense and that meant they were weakening their defense. We had to take advantage of that.

Anyway, I've got Felipe Alou in the outfield on my all-underrated team. And Jim Davenport is at third. Davenport, who played with the Giants from 1958–70, could do everything but run the bases and steal. He was an outstanding hitter, an excellent third baseman and a smart baseball player. He hurt us as much as anybody on the Giants.

At shortstop would be Bobby Wine of the Phillies. This guy could really pick it. He's the best shortstop I ever saw. It was just too bad he and Ruben Amaro played shortstop on the same team and had to share the position. You'll never see those guys in the record books, but they were good players.

Glenn Beckert, who played for the Cubs is at second base. He used to wear Sandy Koufax out. He hit .283 for his career but he must have hit .600 against Sandy.

I played with Charlie Neal at second, and he was awfully good. If it weren't for Bill Mazeroski, who I played with for two years in Pittsburgh, I'd say Charlie Neal was the best. But Maz could play. He should be in the Hall of Fame.

I like Norm Larker of the Dodgers at first base. The man could hit and he could field, too.

Dick Selma would be pitching. As I said earlier, he once threw the ball so hard that when it hit the catcher's mitt, my ears rang. Chris Short, who went 55–30 for the Phillies from 1964–66, was another outstanding pitcher. He never got much credit, but he could play.

Put these guys on a team like the Dodgers with spirit and tradition and they might have become players of note in baseball history. These are guys who, for the most part, performed against us. Playing against the Dodgers they got all geared up. And when I say they could hit, I think of big hits in pressure situations. The guy may have hit .200 for the year but .800 in the eighth inning. That's what you remember. Except Felipe Alou. He did it against everybody all the time, but was overshadowed by Mays and Aaron.

# Chapter 39: Clemente

I've been asked if I ever saw anyone better than Willie Mays. The answer is, yes. Roberto Clemente was *much* better than Willie Mays. It wasn't just his arm. He could do everything better.

Clemente had a tremendous arm. He took great delight in fielding a base hit in right field with a man on first base and pausing. He'd just stand there, sometimes in deep right, and hold the ball saying, "Go ahead to third." Runners wouldn't dare go because Clemente nailed them every time. The crowd at Forbes Field would cheer, and Clemente would lob the ball back in to second.

I didn't go from first to third on a single to right against Clemente, either. Except one time.

I'll never forget the day. It was a Sunday afternoon in Forbes Field. I always loved Sunday afternoon games. Baseball was meant to be played in the daytime. Goddam! My legs always felt like feathers, and, man, they would move. When I'd get back to Los Angeles, my legs got heavy from the humidity. I really had to work to loosen them up. But on the East Coast, my legs always felt great.

I was one of the first guys to cut off the shirt tails on my uniform. The shirt tails used to have a vent on the side and they went halfway down your thighs inside your pants. I cut them off at the vent. I didn't need that extra material. Early in my career, I wore sliding pads because I was so skinny. But I noticed that the pads didn't prevent me from getting strawberries. So I got rid of the sliding pads. They just made me heavier. When I first came up, I used to wear two pairs of white sanitary socks because my legs were skinny and I wanted to puff them out a little bit. I got rid of that vanity and wore one pair to be lighter. The old-style baseball cleats we wore had an innersole glued inside. I ripped that out. I always had to have about 10 pairs of shoes—size 9, a size and a half smaller than my dress shoes—because after a while, the spikes would come through the sole into my feet.

In streamlining my clothes, I was doing what some football players do today. The pads are much slimmer and lighter than they were when I played. Some guys don't even wear hip pads and no one wears the kind of kidney pads we wore. You want to get as light as you can.

So there I was on first base, feeling as light as a feather, when somebody hit a shot to right field right at Clemente. He picked the ball up to dare me, and I rounded second. As I rounded the base, I looked back at him over my shoulder as if I were going to honor his arm. And when I looked, I just shifted into high gear. He saw that and came up firing. He made a clothesline throw, all the way to third in the air. It wasn't even on one hop. I slid à la Rickey Henderson and Pete Rose—head first. I don't mean I put one hand down to break my fall. I mean I was stretched out parallel to the ground with both hands out as if I'm diving into a swimming pool.

SAFE!

In Forbes Field, the dugouts were like pillboxes. Standing in the dugout, your shoulders were at field level. When I beat the throw, all my teammates were at the top of the dugout applauding. We hated Clemente's guts because he was so good. He had a style about him of arrogance, cockiness and defiance.

Sandy Koufax couldn't get him out. Don Drysdale couldn't get him out, so we didn't worry about getting him out. Clemente hit right-handed, and he would stand as far from the plate and as far back in the box as anyone. From there, he had no coverage of the outside of the plate. So you'd throw him a perfect slider from a right-hander on the black of the plate, or a screwball or fastball riding away from him by a left-hander on the outside corner, and Clemente would hit the goddamnedest line drive down the right field line. Then you'd throw him inside and he'd still hit a screaming line drive down the right field line.

You'd try to change speeds on him and he'd top one through the infield. The only time we'd get Clemente out is when the pitcher would wave me over behind second base and leave a big hole between short and third.

Clemente naturally hit to right field, but he'd see that hole and his ego would say, "Okay, you're going to play me over there? I'll show you I can pull that ball." A lot of times your strength is your weakness. His arrogance was his strength. But Clemente's arrogance made him want to show us he could pull the ball, but he couldn't. He'd end up topping the pitch between short and third and I had plenty of time to go over there and get it.

Ted Williams' arrogance worked just the other way.

Clemente was bitter all of his baseball life. He didn't get the attention that Mantle and Mays got. He goes on my team of underrated players. Can you imagine a player of his caliber—Hall of Fame, 3,000 hits—being underrated? But he was.

Roberto Clemente played in Pittsburgh, and very little word got out of Pittsburgh in those days. Willie Mays and Mickey Mantle got all the headlines. Especially Mantle. Clemente just hated that. I played with him for two years. I know.

Clemente would be in the clubhouse reading in the paper about Mantle's knee problems, and Clemente would be muttering, "Bullshit! Bullshit! What about me? I hurt all the time. Nobody ever writes about me being hurt."

## Chapter 40: A matter of style

They say that every man puts his pants on one leg at a time. I will go so far as to say that most people put them on left leg first. I will say that most athletes put on their uniform top before their uniform bottom.

I don't know if that's superstition, but it is ritual. Some people always do certain things the same way. Or maybe they wear a lucky piece of clothing. Walter Alston had a sweater one year that he decided was lucky. He wouldn't take it off. By the time the season ended, it could stand up by itself.

Some things are mannerisms. The way a guy goes up to home plate and takes his swings, tugs at this and that, adjusts various parts of his body, makes the sign of the cross—those are all mannerisms. They help the hitter get his concentration.

Don Sutton went beyond mannerisms. He was downright superstitious.

When a pitcher makes the last out of the inning, he runs back toward the dugout and somebody usually throws him his glove. Not Sutton. From the day he came up from the minors in 1966, he didn't want anybody picking up his glove. It didn't matter if he had run all the way to the right field bullpen. We had to wait for him to run all the way to the dugout and pick up his glove himself.

Another thing players will do for a pitcher is pick the ball off the ground and toss it to him as he comes out to the mound to warm up. I went to do that one day, and he started yelling at me: "No! No! No! Don't touch it!" No one could pick the ball up but him.

I would hang on to a favorite pair of pants. Most players get two home and two away uniforms. I usually had three or four because I was always tearing them up sliding. But if I had a pair I liked and they got torn, I'd give them to Nobe Kawano, who is still the Dodger equipment manager, and Nobe would stitch them up for me.

Every year, players got measured in spring training for their uniforms, which were supposed to be custom-made by Rawlings. Then the uniforms would come in and we wondered whether they hadn't just taken them off the shelf. They never fit right. Nobe would take them to a tailor for us. I'd have the legs altered to fit tighter. I didn't want a baggy leg catching the wind and making me slower. And my inseam had to be 23 inches. Sometimes they would come in at 22 and Nobe had to take them down. Or they would be 24 and Nobe would take them up. That inch made a big difference. I had to feel right in that uniform.

That's the kind of world I spent all my adult baseball life in. It was a world where those kinds of things were a big part of my life. They were a part of what made me happy and what didn't make me happy.

Feeling good in a uniform is the first thing about being able to perform properly. If you look good, you feel good. It's all part of the concentration. And thc concentration has to be total.

People will say about their son that "Billy" could have been a great athlete, but he didn't want to play ball. But the truth probably was that he liked baseball, but didn't like all the things that went with it.

My first son, Barry, was like that. He didn't want to play baseball because he saw his mother sitting around a lot with his father gone. It wasn't the game he chose not to get into. It was the lifestyle.

My second son, Bump, chose to adopt that lifestyle because those things were okay with him. But, like his dad, he paid a price in his personal life.

## Chapter 41: Plunka-plunka-plunk

The first time I went to Las Vegas was after the 1962 season. I had just stolen 104 bases and I was a celebrity. The Dodgers had played their first year in Dodger Stadium and lost the pennant to the Giants in the last game of a three-game playoff, and they were celebrities, too. That was when Milton Berle asked a group of us to come to Las Vegas with him and put on a show.

It was Sandy Koufax, Duke Snider, Willie Davis, Frank Howard, Don Drysdale and I. I sang—if you can call it that—and played the banjo.

I had become interested in playing an instrument almost by accident when I was with Spokane in the minor leagues. One of the team's sponsors started a promotion where if a player got four hits in one game he got a Japanese transistor radio. This was in the late Fifties, when transistor radios were new.

Anyway, the first two nights of the promotion, I got four hits in each game and won two radios. Dick Young, one of the reserve players on the team, asked me if I would sell him one. Now the guy had a ukulele—a Martin. He could really play that thing and sing cowboy songs. I was fascinated by it. I told him I wouldn't sell him the radio, but I'd trade it for his ukulele. He said okay, and, as part of the deal, I made him show me three chords—C, F and G7. That was all I needed to start strumming away.

I played that ukulele on the bus on road trips. All of a sudden I didn't mind those 20-hour trips. I played in the hotel room. I played from the time I woke up to the time I went to the ballpark —C, F and G7.

I fell in love with that thing. I went out and got a "Ukulele Ike" book. They had a whole bunch of chords in there. Now I was obsessed.

That was around the time the Dodgers called me up. I took my ukulele with me to the big leagues. After that first season in 1959, I went to a Shakey's Pizza parlor in Spokane in the off-season and heard a guy playing the banjo. I realized right then and there that was what I wanted to play. I went up to the guy and asked him if he could teach me to play the banjo. He said he didn't have the time, but he referred me to his teacher, Dutch Groshoff. Dutch was 77 years old. I spent two months on that banjo—a four-string model—and said, "No way. This is impossible." I didn't see how my fingers were ever going to stretch to make the chord changes. But they did.

When I first started playing, the banjo was a source of relaxation. Later, when I became a superstar and my life became more complex, I often had troublesome decisions to make. I'd pick up my banjo and start to play and before you knew it, an answer would come to me. I learned to play well enough that all of a sudden, I started getting on the shows and I made money with it.

The greatest service I performed with my banjo, though, was probably on the Dodger team plane. At one time, the Dodgers had their own Elektra. It didn't fly high enough to get over the storms, and you couldn't always fly around the storms, so we were always being tossed around. One day, we were caught in terrible weather. The plane was bounding all over. Lightning was hitting it, which doesn't do any damage, but it sounds as if the plane is scraping the top of a mountain. You're in this thick soup of rain and clouds and you don't know how high you are. You start to think that a mountain could be right in front of you. Those were the times I'd start getting closer to my Creator, and asking him, "Lord, just let me live."

Through all this, I'm picking my banjo: PLUNKA-PLUNKA-PLUNK-PLUNK. PLUNKA-PLUNKA-PLUNK. It was relaxing.

All of a sudden BOOM! Another shot of lightning. I stopped

playing. It was real quiet in the plane when a voice cried out from somewhere: "Play that banjo! Don't stop! Please don't stop!" So I had to start again. They didn't want it to go silent.

In 1962, my banjo and I went to Las Vegas with Milton Berle. That opened up a new world for me in the off-season.

After the next season, 1963, I went back to Las Vegas on my own and worked at the Sahara. I had my own little group of three guitar players and two girl singers with tambourines. I worked the big room at the Sahara with Connie Francis. My name was up on the big marquee—"Maury Wills and Company" and "Connie Francis." I thought I was hot shit.

People came in, but I didn't know that they were already in Las Vegas and they would come into the room regardless of who was playing. I thought they came to see me because they enjoyed my show, but if they came to see me it was because I stole 104 bases.

As long as I was having good seasons, it was fun. I was still Mr. Baseball on the West Coast. When I stopped stealing as many bases, it wasn't as much fun anymore. It was a job.

The greatest natural high I ever had was when I went to see Frank Sinatra one night at Caesar's Palace. He was there for only one week, and he did one show a night. The tickets were by invitation only and the shows were sold out before he gave his first performance.

I had met Frank before. He had seats at Dodger Stadium right behind the visiting dugout where we could see him from our dugout on the third base side. He was a big Dodger fan, and he was always there. And here I was doing all this running and Frank was clapping for me just like everyone else. I was to find out that I was his favorite player.

When Frank came to Caesar's I thought I'd try to see his show. I went to his opening show after my show was done and got there about 10 minutes after he had started. I didn't have a ticket and nobody knew I was coming. Heck, I didn't know I was coming myself.

When I got to the door of Caesar's big room, the maitre d' greeted me as if I were royalty. "Mr. Wills! We've been waiting for you. I'll take you right to your seat."

He took me in, and every star on the Strip was there. Frank's show started after all the other shows were over so everyone could be there. The place was packed—2,000 people and all the stars.

The maitre d' led me in and took me to the lounge booth right on the 50-yard line, level with the stage. It's the best seat in the house and I'm there all by myself.

At the end of the show, Frank said he wanted to introduce one person. For four minutes he went on about this guy who's a pure athlete and how he loves watching this guy perform and so on and so forth. While he's talking, I'm looking all around to see who he's going to introduce.

The spotlight swung around and stopped on me as Frank was saying, "Maury Wills!"

Wow! I slithered around from under the table and stood up in the aisle. I had been with Milton Berle and was doing my own show, so I knew how to acknowledge a crowd. I didn't just get up, wave and sit down. I acknowledged everyone: Frank first, then one side, the other side, the back of the room, the entire room. And they were still going. I threw them a kiss and, oh, God, it escalated.

Finally, before sitting down, I acknowledged the host again. And Frank said, "Hey, Moish,"—that's what he called me—"c'mon back after the show!"

It was just like that. Here were all these high-powered people from the business and entertainment worlds, and he singled me out. That was a thrill.

Another time, I went to the Sahara to catch Don Rickles' last show of the night. It was late and I was alone. It seemed I was always alone. After the show, I was leaving the Sahara lounge when I saw Frank Sinatra sitting in the middle of a big banquette behind a table with 10 people on either side of him. Frank saw me and made 10 people clear out so he could slide around and come out halfway across the room to greet me. He threw his arms around me and said, "C'mon and have a seat, Maury."

God! Frank Sinatra! Here he was with all these highfalutin people and he came out just to say hello to me. He wanted me to sit down and join him!

I felt so out of place. I sat there for about 30 seconds and then made up some big lie about why I had to get going. I would have liked to have stayed there all week.

Then there was the time I saw Frank in Las Vegas when he

had his daughter, Nancy, with him. She had just recorded the song "These Boots are Made for Walking." It was a big hit and she was doing her own act. She was so pretty, I kept looking at her to the point I got scared and got the hell out of there. She was real nice to me, but I wasn't taking any chances on Frank misunderstanding anything. The rumor was already out that I was looking at women and had girlfriends. I didn't want him to think Nancy was going to be one of them. I went to see her show, but I slipped in and slipped out without any fanfare. I didn't want Nancy introducing me. I didn't want any personal contact with her.

I got to know a lot of the stars. I got to know Johnny Mathis. Sammy Davis, Jr., put me in his songs. I'll never forget the time I saw him at the Sands and he sang "The Lady is a Tramp" and made up some of his own words. His parody was: "She goes to ballgames 'cause she digs Maury Wills." It went on from there. He was talking about Doris Day.

I went to see Jerry Lewis and he put me in one of his monologues. Dean Martin did the same thing. I was on several of Dean Martin's roasts. One time, we were roasting Howard Cosell and Nipsey Russell told a joke about Howard.

"Black people just love Howard Cosell," Nipsey said. "We love him, love him, love him. We love a white guy who makes an ass of himself."

These people put me on their level. I was in the entertainment field as they were. I was just in a different category. That's why they related to me. At the same time, I was awed by it all. I eventually found out they were just as much in awe of me.

You'd be surprised how many entertainers aspire to be athletes. They would give anything—their talent, fame and fortune—just to be simple-ass ballplayers in the major leagues. Gee, whiz, I couldn't believe it.

Cary Grant was a big fan of mine. The man loved me. I sat on the floor with Cary Grant and Dyan Cannon at a party. I was playing the guitar and singing with just those two while everybody else was huddled over on the other side of the room. And Cary said, "Just keep playing, Maury. Just keep playing." Can you imagine?

I went to Buck Owens' golf tournament in Bakersfield. After

the tournament, we went to one of the big homes there and Charlie Pride and I ended up playing the guitar and singing country songs. Charlie would sing one then I'd sing one, and we'd pass the guitar back and forth. This went on for a while until someone said, "Charlie, give the guitar to Maury and let him do the singing." What an ego trip!

Charlie invited me to his celebrity golf tournament in Albuquerque. Roy Clark invited me to his tournament in Texas. I got to know Johnny Mathis from playing golf in Montebello, Calif., where I went for a charity pro-am tournament. I was in a foursome with Mathis, Lee Trevino and James Garner and played in front of a gallery that covered practically the entire golf course.

I got to know Johnny Mathis during that round because he and I were always in the rough together. I didn't get to talk to Lee Trevino much because he was there to entertain the gallery. He could answer questions and play golf at the same time. I realized that Lee didn't hear much of what was said to him. He would respond by saying whatever he was thinking of. He did a fantastic job.

I had to concentrate just on not hitting the ball into the gallery and killing somebody. James Garner didn't have to worry because he's a very good golfer. But Johnny Mathis and I were suspect on every shot.

Johnny would come down to Los Angeles every year when the Dodgers put on a Hollywood Stars-versus-the-sportswriters game in Dodger Stadium. Dean Martin came four or five years, too. He played shortstop and always insisted on wearing my shoes and using my glove. And every year Dean Martin would make one spectacular play. He felt sure it was my equipment that did it for him.

Some years later, *after I retired,* I had my own golf tournament. The first year, Glen Campbell and Johnny Mathis both agreed to come. After the tournament, we had dinner and then a musical program. I brought my little group that backed me up in Las Vegas—Danny Andrews on piano and John McWorthy on drums. They worked at a little club in Los Angeles called the Hungry Tiger and I used to go in there at night and sit in with them with my banjo.

Mac Davis was there, too. He was good friends with Glen Campbell but they had a fierce musical rivalry. When Mac Davis performed and got a rousing ovation, Glen Campbell went on stage to answer back.

I always say Glen Campbell's my favorite singer. He's one of my favorite people in the world. My own claim to fame as far as playing the banjo goes is that Glen Campbell backed me with his 12-string guitar on a studio record back when he was doing studio work. We joke about that.

I played banjo in Las Vegas at the Sahara, the Desert Inn, the Sands. I played at Harvey's in Lake Tahoe. I performed with George Gobel in Salt Lake City for a week. I was on all those TV shows. I was stealing a lot of bases then. When I wasn't stealing as many bases anymore, it seems that when I played on a show, my playing wasn't as good.

After that first year when I went to Las Vegas with my teammates and Milton Berle, Milton started inviting me to appear on different shows that he hosted. At one time he had a national weekly television show called "Hollywood Palace" and he asked me to be on that.

Buddy Rich was on the same show, and when we took breaks, he and I would go into the parking lot because he was a big baseball fan and wanted to play catch.

They had a couple of other acts on that program. One group consisted of two dirty little hippies with a guitar. They called themselves Sonny and Cher. The other act called themselves Gladys Knight and the Pips.

Nobody had ever heard of Gladys Knight and the Pips, and the producer of "Hollywood Palace" was really disappointed that they had a group with a goofy name like that on his show. He was all over Milton Berle demanding to know who the hell booked these acts?

Milton came to me for help. "Maury," he said, "have you ever heard of Gladys Knight and the Pips?"

"Let me think . . ." I hedged. I hadn't heard of them, either, but Milton was desperate.

"Aren't they a top-notch group?" Milton prompted.

"Yeah. Sure!" I said. "I've heard them. They're good."

"See," Milton said, turning to his producer, "I told you they're good." And that's how Milton Berle sold Gladys Knight and the Pips.

I knew all these famous people and I had no idea they were in awe of me. I thought they all were just being nice to me. You know, patting me on the head before saying, "Now shoo. Run off."

I met President Nixon, and I found out later he was trying to impress me just as much as I was trying to impress him. I realized much later that the lesson in all this is to put aside the person's talent and what the person's known for and be more involved with the person himself. Take away the materialistic things and all the fanfare and hoopla and relate to the individual.

People tend to categorize everybody. When you do that you're dealing with everything but the human element. You're looking at what the person represents rather than what the person is about.

It doesn't make sense to be in awe of a person just because he can play baseball. As athletes we are primarily entertainers. But we bring a lot of joy to people and give them a momentary release from a lot of stressful thoughts.

But if you want a real hero, look to a guy like Othmar Ammann. More than half a century ago he designed the George Washington Bridge, which connects New York City with New Jersey. He built it so that a second deck could be added to handle traffic far into the future. It carries more traffic on more lanes than any suspension bridge in the world. Now that's vision. That's a real contribution to life. There's a real hero.

As for me, I had a nice life, but I grew up in a false world. I don't recommend it.

## Chapter 42: Doris

Doris Day was a big Dodger fan. In 1962 she came to all the games. She sat in the dugout seats behind home plate at ground level. That's where Mike Brito, the guy in the white hat you see on TV holding the radar gun at Dodger games, stands. Those are very elite seats. You can't just walk up and buy one. People die and leave those seats in their wills. People getting divorced fight over those seats.

I was 29, but a young 29. I have no idea how old she was. It never crossed my mind. I know that she was more sophisticated than I, and the friendship and relationship we had was scary to me. It was bizarre to me because she was such a worldly person.

I was electrifying the baseball world, chasing Ty Cobb's record. It was the first year for Dodger Stadium. Major league baseball was still new in the minds of the people on the West Coast. We were the best show in town, and just having people like Doris Day in the stands watching us and cheering us like everyday fans was really a Hollywood scene.

I don't know how it happened. It wasn't as if we'd been catching each other's eye. It was nothing like that. I was busy playing baseball. She was over there. That's all. She didn't hang around to see me after the games. It just happened.

It started at the end of the season. Long before we saw one another outside of the ballpark, it was known that she was fond of me. I was her favorite player. But there were a lot of people out there whose favorite I was.

My teammates never said anything. It was just a rumor. Even after it became known that I was her favorite player, it still fell in the fan category. It didn't become more than that until she and I knew it was more than that.

I guess it started one day when she came to the ballpark early to watch batting practice. She brought her lunch and was having a sandwich or something and I went over and said hi. We talked a little and I went inside and got a baseball, autographed it and gave it to her. I think that's the first time I got close enough to her to see that she was attractive and that I was attracted to her.

I don't think we saw each other until after the season. Then it came to be known that . . . but, you see, we made an agreement that regardless of what happened, we'd always deny it. I've lived up to that all these years.

But now John Roseboro has written about it in his book. He was the first. Whatever John said is all right. He wouldn't lie just to sell a book. Poor John. When he came to the clubhouse on old-timers day just after the book came out, I know he had to be thinking about it. It had been in all the papers. They probably told him to put it in and he hoped it would be played down. It wasn't. It didn't bother me, though. I have such a love for John Roseboro, he can't say anything that would make me change my feeling for him.

But he did broach the subject, so let me say a few things about it.

Doris Day is a lovely lady and we did see each other. And, yes, we were lovers. I was young and still inexperienced. Baseball was the only thing I knew.

With Doris, I was in over my head. I was married at the time, too. My family was up in Spokane. I didn't know what to do. I was scared. What do you do with a princess, a beautiful and precious person? Do you make love to her? Or do you try to just jump her bones like you would anybody else who was a female? Do you kiss her? Do you hold her hand? Do you dare make contact with her in any way?

We talked. I called her by her nickname—Dodo. She's a sweet person. Not one negative word or thought ever came out of her mind. She said one thing to me that was valuable. I don't even know how it came up. We were discussing somebody who wanted to borrow some money from me. She advised me against it. She said she never lends money to anybody for anything. If anything, she said, just give the person the money if you want to help him. Lending is only setting yourself up to disrupt a good friendship, she said.

That always stayed with me. From that day on, I've always given to people instead of lending. When it's given it's all over.

She brought me gifts. She would bring a lunch for me in a nice wicker basket. I had never experienced that before. One day she gave me a little, 45-rpm, battery-operated record player. It looked like a little suitcase. It was made in France. It was the first time anybody ever gave me a gift with such lovingness about it. You could tell that it was a gift—an expression of love. She wasn't trying to play the big shot. It wasn't that at all. She gave it to me because she really loved me.

That only made me more scared. I didn't know what love was all about. The only love affair I'd had was with baseball.

I'd have loved to have gone to dinner, but we couldn't go out in public.

That winter, the rumors began to fly. They started one night at the Friars Club when I was being roasted. She knew I was there and she called me. They told her I was in the middle of the program and couldn't come to the phone. She left her phone number and somebody recognized it.

After that, when I went places, the interview was about Doris Day right off the bat. I was the National League MVP and the Hickok Award winner, but when I went places, they didn't ask me about my great season or about breaking Cobb's record. They asked me about Doris Day.

I used to think I had to answer the question. If only I knew what Barbara Walters would explain years later. She was being interviewed herself and the interviewer asked her why all these important people she interviewed—kings, queens, prime ministers, presidents—answered when she asked such personal questions. Was it because she was a woman?

Barbara Walters said, "No. If only these people knew all they have to say is, 'It's none of your business.' But people feel like they have to give an answer."

I thought I had to give an answer. I was stuttering, sputtering and stammering trying to give an answer when I really didn't have to.

I got through the winter, though. I caught most of the hell at the beginning of the 1963 season. By then the rumors were really flowing.

KFI carried the Dodgers games at that time. They asked me to come in to do an interview, and I left home in the middle of the afternoon on a torrid day. It was so hot it was disgusting to travel. But it was the Dodger station. I figured it was something I was obliged to do, to give back something to the fans.

So I drove to the station and parked the car. They got the camera ready and the sound level set. Ready. Roll.

The guy put the microphone in my face and the first thing he asked was: "What about you and Doris Day? How are you two getting along?"

Oh, God! That was one of the most trying moments I've ever lived through. For about five minutes I sputtered, trying to answer this guy's question. It wasn't live. It was being taped. All I had to do was say, "Fuck you," and walk away, but I didn't do that.

I would call her and talk to her on road trips. I had to explain to her I couldn't go on with it. It was tough for me. It was tough for her. I found myself always distracted from my playing. So after a little while we just didn't see each other anymore. I think she stopped coming to the games, too.

I haven't seen her since.

Many times in my later years, I thought I'd try to look her up, but I never went through with it. I might now. I feel cleansed. I feel I've made amends. I feel I could go back now and try to find her. I might have to make amends for saying this now. I made an agreement with her I never would. But I don't feel like I'm telling tales out of school. It's part of what happened to me in my life.

I really cared about her. We had a mutual need for one another. We were in love—as I understood it at the time. I only had so much love for another human being because I was so much in love with baseball. As much love as I had, it was extended to her, but it was too much for me. I couldn't handle it. I was a baseball player. I had this fantasy that baseball players are all-American people and aren't supposed to know women, especially famous women. There was a bad connotation to that.

## Chapter 43: Edie

Edie Adams was the favorite of all the women with whom I've been personal.

I met her while I was working in Las Vegas. I had gone to the Riviera to see Lionel Hampton, whom I'd met some time before in Los Angeles. He was cutting a record in a nightclub in Los Angeles and he had this big, mobile studio parked outside the nightclub with all the recording equipment inside. Hamp met me and took me outside and made me cut a 45-rpm record with him right on the spot. We sang "The Crawdad Hole." It goes: "You get a line, and I'll get a pole, honey, honey. You get a line and I'll get a pole, ba-abe, ba-abe. You get a line and I'll get a pole. We'll meet down at the crawdad hole." I was singing and Hamp was playing and going, "Yeah, yeah, YEAH," in the background.

So when he came to Las Vegas, I went to see him. He had a young, pretty black girl singing with his band. Her name was Freda Payne. When the show was over, I went backstage to Hamp and asked if he would introduce me to his singer.

"Sure, her name is Freda," he said.

"Will you ask her to have coffee with me?" I asked him.

Hamp did and she accepted. We went to the coffee shop and sat down. As we were sitting there, Edie Adams came in after her last show and sat at the counter. She let me know that she liked me, and I ended up going with her instead of going with Freda.

Edie was hurting at the time. Her husband, Ernie Kovacs, had just died. She was performing on stage and on television to pay the bills. That was when she started doing those sexy cigar commercials. She had a lot of sorrow in her life. I felt closer to her for that. I got to know her well. She even took me home once to meet her children. That was tough. I could tell her children didn't approve. But she really cared about me.

Again, I was so wrapped up in my baseball life I didn't have the capacity to understand what I really had. I would go to her shows at the Riviera and she would introduce me to the audience every night. She would call me out of the wings. She insisted that I be there. She'd call me out on stage, put her arms around me and introduce me. Shecky Greene, a comedian who worked Vegas, and all the other guys used to kid me about it.

She had a big Bentley and she let me drive that sucker. It was another world. It was just too much. I couldn't cope with that, either. It felt good when I finally got back to Los Angeles.

I flew to New York with her one time. She had to go there on business. I spent the whole week inside the hotel, waiting for her each day. I didn't go out because I didn't know what to do in the city.

Her job was threatened because I was black. I had heard rumors that I was going to be banned from baseball because of my affair with Doris Day. And now I was seeing Edie Adams. Buzzy Bavasi, the Dodgers' general manager, called me into his office and questioned me about it. Things were different than they are now.

But Edie Adams was one terrific lady. The first time she saw me, she knew she wanted me in her life. She was great, but when I went back to Los Angeles, we lost contact. It just faded away.

It seems everybody knew about Doris and Edie. There were other women, some of them famous, but I don't need to talk about them. I know a lot of former athletes would sit here and try to name every woman they ever made love to. But with my approach to life today, that wouldn't serve any purpose.

## Chapter 44: Why white?

I had a problem with black women. It's all psychological. I haven't gotten over that.

Most of my girlfriends were white, but it wasn't that I sought white girls. I never even liked blondes. I always liked brunettes. But somehow I'd always end up with a blonde. If she wasn't blonde when I met her, she certainly became a blonde shortly afterwards.

It wasn't my choice. If you line up a number of women and ask me to choose, it would definitely be a black girl. If she had to be white, she would have black hair. I'd rather have a darker-complected girl. But they always ended up being fair-skinned California blondes. Every time. One of the old truisms is: Whenever a black guy has a little success, the first thing he does is get himself a blonde. I typified that statement. But it wasn't by choice.

It had more to do with an attitude that I liked better and that was different from the attitude of women from my culture.

Black women were always hard. When you go back to the days of slavery and think about it, they were always the most oppressed. They were snatched out of the fields and used. And black men kept them barefoot and pregnant. We were hard on them, really hard on them. They had no skills to take out into the world to get a job. All they did was get married young and have a lot of babies.

My own daughters were like that. My eight sisters had an adverse effect on me, too, in the way they related to my brothers-in-law. I saw my brothers-in-law become whipped. Some became alcoholics. They changed in a matter of a year or two after they got married.

I was just a kid when one of my older sisters married. The guy she married was really sharp. He had a '39 Ford that he shined like his shoes. He had style. I admired him. I wanted to be like him. And within two or three years he was an alcoholic, a vegetable. He withered away in his relationship with my sister.

That hurt me. I was just a kid seeing this for the first time. I heard the fights. And then, all of a sudden, I saw boyfriends. She'd come around with them and I knew this was wrong. I saw this stuff going on and it bothered me.

I saw my oldest brother, Guy, who was a sharp man and a tremendous athlete, go to war after he married this beautiful black girl. Her name was Cleo. He left her with a nice apartment and he got a "Dear John" letter from her. He came home in 1945 and he never recovered. He's had emotional problems all his life because of that.

I saw my other older brother, Duke, marry my sister-in-law, Elaine, and give her eight or nine children and stay drunk all the time. He was in the Philippines in World War II. One day, he was sitting on a stump with a buddy when a Japanese sniper picked off his buddy. From that day on he fell apart. This was the world I grew up in. I knew nothing else.

When I started playing baseball, I started traveling. I saw what white society was like and I wanted it. It was an escape. It educated me. I learned more than I learned in my neighborhood. That's why I was so aggressive as a player. And that's why I was always running around before the game trying to round up tickets. It was my way of getting involved with people. As a result, I gained enough skill and confidence so that it was no problem for me to approach a young, attractive white woman. It had nothing to do with her being white; it was an attitude.

I'd try to approach black girls, too, and it was: "Don't you come over here and bother me. I know you've been spoiled. Don't get so close. Don't be looking at me like that." This was the attitude of the black girls I'd try to talk to.

Judy, the girl who was my downfall, was a strawberry blonde. Angela, my drug wife, was a blonde. The lady who rescued me after my last relapse in 1989 is blonde.

I can't have another white woman. I've got to have a black woman. I have to face up to and get over whatever the hang up is that has prevented me from having a black woman in my life. At this stage, I've got to stop and be racially conscious of my next relationship. I can't be so independent anymore, so much of a maverick.

I said that black women are hard. Maybe I ought to start looking at myself. Maybe I give them reason to be hard. Maybe with my new approach to life I won't be such a hard-nosed brother.

You'll hear some black men say that white women are better in bed. I wouldn't know. I have nothing to compare them to. You'll hear white women say that black men are better in bed. Some of my white teammates thought that black women are great. They'd be going crazy over chicks that I'd say, "What? What do you see in her?" That's a lot of bull. But black men think that white women are more innovative, more imaginative, and freer spirits in bed. Black women have more hang ups about showing their bodies, not to mention oral sex and stuff like that. They're just not innovative. If you get one who wants to get it on with you, it's just the plain, old missionary position, but waling away—Screw your brains out, Mister, and you better measure up.

Goddammit! I tried my best to have a black girlfriend. My preference initially was that she be pretty and at one time I would have preferred that she be fair-complected. Then it didn't matter if she was so black she was blue. That wasn't important so long as she was sweet and she was attractive.

I never had the luck. It seemed the black girls were always tough on a black athlete in particular or on any black man who had some success. They seemed to harbor some deep bitterness. That bitterness came out and it was just too tough getting to know them, getting them to relax and getting them to trust you.

It seemed that every white girlfriend I ever had was pleased and happy to be with me and trusted me from the very beginning. That made me relaxed and comfortable.

But black girls had a toughness that came from being raised as second-class citizens. Once they were in your corner, you had somebody. You had a strong partner, but it was hell getting that far. Being a spoiled athlete, I didn't have the time or the patience or the energy to cultivate a relationship with a black woman.

# Chapter 45: Racism

I didn't have to date white women to find prejudice. I found that in Spokane, where I made my home.

Black people didn't run into racism in Spokane if they weren't interested in going to certain places. But I started to run into it because, when I started playing major league baseball, I got exposed to the finer places. I thought I could go to those places and I found out I couldn't.

I was a hero in the city after 1959. They were making all this hoopla about me being Maury Wills from Spokane. But when I got my check from the World Series and tried to move my family out into the valley where we found a little ranch house with a couple acres around it, they wouldn't sell. A white realtor, who was a hunting partner of mine, tried to buy it for me, but they didn't want to sell because it was for a black man. The seller of the land asked for some more information on me: "How black is he?"

We finally got the house. The people who sold it didn't live in it. They lived in a second house they owned up the road. We became neighbors and then we became best friends and hunting partners. People fear things they don't know. A lot of prejudices are based on that. But once we got to know each other we were in one another's homes all the time. That's progress.

So we moved out there and the next thing I knew, I was Man of the Year in the State of Washington in 1962. They took me to Olympia, the state capital. I spoke before the state senate. Then I came home to Spokane. A friend wanted to take me to the Athletic Roundtable. That was a very elite club for sportsmen in the city. They told my friend I couldn't go to lunch there because I'm black.

Then a performer I had met when I was in Las Vegas with Milton Berle came to town. He was going to put on a show at the

Elks Club, and he asked me to be his guest. I accepted and came to his opening night. The Elks refused me admission. The man who invited me was at the front door explaining that I was his guest. They said blacks weren't allowed in. So I had to leave.

I felt bad when something like that happened, but I got over it. I was pretty naive. They let me know where my place was and I stayed there. I found out that no matter how much of a star I was there was always a limitation, even in Los Angeles, on where I was invited. All those years that I was acclaimed, I was always reminded I was just a nigger, just a baseball player.

I bought a bigger place in the valley, a ranch. It had a long driveway, about 500 feet, going up a hill and then back down to the house. At the bottom of the driveway, I put up a two-rail fence that was wide at the road and narrowed like a funnel to the drive. I put a post up and hung a little sign on a chain. Somebody came and wrote on the sign: "Nigger Gulch."

I laughed about it. I figured it was said with amusement more than anything else. For some reason, I didn't get the feeling it was said in a malicious way. The people out there knew us. They knew my kids. They loved my kids. I figured it was more envy than anything, because the ranch was a nice place on a good piece of acreage. If we were Italian, they probably would have written "Dago Dell" on the sign.

I like to feel there's not one prejudiced bone in my body, but I am always aware that I am black. When I was involved with Doris Day, I was always being reminded of it.

That doesn't bother me. That's not so bad. In fact, if I weren't black, it might have ruined my career. I say that as a joke sometimes, but in many cases it's true. A lot of humor is based on truth.

There was a player named Alex Johnson who played for eight teams from 1964–76, including the Yankees and the Angels. He was a good hitter. He was a lifetime .290 hitter and in 1970, while playing with the Angels, he hit .329 and was the American League batting champion. But he was one of the black players who couldn't let go of the years when they were treated badly and subjected to racial prejudice. They held on to it, and when they became stars, they lashed back. They took out their anger on the people around them—the sportswriters and fans who were mostly white. And it never did them any good. It just got them traded and shortened their careers.

If I thought that way, I could have been nastier than they were. But I didn't harbor those feelings. It didn't make any sense. It wasn't from any sense of righteousness. It's just the way I am. I decided it was no big deal and I never made it an issue.

My first experience with real prejudice as an adult was when I got to Fort Worth. That bothered me for the season and I couldn't concentrate. When I got to be a major league star that was the time I could have lashed out and said ugly things. But I never did. I didn't find it necessary. By that time everything was good.

Being accommodating definitely opened more doors for me than if I had been hostile. There was a point in my life when I had to decide whether I was going to march and be militant or lead by example. I decided to let my conduct be my contribution to equal rights.

I'm not racially motivated. Many black people figure that all whites have it in for all blacks. They'll always feel that way. Most of them are people who don't have much going for themselves.

But a lot of black people's racial prejudices fall on individual whites rather than on whites as a race. Blacks, on the other hand, are usually put into a group by whites and experience prejudice as a race. So you don't even have a chance to show you're a decent guy. I know there was a lot of prejudice in this country against white immigrants a long time ago. But at least when you first walked in a room nobody knew if you were Irish, Jewish, Polish, Italian, or whatever. At least you had a chance. Others had to find out what you were before they could express their prejudice. When you're black and you walk into a room, it's instant.

BAM! "You're black. We gotcha."

Martin Luther King, Jr., used to say that black people have better memories than white people. They have to, because white people don't have to remember they're white.

We had ways of checking out white players in baseball. If a guy smoked, you could offer him a puff of your cigarette. Or you could offer somebody a bite of your sandwich or a swig of your drink. The guys who accepted were all right. The guys who were prejudiced would rather die than take a puff or a bite or a swallow.

In the drug scene there were no problems like that. Germs don't have a chance in the drug scene. White people have no problem snorting a black man's coke.

I experienced very little racial prejudice in the big leagues. The one time it affected me pretty badly was when I was with the Pirates in 1968. Martin Luther King was assassinated April 4 of that year in Memphis and things got spooky. We had 13 blacks and 12 whites on the team and the black guys really let the white guys know about it. It was bad. It was strong, hard-core, racial division on the Pirates that year. Some of the black guys even carried guns. It was chaos.

That was the only time in my life it was really frightening to be black. I got involved that year in a Solidarity March during the Poor People's Campaign in Washington, D.C. They put me on stage and I played a folk song on my banjo. The song bombed, but participating made me feel good.

In the minor leagues, there was more prejudice. But everybody was struggling to make the big leagues and we didn't feel secure or prosperous enough not to worry about it. A lot of prejudice comes from intimidation or insecurity anyway, and there was a lot of that in the minors. That's where we always checked out all the white boys on the team to see who, as we put it, the good dudes were.

People call each other ethnic names in the locker room all the time and it's okay—unless it's coming from the guy who kicked the mound when you booted one. If Willie Davis goes from first to home on a short double and wins the ballgame, a white player might say, "Boy, you niggers can really run!" That's okay. But if Willie Davis boots a ball in center and costs us a ballgame and the same guy says something about niggers, that's a different connotation.

It's the same with jokes. Black people don't tell jokes about white people. They don't like to tell Jewish jokes or Polish jokes. Black people tell jokes about black people. But they don't like to hear white people telling black jokes. It's offensive.

When the Redskins played the Dolphins in Super Bowl XVII in the Rose Bowl, some of my family came out to see the game. I gave them my house to stay in and I went to stay with a friend.

This was in 1983 when I was addicted. My friend was also my drug connection. He was the guy taking all my money.

I'd stay up all night in my friend's house doing drugs, then stroll over to my house in the morning to see my family. I'd come in and all the women would be in the kitchen cooking eggs in two inches of grease.

One day, my friend, who was white, came with me. He was a guy who liked to tell nigger jokes. He had told me one that went like this:

"What's the difference between a black chick and a bowling ball?"

"You can only get three fingers in a bowling ball."

I told him to tell the joke to my sister and two of her girlfriends, who were busy frying eggs in grease.

"I'm not telling them that joke," he said.

"Tell the joke, man!" I said. "You told it to me!" I Bogarted him into telling them the joke.

And when he did, my sister threw the whole pan of grease at him. They didn't appreciate that joke at all.

They ended up liking the guy, though. They thought it took a lot of guts to come in there and tell that joke. A man with that much nerve must be all right.

When I was a kid I was colored. Then I was Negro. Then black. Now I'm African-American. To call me colored when I was a Negro was fighting words. Then to call me Negro when I became black, I was ready to kill over that. But if you had called me black when I was colored or a Negro . . . Jeezus Christ. It's amazing, but it wasn't silly. It was an important cultural change. It's growth.

We used to fight in the colored neighborhoods among ourselves. We had our own prejudices. A lot of it came from the complexion of our skin. I'm a fair-complected Negro . . . black person . . . colored person . . .

Being fair-complected meant that you were supposed to be a little better off than the real black. That was a great prejudice. The real black-complected people used to call the light-complected people shit color. That was the prejudice of the dark blacks against the light blacks. Other terms they used were "dirty red" and "high yellow." Those weren't as bad as shit color.

I wasn't supposed to aspire to get out of the projects. Anybody who said they wanted to get out and live on the other side off the tracks was looked down upon or thought of as being a nut: "What the hell are you talking about, boy?"

In a sense, black society helped to keep black people down. It was the same as those people continuing to sit in the right field stands in Vero Beach when they took down the "COLORED ONLY" signs and they could sit anywhere they wanted. You become comfortable. Even if the position you're in is subservient, there's a risk in change. People don't want to take chances. People tend to stay where they're comfortable. Black people had to be encouraged to go into certain restaurants, to sit in the front of the bus.

I have a daughter, Mauricia. We call her Mikki. She complained to me once that she was unhappy. Whenever she went out to parties or social occasions, the other blacks her age—her peers—were really down on her. Those girls were black, but she had red hair, freckles and green eyes. Mikki said she hated herself and wished that she were pitch black. Coal black. She couldn't understand why she couldn't be black like everyone else. She didn't even want to go out anymore. All my kids had the same hang-up. Mikki told me that when they moved from Spokane to Seattle, where there's a bigger black population, they got more into "black awareness." They didn't like their father because they felt I tried to raise them as if they were white. All these years they held that against me, Mikki said.

Black awareness means saying things like: "I don' be doin' that kinda talk."

When Mikki moved from Seattle to Los Angeles, I said to her, "Mikki, you went to college. You can speak better than that."

"You don' be tellin' me how to talk," she said.

I backed off. But after she'd been in Los Angeles a year or two, she came back to me and apologized. She said she didn't have to be like that. That's not what it's all about. In Los Angeles she had an opportunity to see that people were just people. People get along there. They tolerate one another.

I don't know why my kids felt I was raising them as if they were white, because I certainly was always reminded that I was black. But these are things that happen between parents and children, especially when you're away most of the time.

I didn't know how you raise them black. I didn't go into that with Mikki when she told me that. That's another generation telling me this. I didn't understand it myself. I didn't want to be antagonistic and ask her in what way I failed. She just said I didn't give them their black awareness.

I suppose that means I didn't sit down and explain black history week and Abraham Lincoln and the slaves. Jesse Owens. Sojourner Truth. Rosa Parks.

I guess they had that idea because they lived outside the city on a ranch and they went to the schools in the Spokane valley. Those schools weren't totally white—my kids went there. But they lived out there instead of in downtown Spokane on the other side of the tracks where all the blacks lived. They have tracks in Spokane, too. There was more hardship downtown and more black kids. But my kids had everything. All their friends growing up were white—even their little boyfriends and girlfriends.

It was that way until they got to a certain age. It's amazing, but when my kids were 10 years old, the other parents thought it was so wonderful when all the kids played together. When they went to junior high school, it was still nice and wonderful. Then, all of a sudden, about halfway through high school, these parents cut them off. My kids couldn't see their daughters or sons anymore. My kids were really set back by that. They were getting to that age, I guess, where sex comes in, and that bothered the white parents. I had no way of explaining that to my kids.

I didn't set out to conquer with kindness. I was just being myself with my own standards. I believe that people are nice, that people are just people. I didn't let those things affect me.

I didn't become bitter and I didn't practice anger and resentment in my everyday activities, but that doesn't mean I wasn't aware of it. It was there, but I hid it. That's one of the worst things a person can do with any kind of hurt or pain. That's what I always did.

Still, inside, that's the thing I took home with me that caused me to go through the changes I did. I had nobody else to share that with. All the hurt, the knowledge of that kind of prejudice, was all mine. When you get enough of that, when you fill up with it and you're going through some damaging defeats, all that stuff comes back to disturb you.

# Chapter 46: A-hunting I won't go

One year, late in the hunting season, my insurance agent told me he was going to have a venison feed at his office for Christmas. He asked me if I could get a deer for him.

I looked at a map and found one area that was still open for hunting. I went up there and asked the farmer who owned the land whether I could come up there and hunt. "Sure, Maury," he said. "Get up here about six tomorrow morning. About 6:15, they come right down over the field and they're all over the pasture. They meander around there for a little bit and then they drop down into the valley." It was rutting season and the bucks were after the does.

Well, the next morning I got there three minutes late. Three minutes! The deer had just gone down over the hill. Damn! We didn't have any choice but to go down in there and root them out.

So we went down over the hill. The farmer put me on a stand while he went around to try to scare up a deer. I looked down and maybe 40–50 yards away was a little white-tailed deer flagging me from behind an evergreen. I sat there about 20 or 30 minutes but the deer wouldn't come out. He just stayed behind the tree.

I had a .30-06 rifle with 180-grain bullets. I figured I'd just take that damn tree right with the deer. That 180-grain bullet would wipe the tree out and get the deer, too. That's what I did.

BOOM! To tell you the truth, I didn't know if it was a buck or a doe when I shot. That was bad, too, because only bucks were in season. But I pulled anyway. The deer went about five feet in the air, came down, and took off through the woods.

I ran down to the spot where he had been standing and there was blood on the ground. I knew I had wounded him. Now I had to find him.

I looked for about an hour and a half. I couldn't find him, but I'd find blood every now and then. I thought I couldn't let this animal suffer like that. I was just about to give up when I saw him down behind a bush on all fours. He was a little buck with little spikes just starting to grow on his head. He was lying on his side as a dog would, looking up at me with these big, pretty, brown eyes. He had a big hole in his side, and his mouth was open and his tongue was hanging out. He was panting and looking at me as if to say, "Please don't shoot me again."

Damn! I had to put the barrel on him. I pulled on him and hit him in the head. He rolled around and kicked and kicked and kicked. Blood was all over his face now and he looked up at me again with his eyes, those big, pretty, brown eyes, and his tongue was hanging out and he was panting. "Please don't shoot me again."

Jeezus Christ.

I took my knife out and cut his throat. I gutted him out, carried him to the car and drove back to Spokane. I carried him up the steps of the building where my insurance agent was and walked into his office. He was sitting at his desk. I dropped the deer right in the middle of the desk on top of everything.

"Here's your deer," I said.

I went home and hung up all my rifles. I never hunted game again.

## Chapter 47: Getting paid

The more you make, the more you spend. What I did with my money early in my career was move my family out of a dumpy home in the city and into a home in the valley. Finally, we moved to the ranch.

I never was extravagant. I was used to living on $5,000 or $6,000 as a minor leaguer all those years. Not until I got into drugs and alcohol did I get extravagant. I bought the occasional

Dodger-blue sweater. I wore corduroy pants. I upgraded from Thom McAn to Hanover shoes.

I had made $6,000 in 1959. The next year, 1960, I made $12,000 and had a good year. I stole 50 bases and they pulled the base out of the ground at the Coliseum and gave it to me. For 1961, I was raised to $23,000.

After the 1961 season, I went home to Spokane, but I wasn't finding any satisfaction there. My heart was in Los Angeles. But I couldn't persuade my wife to move to Los Angeles. She didn't want any part of big-city life. But I wasn't comfortable at home. Nothing was happening in Spokane for me.

I called Buzzy Bavasi and asked him if I could come down and work out in the Coliseum alone. Today, players regularly work out all winter. Many go to their home stadium to do it. But this was unheard of in 1961. They weren't even sophisticated enough then to have batting cages and pitching machines under the stands.

I drove down from Spokane, and on the way I heard on the radio that Maury Wills had signed his contract with the Dodgers already. "Signed his contract?" I wondered. "I haven't signed a contract."

I got off the road and called Buzzy. "Don't worry about it," he said. He told me he had used me to get some other players to sign. "You know I always take care of you," he said.

I said okay. I really felt complimented. I knew I had a contract for 1962.

When I got to Los Angeles, I went to see Buzzy. He wanted to know what I wanted. I said I just wanted to work out. How much did he have in mind for me? I figured he called all the other shots, he must have a figure in mind for me. But he wouldn't commit himself to a number. I had to give him a figure first.

Finally, very sheepishly, I stuttered, "H-how, how about $30,000?"

"THIRTY-THOUSAND DOLLARS!!!????" he yelled. "You must be out of your mind! I can't give you $30,000. That's ridiculous."

"Is that a lot of money?" I asked innocently. "Is that too much?" I really didn't know. I just knew I had led the league for the second straight year in stolen bases. I had hit .282 and scored 105 runs. I had established myself as a bona-fide major leaguer.

"I'll tell you what I'm going to do," Buzzy said. He looked around the room and closed the door. Then he called his secretary and told her, "I don't want to be disturbed." You'd have thought he was about to reveal national defense secrets.

"I've never given a player what he asked for," Buzzy said. "I'm going to give you $29,999 and you better not tell anybody what I gave you."

He called in his secretary. "Edna," he told her, "I want you to draw up a contract for $29,999."

Edna looked at him and said, "Huh?"

"That's right," Buzzy said.

She walked off with a sheepish smile. When she came back with the contract, Buzzy got me to sign it and made me swear that I wouldn't tell anybody. If I did, he'd never trust me again and he'd deny it. And that's what I got in 1962—$29,999.

That wasn't so much considering the way Maury Wills was playing, but it was all the money in the world to me. The only guys who were advertised as making $100,000 were Willie Mays and Mickey Mantle. I was on the ballclub. I was the starting shortstop. They were paying me $30,000—less a dollar. I knew I didn't have to worry about winning my job from Charley Smith. I knew I'd be in the major league barracks instead of the minor league barracks. I was tickled like a bee.

"You know, Maury, you better give me a good season," Buzzy told me. "I want you to bust your butt out there."

"You got it!" I told him. "You know I will. I always do. I always will."

I stayed in Los Angeles until spring training, working out three days a week at the stadium. I got batboys to come out and throw to me. Tommy Lasorda was a scout then and he even came down to throw to me. We'd get somebody else to shag balls in the outfield. When I couldn't get anybody to shag, I practiced bunting.

I went out that year and stole 104 bases, won the Hickok Award and was the National League MVP. Now, I'm back in Buzzy's office and this time, my guns are loaded. This time, I know there's not going to be this, "Thank you, thank you, sir." This time, I'm probably going to get a little squawk out of him. This time, I want to know how much he's going to offer me.

He still wouldn't give me a figure. I had to make the first

commitment. At the time, Ken Boyer, the Cardinal third baseman, was advertised as making $50,000. That was a lot of money. That was *all* the money in the world. There was no more money than that. I wanted that much money.

"I want $50,000," I said. "Fifty thousand. Fifty."

"Edna!" Buzzy shouted before I could say another word. "Get in here! Draw up a contract for $50,000."

He got me out of there in a hurry. He shook my hand and he made sure to remind me that I'd better go out and bust my butt for him. And I did, because when I got out of his office, I was glad I was still on the team.

Buzzy Bavasi knew $50,000 was a low figure considering what I'd done. Players had to negotiate for themselves then. We weren't allowed to have agents. If he had $70,000 in mind for a player and the player came in and asked for $60,000, Buzzy would have a fit. "SIXTY-THOUSAND DOLLARS!!!??? You gotta be out of your mind! I'm going to give you $55,000 and you better not tell anybody."

Or if somebody asked for $60,000, he might say, "You want $60,000!? Let me tell you one thing. You're not worth $60,000. But, you know, you have been playing good and you give good effort out there. You really bust your butt. I'm gonna give you the $60,000 and you better not tell anybody."

Then he'd tell another player that you signed for $50,000. He did that to get the price down: "If Maury Wills signed for $50,000, who the hell are you coming in and asking for $60,000."

He played all these little games. I can't say he wasn't a nice man. That was just negotiating. That was his job, to save money for the ballclub.

I didn't know that. I did start thinking after Buzzy was so quick to give me $50,000 after I stole 104 bases that I undersold myself. That wasn't like Buzzy. He had already told me the year before he never gave a player what he asked for. I walked out shaking my head. I never learned.

I was always underpaid, but I was always contented. Who's to say what underpaid is? In 1963, I led the league in stolen bases again with 40. I hit .302 with 83 runs scored. I played in the World Series and we beat the Yankees four straight.

I don't remember what my World Series share was that year. I had money in my pocket.

The only time I held out was in the spring of 1966. In 1965, I had stolen 94 bases and would have broken my own record if my leg hadn't started hemorrhaging. We beat the Twins in the World Series as I got 11 hits. Sandy Koufax had had a pretty good year, too. He set a single-season record with 382 strikeouts, went 26–8, and had a 2.04 earned run average. And Don Drysdale went 23–12 with a 2.77 earned run average. He also hit .300 with 7 home runs.

Koufax and Drysdale shocked the baseball world that spring by announcing that they were holding out together. They reportedly wanted $1.05 million over three years, divided equally. That's $175,000 each per year.

I decided I wanted the same money Drysdale and Koufax got. I didn't know how much that was. I wasn't in with them. I was on my own. I just told the club I wanted whatever they got.

When spring training started, I stayed in Los Angeles. But Koufax and Drysdale were getting all the publicity. There were reports that they were going to be banned from baseball for acting together and for reportedly having an agent advising them. There was a rumor that they were going to play in Italy or somewhere for a bunch of money. With all that going on, the press forgot about me.

Buzzy Bavasi didn't forget, though. He started using his tactics on me.

"Mr. O'Malley knows you're in cahoots with them," he told me. "They're going to get barred from the game and you're going with them."

I swore up and down I wasn't involved with Koufax and Drysdale.

"That's bullshit," Bavasi said. "Don't tell me that stuff. Who do you think you're talking to? I know you're with them. Mr. O'Malley knows you're with them, and he's really upset with you. You can't be fiddling around doing what those guys are trying to do. You could be gone any time.

"You better get down here and talk to me!" he ordered. "Start working out and we can continue to negotiate."

He scared the hell out of me. But he also gave me an opening to get down to Florida. I thought that was a great move on his part. I was getting nervous. I had been out a week or 10 days. That's a lot of time to miss in spring training. I was reading everything in the papers and watching all the news on television from Vero Beach, and I wasn't there. I wanted to be there more than anyplace in the world.

I went. And once I got to spring training and got into uniform, I was a dead duck. The second or third day down there, I sat down with Buzzy.

"I'll give you $85,000," Buzzy said.

"Give me the pen!" I barked. "If that's the way you want to be . . . I just want to play ball. Go ahead and treat me that way. I'll play."

I was trying to put him on a guilt trip, but I was as happy as I could be. So was he.

Koufax and Drysdale ended up getting $125,000 and $110,000 respectively. The papers always make a big deal out of salaries, but the other guys on the team don't really care. They're more concerned about whether the guy shows up on time and gives his best effort. We complained about guys just going through the motions. We didn't complain about how much they were paid.

The reason I held out—wanting as much as Koufax and Drysdale—was status. I wanted more recognition. I wanted to be a big-time, big-salary player. That's why I asked for as much as they were getting. It wasn't because I was envious of Sandy and Don. It didn't matter to me how much money they made. I didn't need the money any more than players today need the money to live on.

A player doesn't need $3 million. It's a status thing and an ego trip.

That's the only time that money and holding out came into play during my career. Playing—just being on the field—was the love of my life. I honestly would have played for nothing.

So I made $85,000 in 1966, and after the season was over, I was traded to Pittsburgh and Sandy Koufax retired. I played for the same money in 1967 in Pittsburgh and hit .302. After the season, I told Joe Brown, the Pirates general manager, I didn't need a raise. Making $85,000, I said, I should hit .302.

I was thinking like management. Only a few guys were getting more than $100,000 a year. I figured I wasn't in a class with them. I didn't know my worth to the ballclub.

Then Montreal, a new franchise, took me in the 1969 expansion draft. When that happened, I decided I wanted to go up to

$100,000. I told the Expos I wanted to be a $100,000 player and they got the idea of paying me $110,000, but in Canadian money. That was worth something like $95,000 American. But I was a $100,000 ballplayer at last—north of the border.

After a horrible start in Canada, I was traded back to the Dodgers that year and was paid the $95,000 American equivalent. After the season, Al Campanis, who was the new general manager, raised Cain with me. He didn't want to pay me that much. He didn't, either. He cut me back to $90,000 for the 1970 season. He beat me down for $5,000. I almost quit, but I took the pay cut.

In 1970, I had another good season and got the $5,000 back. I finished out my career at $95,000. It was reported that I was a $100,000 player, but I never made that much in American money. They didn't want to pay me that symbolic figure.

## Chapter 48: The men in blue

I used to think that certain umpires had it in for me—had a hard-on for me. But I came to realize that no umpire would make a bad call on purpose. He was just calling it the way he saw it. But he saw it the way he felt.

In most instances, giving the batter or the base runner the break on the close plays is contrary to what umpiring is all about. Umpires favor the defensive team because the idea is to get the game over. That's why you see more guys called out than safe on bang-bang plays. If the umpire calls every close play safe, that makes for long games. Most umpires don't want long games. Close plays are automatic outs because umpiring is all about getting the game over with.

That tendency is one of the reasons it's so hard for knuckleball pitchers to be successful. The ball may be hitting the strike zone, but it's dipping and diving and bouncing all around. It's hitting the catcher in the shin guards and bouncing off the catcher's mask. Batters are lunging at it and fouling it off the umpire's throat and shoulders. An umpire can get ticked off from that and start calling the pitches balls because he's ducking and doesn't see it. He'd rather see the blasted knuckleball pitcher out of the game.

On the other hand, a pitcher who's breezing along is a pitcher the umpire wants to see stay in the game. So that pitcher is going to get the breaks on the close calls.

Everything changes, though, if it's Maury Wills stealing or Ted Williams hitting when the count is 3–2 and the pitch is on the corner. Your reputation as a player becomes a point of honor with the umpire to make that call. These are the best players at judging the strike zone. The umpire has to give it his best shot, too. The law that umpiring favors the defensive team goes out of effect. If Ted Williams took that close pitch and the umpire wasn't quite sure, it was a ball. For anybody else it was a strike. If I'm trying to steal and the play is close, the call is safe. The umpire calls it the way he sees it, but you have a lot to do with how he sees it by the way you conduct yourself and the way you play.

I'm witness to that, courtesy of Tom Gorman, a great umpire. Late in my career, Gorman asked me one day for a baseball glove for his grandson. Just that he asked for it showed how much he respected me. Umpires have to be careful. They can't stay in the same hotel as the visiting ballclub. They don't drink in the same bars as the ballplayers. They can't do these things because friendship can't be involved with the way they call the game. To have a drink with a ballplayer or, in this case, to ask for a baseball glove, can look bad.

But Gorman asked me for the glove. I had a brand-new Spaulding glove. I wrote his grandson's name on it and gave it to Gorman before the next game he worked for us.

The game started and in the very first inning I got on first. I took off for second on an attempted steal and the play was the kind of close one that I'd been safe on my entire career. Gorman, who was working second, ran over and made the call: "OUT!"

"Out?" I protested. "Jeezus, Tom, what are you talking about? It was close, but I was in there. I was right under the tag. You used to call me safe on that play all the time."

"Yeah," Gorman said, "but you don't steal them like you used to, Maury."

He meant that when I was stealing them all the time, I had the reputation as a great base stealer. I got the calls. But I had slowed down. This was my next-to-last year and I wasn't stealing many bases. Lou Brock had become the stolen-base king.

One night in Milwaukee, I was in a bar in a top-notch place with a panoramic view of the city. Ed Sudol happened to be there, too, probably because it was the kind of place where he wouldn't normally run into ballplayers. I sent a drink over to him, and he sent one back to me. Before you knew it, we were side by side talking like two old buddies. The next day on the field, I was bitching at him as always: "Goddammit, Ed! Why don't you wake up?"

The ideal umpire has to overcome everything that's happened before. He has to see the play the way it is rather than the way he feels. He's got to forget I chewed his ass out last week when he called me out on a close play and I lost my composure and turned the home fans against him. Most umpires are going to remember that.

The ideal umpire won't remember that because it's over and gone. Shag Crawford fell into that category. So does Doug Harvey. Harvey does not remember what happened yesterday or last week.

Doug Harvey was a nice guy when he came up and he continued to be a nice guy when he became established. He wasn't a nice guy because he called things in my favor. What made him a nice guy was the way he handled things when you disputed a call. I'd be questioning the call and he'd say in a calm, low, sincere voice: "Maury, the way I saw it, he had you. He had you."

"HE HAD ME??!!" I'd scream. "HE MISSED ME TOTALLY!!!"

"I didn't see it that way," Harvey would say. Somehow he could be patient and assertive at the same time.

One time he called me out and I cussed him good. "#%&*!#*&!" I said, or words to that effect.

Doug Harvey could have thrown me out of the ballgame for what I said. But then Walter Alston would have come out and started raising hell because Harvey tossed his star player. So he'd have to toss Walter Alston, too. Then whoever Alston gave the lineup to was going to be on Harvey's butt the rest of the game and the crowd would be on him.

So Harvey didn't throw me out. All he said, with a tone of paternal disappointment, was, "Maury, you're a better man than that."

When he said that, I choked up. I apologized and walked away saying to myself, "Damn. I am a better man than that. He's a nice guy."

Doug Harvey started umpiring while I was playing. We didn't have a nickname for him back then. Years later, I was told, he became known around baseball as "God." I wasn't surprised.

## Chapter 49: One monkey doesn't stop the show

We won the National League pennant in 1966 for the third time in four years, but we lost the Series in four straight games to Baltimore. After the Series, we were scheduled to go to Japan to play a series of exhibition games.

I had injured my knee during the season. After stealing 94 bases in 1965, I stole only 38. For the first time in seven years, I didn't lead the National League in stolen bases. Because of the knee injury, I asked for permission to skip the trip. It was a voluntary trip and I didn't want to go. Buzzy Bavasi said that would be okay.

Then Bavasi called me back and said that when the Japanese promoters of the tour heard I wasn't coming, they wanted to cancel the trip. Because I was a little guy who hit singles, bunted, stole bases and played hard, I was very popular in Japan. Everybody wanted to see me, Buzzy said. He said I wouldn't have to play. They just wanted me to be there. That was his way of getting me on a guilt trip and out-negotiating me again.

The team flew to Hawaii for a few days before continuing on to Japan. But I left late and joined them in Hawaii. I was there only four or five hours, but it looked nice.

When we got to Japan, they started playing me even though they said I wouldn't have to play. It was just because the Japanese wanted to see me, they said. But I hurt my knee again rounding third base. It just locked up on me. I called Walter O'Malley and asked for permission to go back to Los Angeles and have my knee taken care of. He gave me a definite no.

I hung up on O'Malley, sneaked out of the hotel, got a plane ticket and left without telling them.

On the way home, the plane stopped in Hawaii. I'd been to Europe for the State Department. I'd been in Mexico, Venezuela, Puerto Rico and Nicaragua. But this was Hawaii. This was the Garden of Eden. Even the rain seemed to be soft and mellow. I decided to stay for a while.

Nobody knew where I was. Headlines were running in the Los Angeles papers about Maury Wills disappearing. People were calling all over trying to find me. I didn't know anything about it. All I knew was that I was walking past the Garden Bar in the Hawaiian Village and I heard a banjo playing with a Dixieland band.

The music put me in a trance. I went in the bar and found a seat beside somebody named Clint Eastwood. A tourist saw me and came over and said she had to have my picture. She was a Dodger fan from Los Angeles. So she went to Clint Eastwood and said, "Excuse me, sir, but would you mind moving out of the way?" Shortly after that the movie *A Fistful of Dollars* came out, and nobody ever asked Clint Eastwood to move aside again.

Before long, I was playing the banjo with the band and having a great time in Hawaii. I stayed there until one of those tourists got off the plane in Los Angeles and saw the newspaper headlines asking, "Maury—Where are you?" The tourist called one of the newspapers and said, "You people looking for Maury Wills? He's in Hawaii playing the banjo for a Dixieland band in the Garden Bar in the Hawaiian Village."

That came out in the papers. When I heard about it, I got home in a hurry and locked myself in the house. I was sitting in there at one o'clock in the morning when Bob Hunter from the *Herald Examiner* started knocking on my door and walking around the house. He was dying to get in.

When two papers are competing in the same city, it seems the guy from the more established paper is easier going. The guy from the less successful paper is more aggressive. The Los Angeles *Times* was the more established paper and the *Herald Examiner* was the one always trying to get the story.

Bob Hunter was a great writer. Today, he's one of my best friends. Time and maturity have mellowed us both. But back then he was my nemesis.

So he's walking around my house, banging on the doors and windows. He stayed out there for an hour or two begging for a story.

"Maury? Maury? Please, Maury. I'll write anything you want. Please," he's saying. That was really hustling for a story.

Finally, I lifted the curtain by one of the louver windows and said, "Bob, I'll call you tomorrow. I promise. Just leave me alone tonight. Let me think about things. I'm scared."

Bob came back that morning with a photographer. I told him I wanted him to take a picture of me jogging. My story was that I had to come back to Los Angeles because I'd hurt my knee badly and it was the only way I could get ready for the 1967 season. Even though Mr. O'Malley wouldn't give me permission to leave Japan, I had to fight him, I said. I had to come back and that's why I was jogging—to get my knee ready.

It didn't work. The Dodgers hummed my ass out of Los Angeles and I found myself in Pittsburgh. The deal was announced Dec. 1, 1966. Maury Wills to Pittsburgh for Bob Bailey and Gene Michael. I was back in Spokane when the trade was made. Although the mother of my children had thrown me out, I still went up to Spokane at times to visit my children and go hunting with my buddies. I stayed at my ranch, but slept on the couch. Joe Brown, the Pirates general manager, called me in Spokane and gave me the news. The Dodgers didn't call. They never said anything to me.

That was the first time that I really understood the saying that one monkey doesn't stop the show. No one's bigger than the establishment. It had always been said that as Maury Wills goes, so go the Dodgers. But the Dodgers continued to exist without me.

Being traded was my first major defeat in my adult years. I knew I still had talent and that my career wasn't over. But I cried. I really cried.

I was traded and this was real pain. It was the type of pain that later in my life made me drink and use drugs. If such a thing had existed in my life then, maybe I would have drunk and used drugs. But I just had to take it.

Joe Brown, the Pirates GM, helped make me feel better. He was a fine man. He called me and told me he wanted to come up to Spokane to spend some time with me and sign a contract.

I went to spring training with the Pirates and put on a Pirates uniform. It was a brand-new feeling. The pain of being traded went away and didn't come back until the Dodgers came to Fort Myers, where we trained, to play the Pirates.

I was in the dugout before the game when Vin Scully and a group of Dodgers and Los Angeles sportswriters came over to give me my World Series watch. That was one year they didn't give out rings. They gave watches instead, and that's how I got mine. Vin Scully handed it to me. I guess Walter O'Malley was really indifferent to me by then.

When we came to Los Angeles to play the Dodgers once the season started, I felt like a hero coming home. I figured I was supposed to get a hero's welcome. It's nonsense to think that way, but I got the reception and I had a good game.

I hit .302 that year and was in the top 10 hitters in the league. The Pirates were a hitting team and nobody took a pitch for me so I ended up with only 29 stolen bases. The next year I stole 52.

When a good player is traded, that first year with a new team he can look for a real good year. You saw that from Kirk Gibson when the Tigers traded him to the Dodgers in 1988. He led the Dodgers to the World Series and was MVP.

So I had an excellent first year with Pittsburgh. I did well against the Dodgers. I didn't do it vindictively. I did it out of pride. To tell you the truth, I was playing as a Dodger. I only had a Pirate uniform on. And I remember Vin Scully saying, "Now the Dodgers know what it feels like to be under the wrath of Maury Wills." I was all over their ass.

Yeah.

## Chapter 50: Harry the Hat

Harry Walker, brother of Dixie Walker and manager of the Pittsburgh Pirates in 1967, was a fine person. He had been a good player and he was a capable hitting instructor. But as a manager, he wasn't Walter Alston.

Alston was laid-back, low-key and low-profile. He didn't bother you. He seldom lost his temper. Harry the Hat lost his temper frequently. As calm as Alston was, Harry was intense. When I joined the Pirates, Harry Walker was entering his third year as manager. He wouldn't finish the season. After splitting the first 84 games of the season, Danny Murtaugh was brought in to replace him.

Harry was known for governing his players by policing them. He policed me out of $800 that year, and I don't know whether it would have happened if it hadn't been for the two girls who disappeared.

Harry thought we had a good club on paper, but we were losing and we weren't playing well. He figured he had to do something. And he knew he didn't want players breaking curfew and he didn't want girls in the rooms.

One night when we were in St. Louis, Harry was waiting for the elevator in the hotel to go up to his room after a game. As he was standing there, he saw two girls coming out of the bar with drinks in their hands. The girls headed for the elevator and got on. Harry got on after them. Suspecting they were up to no good —or too much good—he watched to see which floor they pushed. He pushed the same one.

When the elevator arrived at the appointed floor, Harry was the perfect gentleman and let the two girls off the elevator first. Then he watched to see which way they went. He went the other way, but he stopped at the end of the corridor and peeked around the corner to see which room they were going into.

Sure enough, they entered a room containing two of his ballplayers. Harry waited about 10 minutes until he figured they were settled in, then went down to the room and started banging on the door with both fists.

"OPEN UP!!!" Harry shouted.

Nobody opened the door, but male voices from inside were saying, "Who is it? Who is it?"

"YOU KNOW WHO IT IS! IT'S ME! THE HAT! OPEN UP!!!"

The two players didn't know what to do. They were on the fifth floor of the hotel. They couldn't slip the girls out the window and they didn't know where to hide them. All of a sudden they got this idea. They had these little studio cabinet-couches in the hotel rooms. To make the couch into a bed, you pulled it out from under the cabinet. The two players pulled the couch out, stretched the girls out lengthwise behind the couch, and pushed the couch in again. Finally, they opened the door.

The Hat burst into the room and he was foaming at the mouth.

"I GOT YOU!" he shouted in triumph.

He dashed over to the closet. BAM! He pulled the door open and rummaged through the clothes. No girls. He went to the bathroom and ripped the door open—BANG! No girls. He ripped open the shower curtain—CLACK! No girls.

Now Harry's going crazy. He went to the window and threw it open. He's hanging out of the window looking to see if they're hanging on the window sill or standing on the ledge. No girls.

"I know they're in here someplace," he's fuming in frustration and rage. "I know it. I saw them get off the elevator. They had the nerve to offer me a drink. Where are they! WHERE ARE THEY!!??"

"There's no girls in here, Harry," the players said innocently.

"YES THERE ARE!!!" Harry shouted, on the verge of apoplexy. "I know they're here!"

He finally had no choice but to leave. He couldn't find them. But as he left, he pointed his finger at the two players and gave them a warning: "Someday I'll get you. I'll get you. I'll dedicate myself to it."

Those players were married, so I'll leave their names out of this. But I've seen them since. We still laugh about it.

I didn't know about their little adventure that night, though. I was down at the local banjo place, playing. I had the whole place going, singing along to the Crawdad Song. Finally, I told the audience I had to go. It was a quarter to one and curfew was one o'clock. "I'll get fined," I told them.

"Don't worry, buddy," the guys in the crowd were saying. "We'll pay the fine for you. Play another song."

I played another song and now it was five minutes to one. I got up and announced, "I gotta go."

"C'mon, Maury," they begged. "One more. Don't worry about the fine."

So I got to playing and when I looked down at my watch again it was 20 minutes after one. Now I really gotta go. I grabbed a taxi and went back to the hotel. I told the cab to let me off a block from the hotel, which had a big park in front of it. The border of the park facing the hotel was lined with big, old trees.

I got out of the cab and sneaked from one tree to the other like Sylvester the cat. I didn't want anyone to see me going through the lobby, so I went around back, slipped onto the freight elevator and went up to my room. I figured I was safe.

Until the next morning. That's when Harry called a team meeting. During the meeting, everything came out about the two girls. I was just sitting there. Suddenly, Harry pointed at me and yelled, "AND YOU WILLS!! WHERE WERE YOU LAST NIGHT?? You weren't in your room!"

"What do you mean?" I said innocently.

"You know what I mean," he growled.

"How'd you know?" I asked.

"Because I was across the street," he announced triumphantly. "Behind a tree!"

The poor man. He was standing out in the park hiding behind a tree trying to catch players coming in late. I thought, goddam! It seems we can do better than to put him through this.

I had stayed out late from time to time with the Dodgers. The banjo kept me out. It was good, clean fun. Banjo music and sing-alongs were big back then, and the banjo places in the towns we went to kept a banjo for me so I'd come over and play after the games. With the Dodgers it was never a problem.

But Harry fined me $800. That was a lot of money in those days. After he announced the fine, I figured I'd go out and bust my butt in the game. Maybe he'd change his mind and not go through with the fine. He said he was going to take it out of my check.

I always felt I gave 100 percent, but for the next week, until payday, I gave 150 percent. Everything I had and more. We won some games. I was playing well. I thought maybe he wouldn't take the money. But when I got my check, I was $800 light.

Then I figured maybe I could get it back at the end of the season. Some ballclubs do that. They give the fine money back when the year's done if you've had a good season. I didn't miss any more curfews and played hard all year. I batted .302 and scored 92 runs. I had a real good year. But I didn't get the $800 back.

## Chapter 51: And give me a couple dollars

When I was with the Dodgers, I was chairman of Athletes for Youth in California under Governor Reagan. I was also chairman of a similar program in Las Vegas. So when I went to Pittsburgh and Mayor Joseph Barr asked me to go to the depressed areas of the city during the 1968 season and work with deprived children, naturally I said no.

I told the mayor I didn't want to deny any kid the opportunity to have Maury Wills come to his neighborhood the way Jerry Priddy had come to mine simply because a kid lived in an affluent area. I said if I was going to participate in the program, I wanted to go to all areas of the city, rich and poor. That's what I did.

I tried to get some of the other Pirates to go with me, but they wouldn't. We ran the program in the daytime in the summer. It was hot and my teammates wanted to rest for the games at night. I did it anyway and still went to the ballpark and played well.

The city assigned four playground directors to work with me. Together, we went to 12 areas and worked with 4,000 kids. I always started by talking to all the kids first for five or ten minutes. Then I would split them up into groups—outfielders, first basemen, second basemen, shortstops, and so on. The playground directors supervised the groups and practiced with them while I went from one group to another giving individual instruction.

When the session was over, I called them all together and gave them a few parting words. I always ended my little speech by saying: "Whenever you see me around town—at Forbes Field, shopping in a store, at church, in a restaurant—don't stand back and stare. Come up and say, 'Hi, Maury,' and ask for an autograph . . . And give me a couple of dollars."

I'd always get a nice laugh from that. It became a big joke around Pittsburgh. Whenever anyone saw me around town, they'd yell, "Hey, Maury! Here's a couple of dollars."

Some of those kids today are executives in the corporate headquarters in Pittsburgh—U.S. Steel, Westinghouse, PPG. Even today in my traveling, I come across some of them, and they say, "Hey, Maury. Here's a couple of dollars." It might be a 40-year-old man. He'll whip a business card out, hand it to me, and say, "Maury, if you're ever in need, just let me know. I remember when you came to my playground."

At the end of that summer, the mayor's office unveiled a painting and gave it to me. It shows me in my Pittsburgh Pirates uniform sitting on the ground. I have about five Little Leaguers, white and black, around me. They're all looking at me. One has his hands behind his back with his glove on. Another one has his bat on his shoulder. I'm talking to them. The painting must be at least five feet square. I didn't keep many things, but I kept that painting.

Those are the kinds of things that I cherished and reflected on when things got so bad that I had to think of some good things in my life in order to stay alive.

## Chapter 52: Back from the moon

Getting traded to Pittsburgh was the first time I had experienced defeat. The only other time that happened to me during my playing career was in 1969, when the Pirates left me unprotected and I was drafted by the brand-new Montreal Expos.

I couldn't play at all in Montreal. I was lousy. Fans were booing me like you wouldn't believe. For about four days I actually quit. I didn't want to play baseball anymore.

By June, things were so bad I announced my retirement. I had a press conference, the only press conference I ever had in baseball. I called my wife and told her I was retiring. "Sure. Sure," she said. She didn't believe me. I told her I was coming back to the home I had left in 1965. "Look," she said, "you're not coming back here." I got the feeling I wasn't wanted back there.

Then Jim Fanning, the general manager of the Expos, told me to come to his office and talk to him. He told me there was a deal cooking with the Dodgers and I'd better get back on the team so they could complete it. We were taking a road trip to the West Coast and he told me I wouldn't come back to Montreal. That made me feel good.

We flew to San Diego and on June 11, 1969, they clinched the deal: Maury Wills and Manny Mota to the Dodgers for Ron Fairly and Paul Popovich.

Manny and I flew to Los Angeles and went straight to Dodger Stadium. The Dodgers were playing Philadelphia that night. I went into the clubhouse and there was my uniform hanging in the same locker I had before. I just stood there and looked up at the locker and uniform. It was like coming back from the moon.

Walter O'Malley sent a note down to me that said: "Welcome back, Maury." Then he came down to the clubhouse to see me. They said it was the only time Walter O'Malley had ever been in the Dodger clubhouse.

Walter Alston asked me if I wanted to sit that game out. I'd been off about four days and wasn't in shape. Walter knew that, and he wanted to know if I wanted to work out a couple days before I played. I said, no, I wanted to play.

I led off in the bottom of the first and the fans went crazy when I was announced. I got on first base and there was another ovation that went into a "GO! GO! GO! GO!" chant. I didn't want to go. My legs didn't feel good, but I took off anyhow and I made it. The place went wild.

That was a great moment, but it wasn't in my top three. The first two on that list were the 85-yard touchdown in high school and my 97th stolen base in St. Louis. The third one happened later in the 1969 season.

As part of the 100th anniversary of professional baseball, the Dodgers honored a Centennial Celebrity at every home game of the 1969 season. They had people like Stan Musial and Sandy Koufax, who were retired, and active players like Willie Mays. The ovation most of those people got was maybe 30 seconds of courteous applause. Sandy Koufax had an ovation that lasted maybe a minute and a half.

One day Red Patterson, the Dodger publicist, came to me before the game. "Maury, we want you to be the Centennial Celebrity tonight," he said.

"No, no," I protested. "That would be embarrassing. I'm not a celebrity. These are my teammates. I'm an active player. I can't do that."

Red left and came back about 20 minutes later. "Mr. O'Malley thought it would be a good idea," he said, using the most persuasive argument any Dodger ever heard.

"What time do you want me?" I asked.

They announced the Centennial Celebrity at the top of the fifth inning. They'd run some credits on the left field message board, then John Ramsey, the Dodgers' public address announcer, would introduce the person. That was the extent of it.

I was at shortstop getting ready for the inning to start. I could tell by the murmur of the crowd that the credits were going up on the message board behind me. Ted Sizemore, my second baseman, and either Bill Grabarkewitz or Bill Sudakis at third were trying to get my attention. I was trying to ignore them. They kept telling me. I shook my head: "I know. I know. I know." I was just trying to pretend I didn't.

Hank Aaron was waiting to step in to hit. Al Barlick, who was elected to the Hall of Fame in 1989, was the umpire. All of a sudden, John Ramsey's great voice came over the public address system.

"And now, ladies and gentlemen, the Centennial Celebrity of the night . . . Captain . . . Maury . . . WILLS!"

The people stood up, started applauding, and wouldn't stop. Vin Scully was looking at me with his binoculars and describing my reaction on the radio. The people in the stands with their transistors could hear him. He said, "I do believe the tears are welling. He's choking up . . ."

The crowd applauded louder. Shucks. I took my cap off and waved and the noise escalated. It went on for three and a half, four minutes and it was still going. Al Barlick was trying to get Hank Aaron to get into the batter's box, but the fans wouldn't quit and Hank wouldn't get in there. He was acknowledging the moment. I threw the crowd a kiss and then—Jeezus Christ—it escalated again. Vin Scully was right. I was choked up.

I had time to do a lot of reflecting standing out there with the cheers washing over me. I came to feel that these people weren't applauding me just because I was back with the Dodgers or because I'd stolen 104 bases or whatever. There was something about Maury Wills that they liked as a person. A lot of great players, including Sandy, had been introduced and the fans didn't respond like this.

It was the first time in my life that I realized what life is really about. It's not how good you are at what you do, but it's how good you are as a person that really matters in the end. The autographs I signed in the parking lot, the appearances I made, the clinics I ran all meant something. People are for me. They wish me luck.

I felt that on the field in 1969. It was one of the greatest moments of my life.

## Chapter 53: Last days of a Dodger

The Dodgers had a day for me in 1971 when I was still playing. It was a fine year for the Dodgers and for me. We came within one game of winning the division. I hit .281, scored 73 runs, and hit the last three of my 20 career home runs. I was named Major League Shortstop of the Year. So when they had a day for me, I said in my speech: "I really appreciate this and it looks like when I get a day like this, I'm finished. But I'm not done yet. I'm going to be around a while."

The Dodgers knew what they were doing, though. The next year they sat me on the bench because they wanted to rebuild. They didn't keep me as insurance. They just put me on the bench and paid me. Bill Russell was the new shortstop.

It's amazing how your body deteriorates sitting on the bench. When you lose your drive mentally everything else goes. I was 39 years old. Steve Garvey was playing third base. He was quiet and shy. They put him at third base but he couldn't throw. It was sad to see him suffer in the field the way he did. The next year, Ron Cey took over at third and they moved Garvey to first. When he didn't have to worry about throwing the ball, Garvey was able to become a tremendous hitter and an outstanding player. When Davey Lopes came up in 1973, the Dodgers infield was set with Garvey, Lopes, Cey and Russell. And I was gone.

I never retired from baseball. I got released. The handwriting was on the wall during the 1972 season, so I knew it was coming. It wasn't a devastating blow. I had already felt and accepted the pain of knowing that would be my last season.

I had asked the Dodgers if they could end my career with some dignity—call in a few writers that we all knew and make it formal. They assured me that was the only way they would consider doing it.

I requested that because I had seen established players, good players, even stars go out of the game in such a poor fashion. They heard about it on the radio or had a writer call them or read it in the paper.

In 1968, my last year in Pittsburgh, one of my teammates was Bill Henry, a very fine left-handed relief pitcher. One day, I was getting dressed in the clubhouse before the game when Henry rushed in. The pitchers were already taking their batting practice and he was a little late. He ripped his clothes off, put his uniform on, and rushed out to the field.

Just after Bill Henry left the clubhouse, the equipment man came through and followed him out. I was still getting dressed. A minute or two later, I saw Henry come back in with his head hanging and his whole body slumped. I went over and asked him what was wrong. He told me that the equipment manager let him know that the Pirates had given him his release. He had played 15 years in the major leagues. That means you have talent. It means you deserve to be shown some courtesy. The general manager could have at least called Henry in the afternoon and said, "Stop by the office before you go down to the clubhouse." They could have just told him over the telephone. But they had the equipment man tell him that they needed his uniform for somebody who was coming in.

I also saw Duke Snider suffering toward the end of his career. Snider went to the Giants. Gil Hodges went to the Mets. Charlie Neal went to the Mets, too. I saw these guys end up with another ballclub before I even knew it. There was nothing formal about the release or the trade. Nobody knew anything about it, and these were great players who made contributions to baseball.

That's why I asked the Dodgers for consideration when it was time for me to go. They assured me they would handle it with dignity. That was at the end of the season. I felt very good.

About a month later, I was at Yorba Linda Country Club. It was Dodger Day, and I was having a lot of fun. All my golfing teammates were there playing with members of the club.

I was playing on the back nine and having a good round. Afterwards, there was going to be a banquet and all the Dodgers would be introduced and each of us would be called up to say something.

I was getting ready to tee off when all of a sudden over the hill came this camera crew. I said to myself, "Oh, my God. All right! These guys came to cover my game. Let me get ready with my swing." I wanted to tell them to be sure not to follow the ball and to just watch my swing. I was going to make my swing look pretty and I didn't care where the ball went, so I wanted them to shoot it from the side and not the back.

The reporter came up to me and said, "Maury, can we have a couple of words with you?"

"Certainly," I said.

"Maury, you've just been released by the Dodgers . . ."

My mouth flew open. Bitter disappointment, not anger, hit me. I mustered all the control and love for the Dodgers that I ever had, and all the maturity that I could.

I said all the right things. "These things happen," I said. "I've had a fine career. I'm happy to have been a Dodger. I love the Dodgers. I loved being a player."

I didn't say, "But life goes on." I didn't even know the expression then. I didn't know any such thing as life going on. All I knew was life playing baseball—in particular for the Dodgers.

The reporter pulled the microphone back and asked, "How do you feel finding out about it like this?"

"It would have been nice if I could have known first," I said, "but, hey, what's the difference? I know now."

I finished the round of golf, but I was numb. I guess I went through the round putting on a big facade. The other men in my foursome were congratulating me on saying such nice things about an organization I spent my life with and being so classy about it.

I didn't mean one word I said. I felt like saying, "Fuck 'em." That's how I really felt.

I think we have the right to think what we want, but it isn't always right to say what we feel. So I just thanked everybody for saying nice things.

I didn't go around the course and check with my teammates. Maybe they knew and maybe they didn't. Nobody came up to me and said, "Sorry, Maury." I don't think anybody felt they had to feel sorry for me. It was obvious it was going to happen. They knew I had had a fine career. But the team never did get in touch with me.

I never figured out why teams act the way they do when releasing a veteran player. It seems they don't want to face you. I was sensitive to it because I had seen it happen. I asked them not to do that with me but they did it anyhow.

## Chapter 54: Ink stains

If I miss any part of baseball, it's the fans after the game in the parking lot. They came there for autographs. It was common to complain about signing autographs. That was part of being a big-league player. You didn't want to take the time for small stuff like that.

I never felt that way. I enjoyed it. I was flattered that they would ask.

Sunday was autograph day. The other days of the week we played night games. By the time we got out of the ballpark and got home it was after midnight. You didn't have to dress up to come to the ballpark. But Sunday games started at 1:30 in the afternoon. By 4 o'clock, the games were over and you had five hours of daylight left. Sunday was always special.

All the things you couldn't do on the other days you did on Sunday. And it had to be the best. If you were going to have a girlfriend come to the game, it was your *special* girl. If you didn't have a girlfriend and you were going to meet somebody, on Sunday she had to be a queen. That was the thing about Sunday. Everything was all dressed up.

Very few of the players parked their cars in the players' parking lot at Dodger Stadium because the kids knew where it was and they'd trap the players there. So we parked all over the place. I parked in the players' lot regularly, but many times I parked in another part of the lot because it was closer to an elevator I took to get out of the stadium. You couldn't fool the kids, though. They combed the parking lot and they knew every player's car.

One Sunday, I came out of the stadium and the kids were by my car. I was wearing white shoes, nice white slacks, a blue blazer and a white sport shirt with the collar out over the coat collar. That was the way to dress then, and I was sharp. Yes, sir. I even showered longer than usual on Sunday. I had iced my leg down so I was late getting out of the park.

When I got to my car, kids were all around it. They had these blue felt-tip pens, and after signing a few, I looked down and I had ink all over my white pants. The kids were stepping all over my white shoes.

"Hey," I said. "I'll tell you what we'll do. Let's just line up, single fine, according to height, shortest guys first. I promise I'll stay here until I sign everybody's autograph book." There must have been 80 kids there.

They lined up and I stayed and signed for everyone. The kids kept order. The adults were the ones who broke into the line and came at me from the side. It was hard for me to refuse the adult. I just assumed it was all right for an adult to break in and make a kid wait. I was brought up that way. We didn't speak unless spoken to.

Today, I don't let the adults break in and get an autograph when kids have been waiting in line a long time. I don't think that's right anymore.

Anyway, the very next Sunday at Dodger Stadium, I came out to my car with my white shoes, white pants, blue blazer, and white shirt, and there was another gang of kids. This time, they were all lined up by height. I could see them standing next to each other seeing who was taller. It was one time when everybody wanted to be short. I heard kids complaining that somebody was getting in front of them and other kids telling them not to worry, Maury won't leave until he's signed for everybody. That just cemented for me the importance of staying there until every kid had an autograph.

Sandy Koufax would sign autographs. I never saw him push anyone aside. But he would sign until he got to his car, like most of the guys, then he would get in and drive away. I went beyond that. I stayed.

I was always overcompensating like that. That's one of my character traits. Sometimes, I pay people back many times. I can't just let somebody do something for me and accept it and say, "Thanks." I can't let them have the satisfaction of doing something nice. I don't give someone something that I was going to throw away anyhow and doesn't mean anything. I give away things like the last uniform I played in, my Hickok Belt, the last cap I wore, my glove, the shoes I wore to steal my 97th base.

At the time I was giving my things away, people weren't selling baseball memorabilia. That started later. But I would have given them away just the same.

I do autograph shows now. One of the first shows I went to when I was starting my recovery was at Disneyland. The promoters of these shows pay you a certain amount to stay there for a certain length of time. The faster you can sign, the more money they can make. They don't want you staying longer because they don't want to pay for an extra hour.

I went to that first show and I was giving high fives to the kids. I was looking at them and talking to them. The promoters were beside themselves. At that rate, I wasn't going to get to everybody in the time I had and they didn't want to pay me for another hour. I told them not to worry. I don't do things that way. I'd stay as long as it took and I wouldn't charge them any more. I wanted the money but I wasn't there for the money. I was there for the people. I was there for myself. I wanted to talk to the people. They were standing there in line and waiting. How could I not look up at them when I signed my autograph?

I don't think people come to get my autograph as much as they come to get the autograph from me. And I'm not giving them me if I just give them the autograph and don't even look up and acknowledge them. Little boys come and their fathers tell them all about Maury Wills and how they're going to meet this great baseball player and get his autograph on a picture.

So the kid gets to me and he's standing there with his eyes open wide. He doesn't know if he's supposed to talk to me. I have to look up and acknowledge the kid. I say, "Hey, how're you doing?" I play a little hand-slapping game with them: "Give me five. Up high. On the side. Down low. Too slow . . . oops, you got me!"

The kids say, "Thanks, Mr. Wills."

"You can call me Maury if you like," I say, "if it's all right with your father. And thanks, John." I know the kid's name because I always personalize the autograph. "Bye, John."

"Bye," the kid says.

"Bye, who?"

"Bye, Maury!"

The next thing I know I look up and that same kid has dragged his father over just to say, "Hi, Maury" before they go home.

I say, "Hi, John," and the kid goes home telling his father, "He remembered my name!"

That's a day for the kid. The autograph is just a byproduct. If he got my autograph and I didn't even look up, that wouldn't mean a thing to that kid down the road. I wanted to be that kid's Jerry Priddy—to have a positive impact on him for the rest of his life.

Athletes make lifelong impressions on kids. I never smoked in front of a kid. I didn't drink in front of kids. I never cussed in front of them.

The really unfortunate part is the athlete who says, "I don't know why they're putting the pressure on me to be a role model. That should start at home."

You can argue that point for a lifetime. But people remember. Almost 30 years later, I would run into people who came to see me play when they were youngsters, the same people who stood in line when I took my time and signed autographs until everybody had one. They never forgot.

## Chapter 55: Hunting duck—bagging peacock

In the winter of 1972, after the Dodgers released me, I was asked to go on a duck-hunting trip to Alamosa, Colo., for an edition of the "American Sportsman" television series with Curt Gowdy. I was still an avid duck-hunter and eagerly agreed.

It wasn't even a hunt, though. It was all a show. They had a local guide there to call the ducks in. "QUACK. QUACK-QUACK." We'd be sitting in the duck blind and the ducks would start coming in. All of a sudden, the stage manager would stand up in the blind with his slate and say, "Ready! Take two!" SNAP! The next thing you knew the ducks flared off.

Finally, we got the stage manager to stay down in the blind. The local guy started calling the ducks in again. "QUACK-QUACKQUACK. QUACK. QUACKQUACK." The camera started rolling again and they told us to start talking.

"Yeah, Maury, here they come," Curt Gowdy said. "I think they're turning. They're northerns."

"Oh, boy. Those are nice ones," I said.

The camera is on the ducks. They're taking beautiful slow-motion pictures as the ducks came in low, just a few inches off the water.

I jumped up. WHOOM! WHOOM! I knocked down three of them right on the water.

"NO! NO, MAURY! NO!" The producer jumped up and started yelling at me.

"What's the matter?"

"You ambushed them!" the producer shouted. "We can't show that on camera. If people see ducks that close to the water and you knock them down like that, we'll be buried in letters. You gotta shoot the ducks in the air!"

"Oh."

The duck-caller had a black Labrador and he sent the dog for the dead ducks. They ended up using the retrieving shots. But we still had to have some kill shots.

The guide started calling again and pretty soon a big flock—there must have been 40 ducks—started turning and coming in The stage manager told Curt and me to start talking again.

"You do much duck-hunting, Maury?"

"Yeah, Curt. Up in Spokane in the winter, all I do is hunt. Walking over the hills is how I keep my legs in shape."

WHAM! WHAM! This time I knocked them down in the air.

"Great shot, Maury! Great shot!" Curt exclaimed.

I was so proud. I must have bagged 40 ducks during the week we spent shooting the show. And in the whole episode all they used was one kill shot. "People watching TV don't want to see kill shots," they explained. "They don't feel good about it."

Curt and I had a lot of time together while the crew was getting shots of the Indians' adobe dwellings and the southern Colorado scenery. The rest of the show was just talk. They showed us getting ready the night before the hunt. They showed us cleaning our guns. They showed us having coffee. There was no script. We were supposed to ad-lib.

During the breaks in filming, Curt said, "You're good at this. You should be on the air for somebody."

When we were done, we flew to Denver and then split up. Curt was going to Wyoming for the next episode. I was going back to Los Angeles. We had gotten to know each other so well we embraced.

Just before he left, Curt told me, "No one knows this, Maury, but Sandy Koufax is resigning." Sandy had been working on NBC's "Game of the Week" baseball telecasts. "I'm going to talk to a man named Chet Simmons when I get back," Curt said. "Chet's president of NBC Sports."

"Will you put a word in for me, Curt?" I asked.

"I'll tell him he should hire you," Curt said.

I went back to Los Angeles and playing golf, having brunch, and living the good life. That January, the Super Bowl was played in the Los Angeles Coliseum. NBC did the broadcast. Sometime during that week, Chet Simmons asked me to come down to his hotel to see him. I took Bump with me. Chet and I talked for about three hours. He was feeling me out.

"I'll let you know when I get back to New York," Chet said. When he got to New York, he called me back and told me I had Sandy's old job. Just like that.

I jumped on the phone and called Curt Gowdy. "Curt, I got the job!" I said, all excited.

"I know," Curt said.

"You must have recommended me," I said.

"Yeah," Curt admitted. "I told him how good you were out in the blind with me."

That was a case of being in the right place at the right time. There were a lot of former athletes who could have got that job in the booth, but I stepped right into it.

So I went straight from baseball to the "Game of the Week" making about $80,000 a year. I was good from the start. I was kind of brash, cocky and free-spirited. I said things.

I didn't really have mike fright except for the first game we covered. The Cubs were playing in Wrigley Field and Rick Reuschel, who was with the Cubs then, had been the star of the game.

They sent me down to the field to do the post-game interview with him. It was my first live interview. They didn't brief me and run me through the mechanics of interviewing somebody. They just sent me down there.

They told me I'd have three minutes for the interview. On the way down to the field, I got together four questions to ask Reuschel. No matter what the answer was, I figured I'd go right to the next question and then the next one after that.

So I got Reuschel, the camera was on, and I asked him the first question.

"Not necessarily," he said in a little voice.

I asked him the second question.

"Maybe," Reuschel replied after a little thought.

I asked the third question.

"I don't know," Reuschel replied.

I looked over at my stage manager. He was pulling his hands apart as if he were pulling taffy, the signal to stretch, stretch, ssstttrrreeetttccchhh.

I asked Reuschel my fourth and final question.

"Mmmmm . . . ummmm . . . I'm not sure," Reuschel said deliberately.

It was early in the season. The weather in Chicago was chilly, but I was sweating. The red light was still on the camera. All my questions were asked and Rick Reuschel hadn't answered one of them.

"Thank you," I said, doing the only thing I could think of. "Now let's go back upstairs."

Whoever was announcing the game took over and filled out the rest of the time. I think he gave the scores about seven times.

I was scared. But the producer was nice about it. "Don't worry, Maury," he said. "But you didn't look very comfortable out there."

"He wouldn't talk!" I said.

"Keep prodding him," the producer advised.

"But I had four questions for him."

"Listen to the answers," the producer said. "Get some follow-up questions from his answers."

I was being mechanical. On the other hand, I didn't know you couldn't get much more from Rick Reuschel if you prodded him with a branding iron. He's a nice guy, but he just doesn't talk much.

The next game we did was at Shea Stadium. I had to interview a kid who had just come up from Tidewater and had pitched a good game.

"It's early in the season. You just got called up and you pitched a great game on national television," I said to him. "Are you nervous?"

"Yeah," he said.

"I am, too."

That broke the ice for me. We got through that interview and I began hoping that the games would end at a time that allowed me to do a post-game interview. If a game ended right on the hour or half-hour, for instance, they'd switch to the regular programming and they'd skip the interview. When that happened, I felt bad because that was when I got to be on camera. I'd go down in the bottom of the eighth inning and wait by the camera on the first base or third base side of the diamond. Depending on the time, I'd find myself hoping for double-play grounder to end the game quickly, or for a rally to make it go a few more minutes so I could do my interview. Meanwhile, I'd decide with the producer who I was going to interview.

One time, I had Bob Gibson and three minutes to interview him. Gibson had just broken some kind of record. It was a big deal. I figured that with three minutes I would ask one question to warm him up and then go to my big question about the record. So I asked my first question, and while he was answering that, something changed and the producer told me to cut it off and send it back upstairs to Jim Simpson, the announcer.

I sent it up, and Simpson wrapped it up. Then the producer chewed my ass out good. Gibson had just broken a record and I hadn't asked him about it.

"I had three minutes," I protested. "I just wanted to warm him up before going to the big question."

"I told you to lead with the main question," the producer said.

"I know," I tried to explain, "but you said I had three minutes."

"You see what happened? You wanted to do it your way and the time slot shifted on us and we had to take you off. All these people are watching all over the country. They saw the record.

They see Maury Wills go to Bob Gibson to interview him and Maury Wills never asks him about the record. Doesn't that make you look a little stupid, Maury?"

"Yeah."

"So when I tell you what question to lead with, you lead with it. Okay?"

"Okay."

That's when I started listening long enough to learn the trade. I was like the baseball player who comes up and after a month in the big leagues is ready to manage and run the front office, too. I had been on the job only about four weeks when I got chewed out the first time by a producer. After that, I asked Chet Simmons whether a producer on the field was really necessary.

"Yes," he said with finality. "Why?"

"Just asking," I said.

Chet Simmons was a good man and I really liked him. He got upset with me, though. It was over an interview I did in Baltimore. A writer had been hounding me. As I remember, he worked for the Washington *Post.* He was one of those guys who only got a chance to write a story once in a while and when he did it had better be good. He had been calling me all season trying to interview me. He was so persistent I got suspicious. What could he want? I couldn't be that hot an item. I asked him whether he had anything better to do. He said his editors just wanted to make sure the article was accurate.

He ended up writing something controversial about racism. The way he wrote it, it sounded as if I knocked Jim Simpson, my partner. He made it sound as if I didn't like Jim because I'm black and he had a hang-up about that. The writer must not have liked Jim Simpson. He used me and tricked me. He took the things I said out of context to make it look as though I thought Jim Simpson didn't like me because I'm black. It wasn't true.

But the story went in the paper because it was juicy and because Jim Simpson was well-known and well-liked in that area. They made me look dumb.

Chet Simmons almost fired me over that. He asked Jim Simpson: "Just tell me, Jim, if you can't work with him, we'll let him go."

"No," Jim said. "I'll work with him. I'll forget it, but I won't forgive him."

Jim Simpson saved my job. We continued to work together, but our relationship has been strained ever since. I can't blame him. I told him I was sorry, but what was he going to do? You slap somebody in the face and then turn around and say, "Sorry. I didn't mean to hurt you."

I had been around long enough not to let that writer get enough from me to write that kind of article. He was calling me for three weeks. I had plenty of time to get to the bottom of it and see that it wasn't quite right. And when he did ask me some sensitive questions, I should have handled it better.

My ego kept me from wanting to consider Jim Simpson. It kept me from seeing what could happen.

Later I concentrated more on not doing anything wrong to a person than on doing the right thing. I found that as long as I could be careful not to do anything to offend or violate a person, I didn't have to worry about what the right thing was.

## Chapter 56: Fowling Street

When NBC hired me, I was living in an apartment on the beach in Marina del Rey. One day before the season began, a man knocked on my door. I didn't remember him at first, but he reminded me that we had met the winter before at a party in San Mateo. I didn't remember the party very well, either, but I could tell he was okay.

He said he lived in the neighborhood and when he heard I lived nearby he was determined to find me.

"I live on the hill up there," he said.

I looked out my window to the southeast at these rows of beautiful big houses on the bluff looking down at the ocean. "You live up there?"

"Yeah," he said. "Why don't you come up and see the house?"

I said okay. I got in my car and followed him. The house was at 245 Fowling Street, a residential road that winds up the bluff in Playa del Rey. I walked into that house and thought, "Wow! What a nice place." It was two levels from the street and three facing the ocean. The top two levels opened out on decks. The bottom level opened on a patio. You could see all the way to Santa Barbara.

The man's girlfriend owned the house. She had been married to a popular bartender in the area who raced sports cars. He had seen the house and decided he had to have it. He worked three or four jobs until he had enough money to buy the house. Then, shortly after he bought it, he was killed in a racing accident. Now the girl had the house, but it was too big for her. Bills were piling up, but they weren't thinking about selling it yet.

Out of the clear blue, I said, "If you ever decide to sell, I'd sure like to buy it."

The couple just laughed.

I went to work for NBC and didn't think of it again. After the season was over, I went down to Mexico to manage Mazatlan in the winter league. I still had a dream of managing in the big leagues, and I wanted to stay in uniform and get experience. While I was in Mexico, I had a business manager who took care of my finances for me in California.

One day my manager called me in Mexico. "Maury," he said, "do you remember that house up on the hill you liked so much?"

"Yeah, I remember."

"Guess what? You own it."

"You're kidding," I said.

"No," my manager assured me. "I bought it for you."

"You bought it! How the heck did you buy it? I don't have that much money." This was a 14-room house.

"I got it for $120,000," he bragged.

"Where did you get $120,000 of my money," I demanded.

"I only had to put $5,000 down with some creative financing."

All I had to do was make a lump-sum payment of about $5,000 each year for four years. My mortgage payments were $744 a month. And I owned my dream home.

Life was good. I had a good job with NBC. I stayed involved with baseball by managing in the winter and working with teams in spring training. I played a lot of golf. I learned how to make stained glass windows and replaced the windows in my new house with windows I made myself. I built and flew radio-controlled gliders. I had a lot of time, but no problem filling it. I became interested in antiques and filled my house with them.

People might have looked at me and figured I was living the good life. And that's exactly what it was. No one could know, least of all myself, that the house on Fowling Street would one day become a prison of my own making.

## Chapter 57: A broken record

The last year I led the league in stolen bases was 1965, my sixth straight year as the league leader. The next year, Lou Brock stole 74 and took over the league lead. He led the league four years, finished second one year, then led for three more years. During all those years, though, he never stole more than the 74 he got in 1966.

Then came 1974 and Brock started chasing my record of 104. The record was my identity. I was the stolen base king. I didn't want to see my record broken. It meant a lot to me. Records were made to be broken, but not mine.

When you hear guys say that they don't mind their records being broken, that's a lie. If a guy wants to be mushy-mushy, he says, "Records are made to be broken." *Nobody* feels that way. Do you think Babe Ruth, if he were around, would have liked to see Hank Aaron breaking his career home run record? Nobody likes to see those great records broken. That's part of baseball's tradition. Those great statistics are a key to the popularity of the game. I don't think anyone wants to see Joe DiMaggio's 56-game hitting streak broken.

As the season went on and Lou Brock got closer to my record, I found myself watching the games on TV and rooting for the pitchers. "HOLD HIM ON! THROW OVER THERE! MAKE HIM STOP! MAKE HIM STOP!!!" It didn't work.

Nothing worked. Lou used to call me for advice. "My legs are hurting, Maury," he'd start. "What should I do?"

"Ice them down, Lou. Take a couple weeks off. Then quit," I kidded him.

I wasn't at the game when Brock stole his 105th base. I was at an NBC studio waiting to comment on it. When it happened, they asked me how I felt about it.

"I don't like it at all," I said honestly. "I wasn't pulling for him. I wasn't wishing him any bad experiences or any harm, but I wasn't pulling for him."

Ty Cobb's stolen base record was 47 years old when I broke it. My record lasted 12 years before Brock set the new standard of 118. Besides myself, Brock was the only player ever to steal 100. I was still the only man ever to steal 90 or more twice. Cobb and I were the only ones to steal 80 or more twice.

The game was changing. In 1979, Willie Wilson stole 83 and the next year, 1980, a kid named Rickey Henderson became the third member of the 100-stolen-base club with an even 100. In the American League that same year Ron Leflore swiped 97. Then, in 1982, only eight years after Brock stole 118, Rickey Henderson broke his record by stealing 130. Vince Coleman soon joined the 100-stolen-base club.

Someday, somebody's going to steal 200 bases. It won't be that long from now. I really believe that. Somebody's going to come along and steal second and third all the time. I was successful because I worked at learning the moves of every pitcher. Guys like Brock and Henderson and Coleman succeed because they simply outrun the ball. You just can't throw them out, even on a pitchout. It's one of the only areas in baseball that could endanger the competitive balance of the game. It could be a problem if guys start stealing 200 bases. You can solve it by not letting the guy run until the ball's released by the pitcher—like fast-pitch softball. It seems far-fetched, but it could happen.

## Chapter 58: Dropping in

I wasn't playing baseball anymore, but I didn't stop over-achieving. I still pushed the limits. That's me.

One day in the late Seventies, I was going to Tijuana with Judy and another couple. We stopped for lunch in San Clemente, where Richard Nixon had been living since resigning the presidency. We were joking around and one of my friends said, "We ought to stop and see the President."

"Would you like to?" I said.

"What do you mean, would I like to?"

"We can, if you like," I told him.

"Oh, sure, Maury," everybody said sarcastically.

Nixon was a big baseball fan and I had met him before. I had met President Kennedy and his family, and I had slept in Buckingham Palace. President Nixon and I corresponded from time to time, and he had recently named me to his own all-time baseball team. But I had never dropped in on a former president. When my friends thought I was just shooting the bull, it became a challenge.

We drove to Nixon's estate. At the entrance to it was a huge gate. It must have been 10 feet high and 25 feet wide.

"Shucks," I thought, "we can't get in there." Then I saw a phone in a little box next to the gate. I went over and picked it up. A voice came on the other end. I identified myself and said I'd like to see the President.

"What did you say your name was again?" the guy on the phone said.

"Maury Wills."

"Maury Wills?" the man repeated. He told me to hang up and wait for him to call back.

When I walked back to the car, my friends were laughing at me. They figured I'd struck out.

"He said he'll call me back," I told them.

"Right, Maury."

Sure enough, after a little bit the phone rang. I ran over and picked it up. The man told me that when the gate opened I should drive down to the first stop sign, make a left and go to the end of the drive. Somebody would be there to meet us.

I hung up and went back to the car. They were laughing at me again.

"The gate's going to open," I said.

"Bullshit," they said.

The gates parted. Their eyes flew open. I gave directions to the driver as if I went there all the time. As we were pulling up to where a Secret Service man was waiting for us, I realized that one of my friends, who was a Los Angeles police detective, had his gun with him. There was a moment of panic while he slipped it in the glove compartment.

We got out of the car.

"Maury Wills?" the Secret Service man said suspiciously.

"Yes, sir," I said.

The toughest part about being around a president or important government official is the Secret Service men. Now this guy started checking the four of us out. He was smiling and asking me pertinent baseball questions. Finally, he asked us all to come into an office attached to the house. He told us to sit down and relax, and all the while he's talking, talking, talking. After 10 or 15 minutes, he must have decided I was genuine, because he stood up and said, "What are we waiting for? Let's go in and see the President."

He led us into a big office with a view of a huge lawn and the ocean down below. There was a desk in the office that looked about 12 or 15 feet long. We must have stood there five minutes just gaping at everything.

Finally, a door on the far side of the office opened and President Nixon walked in, adjusting his suit and tie.

I took a step toward him with my hands out in the open where the Secret Service guy could see them.

"Maury!" Nixon said, pumping my hand for what seemed like five minutes. "Nice to see you! How nice of you to come out to see me." When I was growing up in Washington, D.C., the White

House may as well have been in a different state. And now I was dropping in on the President.

I told him how my friends and I just happened to be passing through on the way to La Jolla and decided to drop in. We had decided not to tell him we were really going to Tijuana. I thanked him for putting me on his all-time team.

We stayed 45 minutes. I realized he was making just as much of an effort to be on his best behavior with me as I was with him. He never did suggest that we leave. We broke it off because we had to get going. Before we left, he took us out on the lawn and had his staff photographer come out and take pictures of us in all kinds of combinations—the President with the ladies, with all of us and with me alone. When the pictures were developed, he autographed them, had them framed and sent them to me.

We never talked about any of his problems. He was still the President, a great President. I always liked him.

Another guy I dropped in on was George Steinbrenner. He didn't come on the scene until 1973, after my baseball career was over, so I never met him when I was a player. In 1975, though, NBC had me on the "Today Show" before the Cincinnati-Boston World Series. Two weeks later, I got a letter from George. He said he liked what I had to say.

A couple of years later, the Yankees were playing the Dodgers in the World Series, so it was 1977 or 1978. I went to New York with some friends to see the games. I didn't have tickets but I figured it was no problem. I'd get tickets from the Dodgers. They came through, but the tickets were in the upper deck, way down the foul line in left field. They were Bob Uecker seats. They apologized because that was all they had. We didn't care. We were inside the ballpark and that's all that counted.

When we got inside the park, I told my friends, "I think I'll go see George Steinbrenner. I want to thank him for that nice letter I got."

"You're kidding," my friends said.

Getting around Yankee Stadium during the World Series is a real challenge. It's not even easy to get around the stadium during the regular season, security is so tight. Fortunately, enough ushers and security guards recognized me that we got all the way to the door of George's private suite.

We were standing at the door, trying to get past the last guard, who wasn't budging, when George looked up and saw me. I guess George sees everything. He motioned for me to come in with my friends.

George showed us around and introduced us to all these big-time people in his box. He must have had 100 people in there, but he spent about five minutes with us. Then he said, "Just make yourselves at home. Have anything you want." We did that. When we were getting ready to go back out to the stands, he saw us and came over again.

"You got tickets?" he asked.

"Yeah," I said. "We're fine."

"Where are you sitting?" he asked.

"We're all right," I assured him. I was too embarrassed to let him know where we were sitting.

"Let me see your tickets," he said.

"No," I resisted. "We're fine, Mr. Steinbrenner."

"Let me see the tickets!" he said in a voice that didn't allow me to say no.

I pulled the tickets out of my pocket and gave them to him.

"Maury Wills can't sit up there!" he thundered when he saw where our seats were. He pulled his private stock of tickets out of his pocket and gave us four new tickets. We ended up sitting in the very first row behind the Yankee dugout.

George took the tickets the Dodgers had gotten for me and sent them outside to the bus drivers who never got tickets. No one knew about that. He didn't make a big deal about it. But four bus drivers had a ball courtesy of George Steinbrenner.

From then on, I considered George Steinbrenner a good man. He always had the guts to speak out. A lot of owners hide behind their hatchetmen and keep that facade of being wonderful. George Steinbrenner was The Boss.

## Chapter 59: Judy

I met her in July of 1975. Her name was Judy.

I was in Milwaukee with NBC for the All-Star game. I had gone to the NBC hospitality room when our unit manager brought her and another girl up. They were flight attendants for United Airlines. They were staying at the Schroeder Hotel, where the airline people stayed, and I guess he had gone over there specifically to meet some stewardesses to bring to the party. He brought them into the NBC suite at the Hopkins—two pretty, young blondes from California. I was just standing in the doorway, looking at them both. Everybody was smiling. Everybody was charming. I was looking at one and then looking at the other.

"I don't know which way to go," I said.

Judy turned to me and said, "Straight ahead, baby." Those were her exact words.

I took her by the hand and walked her down the hall to my room. She was 23 years old, 5-foot-7. Beautiful legs. Sort of strawberry-blonde curly hair down to her shoulders. High cheekbones. From Long Beach. Once you saw her, you never forgot her. That's how pretty she was.

She had on her uniform skirt. At that time, the hemlines were just above the knees. Judy wore hers well above the knees. Hot damn! With her height and her heels on, her legs were better than Ann Miller's or Betty Grable's.

She was just a beautiful girl with an uninhibited spirit. Everything about her was electric. I had been through involvements with Doris Day, with Edie Adams. No girl affected me the way this girl did from the very beginning.

There was no problem having sex with her that quickly. We hardly said anything. We didn't need to say anything.

When she said she had to leave, I asked her if I could escort her back to her room. She said no, it wasn't necessary. Could I escort her downstairs? No.

"You can't just leave like that," I told her. "You live in Los Angeles. Do you have a phone number? Can I call you?"

She gave me her phone number.

When I got back to Los Angeles, I tried to call her a couple of times, but no one answered. Finally, I called and a man answered. I asked for Joyce Williams—isn't that funny? I remember the name I used—and I hung up. I hadn't known that she was married.

I called her again and this time she answered the phone. I asked if I could see her again. She said yes. I was excited about seeing her again.

She came to see me straight from LAX Airport after she landed from a flight. I was only seven minutes from the airport. It was about a week and a half since we had first met. She said she had told her husband about the night that we met. Just like that. She told her husband! And her husband didn't believe her, didn't believe that she had been with Maury Wills.

Her husband asked her who Joyce Williams was. She's telling me all of this. She had a way of putting a man in any kind of frame of mind she wanted him to be in.

She hadn't been married that long, but she had a six-month-old baby girl named Angie.

It was odd that she was married and that she had told her husband—Bill—about me. It was scary, a new experience for me. I didn't like the idea of fooling around with a married woman. She said it wasn't a problem. It was all right. She assured me she and her husband weren't getting along.

It was the same old story that I remember using and that I had heard so many times from so many people. It's a problem at home. I'm not happy. My wife's not treating me right. My wife's mean to me. I'm lonely. We're not compatible. It's just not working out. We're going to part anyhow.

We say those things to lessen the guilt over doing something wrong. This was one of those deals. I knew better. I knew this wasn't valid, but my mind said, "Just tell me anything. I'll make sure I believe it." I didn't want to know the truth.

It's amazing that I could think that way at that point in my life. I was a former major league baseball player. I had traveled around the world meeting people from all cultures. I should have had the common sense to know that something like this was not going to turn out right.

What happened to Bill, her husband, happened to me later. My ego told me I could make it right. I was like a ballclub that takes on a good player who is also a problem player thinking that they know how to handle him. Guys like Dick Allen could play, and every manager figured he knew how to handle him. And the player jumps from ballclub to ballclub to ballclub. I was like every manager that George Steinbrenner hired. I thought I was going to be the one who would last forever.

I was the one who was going to make the difference in her life. She wouldn't be with me the way she was with Bill.

She had such an effect on me that I felt I could never again have a complete relationship with a woman. It was that profound. Just as profound was the devastation of it all when it finally ended. That's why I'm afraid to become deeply involved again. I can't stand another defeat like I had with Judy. I don't think I can trust the emotions that I had for her to another human being.

She was my very first true romance. I was with NBC Sports and doing great. I was on top of my game of life. It was the greatest time of my life. But I paid a price for it.

By the second time she came to my house she was staying overnight. It was mad, passionate love. In no time she was seeing me consistently, coming to see me in my Fowling Street house on her way to and from the airport. It was just the two of us in that big house. Her daughter was either with a babysitter or with her husband. It didn't take long before I was pussy-whipped and she had me in her back pocket. She had a chain in my nose and she was leading me around.

That went on for about four months and I was floating on air. I couldn't wait for her to get off a flight and come over. I even took a couple of flights she was working just to be with her. If she wasn't coming right back, we'd stay in a motel overnight.

After the baseball season, I went down to Mazatlan in Mexico to manage again. She'd take her off days down there, and then she'd call in sick and we'd have a whole week.

About six months after I met her, she left her husband and brought her daughter down to Mexico. The excuse was she was going to leave him anyhow and if it hadn't been me it would have been someone else. That's the way she was. I just didn't know it.

At first she continued to fly. I would babysit or she would leave the baby with her father. Finally, she just quit. In Mazatlan, life was easy. The ballclub rented a nice home for me on a golf course. We had a maid and a cook. All Judy had to do was go to the beach, do her nails, do her hair, and drive a nice car. She didn't mind that life.

We spent three winters in Mazatlan—1975–77. The rest of the year we lived on Fowling Street. I got to meet her husband when he came to get Angie, Judy's baby girl, on weekends. He turned out to be a sweet guy, the kind of guy that this sort of thing's not supposed to happen to. He just accepted defeat and succumbed to his humiliation. There was a custody case and Judy won custody of Angie. Bill was just glad to be able to see his daughter once in a while. He loved Judy dearly, but he was in over his head. I know that because I was in over my head and I was more worldly than he was. But Judy was definitely not a one-man woman.

Her family knew what was going on and they strongly disapproved. Her folks were from Texas. It was the racial thing they didn't like more than the fact that I wasn't her husband. The fact that I was Maury Wills didn't help. All that did was keep them from coming up and hanging me.

I eventually met her mother, and it was cold. Her father wouldn't have anything to do with me. My name couldn't be mentioned in his presence.

Judy wasn't too fond of her father. Her mother was the dominating force in the family. She had more of Judy's respect than her father. Judy used her father.

Her favorite song was "Super Freak" by Rick James, and she really liked "She Works Hard for the Money" by Donna Summer. She sang them all the time. She'd sing "Super Freak" and dance for me throughout the whole song, wearing these tight short shorts. Goddam!

## Chapter 60: The good times end

The first three years with Judy were good. The last three were bad. Real bad.

The day she and Bump fucked in front of me in my own house was when I finally knew that everything was wrong. But that wasn't the turning point in the relationship. The turning point was the day she walked into the NBC hospitality suite in Milwaukee. But the affair gave me so powerful a feeling that I didn't realize it until three years later. It took that long for me to come out of my coma of ecstasy.

Then, all of a sudden, I walked in on them and realized what my life had come to. But by that time, I was so hooked that for the next three years I just watched and suffered. I was aware of what was happening and I couldn't do anything about it. I couldn't leave. I couldn't tell her to leave. I was powerless.

Instead of blaming her or even myself, I blamed Bump. It took a dozen years before I had anything to say to him or showed him any warmth.

After it happened, Bump packed his bags in a huff and left as if I were weird. Judy got on my case, too. For being rude.

After that, Judy would pick an argument with me and go stay with her girlfriend every time the Texas Rangers came to town. I was like a whupped dog with my tail between my legs. I would go looking for her. When I contacted her girlfriend or her mother or whoever, they were all very indifferent to me. They reminded me that I had to treat her better and that we were having problems. I couldn't think of any problems we had other than our whole life together.

And it seemed when the Rangers would leave town, Judy would call and want to know if I'd come to my senses yet. This went on for another three years. She had no shame at all.

But I was hooked. I was addicted to her. And what made it

worse was that now I was in a battle with my own pride and dignity. I was one of those guys who were going to stand in there and take the beating and fight the battle. I was going to make this right. I was going to win. And all the time I was just getting deeper and deeper.

If I had grown up in an environment with guns, at that point I would have killed somebody. But I didn't have the background to think of that. Years later, when I was locked in my house, doing drugs, I was a killer. If Bump had come around then, I would have killed him. I'm surprised I didn't.

I carried my resentment for Bump a long time. It was early in 1990, when I participated in a Texas Rangers fantasy camp in Florida, that I finally spoke with him again. We didn't discuss what happened, but a lot of healing took place. Time had healed, along with the fact that we're father and son. He really had made efforts during the years when I was killing myself to contact me. He left messages and tried to contact me. I had never returned his calls.

I had seen him maybe two times since the craziness with Judy and I hadn't really talked to him. But when I went to the Rangers camp in 1990, he picked me up at the airport. We made amends. I've told him since that what happened with Judy wasn't his fault. It was mine and hers.

## Chapter 61: Liquor by the case

I started drinking with Judy. I had the liquor man come up to the house with big cardboard boxes of whiskey and wine. We were becoming connoisseurs of wine.

We hadn't drunk so much in the beginning. All we did was screw nonstop. Who needs a drink? I was performing in ways I never figured I could. That's how much I was inspired. It was something I'd never known before.

But the honeymoon was over now. The drinking started to fit

in with it. Now, we had to get a little booze before we got going. We were drinking and we were partying. It wasn't that I had to have the liquor. The liquor was just part of the occasion. Then I stopped having people come over. I was so intimidated by her I didn't want anybody around, knowing how she was. She was about where I was with alcohol. To get her hot, she needed stiff drinks.

I didn't have the sense to know that this wasn't a normal woman, that it wasn't a normal relationship. I had never had a relationship that was emotionally important to me. I had always treated everybody nicely. I went overboard being nice. Instead of giving myself and my emotions, my hopes, my everything, I would just be nice. I gave things. It was wrong and misleading to make a woman think she really had a love affair going when I was just going through the motions.

With Judy I didn't have any power of reason. I couldn't think.

I know people who read this are going to say, "The dumb sucker! Couldn't he see what was going on? Why didn't he just leave?"

When you're in the eye of the hurricane, I guess, you don't know the power of the storm. The wickedness of it never hits you. It had gotten to the point where I was just praying that she would never take me on as an adversary, that she would always be my friend.

I couldn't just get the hell out. I was hooked. There was nothing she could do that was so offensive, so humiliating, that it would provoke me to say something about it. She did things to see how far she could push me, like leaving when the Texas Rangers came to town. I wouldn't react. I'd just clam up. Maybe I would just leave the house and walk down the street to a bar to avoid a confrontation. And she would use that as an excuse to leave.

She stayed around strictly for the money. The first half, I think she was there with honesty and sincerity. When the Bump thing surfaced I had an awakening. I saw everything. That made it uncomfortable for her and my house was no longer a place she wanted to be. She continued to see me only for whatever she could get out of it. She left and came and left and came and manipulated me with all her power. She could do anything, which she did. And I couldn't do anything about it.

By 1979, we were still going along. She moved out but she would come back to see me when she wanted to. She came as a single lady. Those were her own words. She picked her times to see me. I had no more claim to her. She gave me sex to keep me corralled. She came to get more money or whatever. If I had known about escort services I could have had the same thing and saved myself a lot of pain and suffering.

## Chapter 62: Signing off

My last year with NBC was 1979. I didn't give the job up. Don Ohlmeyer came in as producer of the "Game of the Week" that year. I worked the one year for him. Then he made a change. After six years with the network, they didn't renew my contract. I ended up working the next year for HBO doing a show called "Race for the Pennant." Tim McCarver is doing everything that I could have been doing with HBO.

I quit HBO in August 1980, when I got the chance to manage in Seattle. I did HBO wrong. When I got the job managing, I had about a week to call HBO and tell them I had to quit, but I didn't do that. I think I told them the day before I was supposed to do that week's show that, by the way, I wasn't coming. They gave the job to Tim McCarver and that's how he got his start. He's still doing things with HBO. He's doing things with everybody. Every time he came on TV, even in my drug days, I told everybody I could have been there. I still feel that way.

My work had fallen off badly in 1979 because I was so distracted with Judy. I had to leave on Friday to do a Saturday game. As soon as I got to town, I'd call her to tell her where I was and the room number at my hotel. But I couldn't reach her. I couldn't find her.

I'd end up calling her all night. I'd call her the first thing in the morning. Finally, it would be time for the limo to come to take me to the ballpark and I hadn't had any sleep. For the first time in my NBC career, the producers were telling me to PERK UP! I was flat. I was late coming in on the replays. I was stuttering.

If you have enough talent to start with it takes a while for the deterioration to show. You don't crumble all at once. At first you have enough to carry you at your normal level. Then you have enough to do a pretty good job. Then you have enough to wing it. When I got beyond being able to wing it, I started falling apart.

One producer chewed me out after a game. He sent a report in to the network and I got chewed out again.

I figured they were picking on me. I wasn't going to admit I wasn't doing a good job. I couldn't let them know what was going on. I figured it was something with Judy that I could fix.

Now the loneliness of going back to my hotel room was killing me. The loneliest time I ever had in my life was a Sunday I stayed at the Sherry Netherland in New York. We had had a Saturday game and we were staying over to do another game Monday night.

I stood at the window looking out all day. There were no people in the streets shopping or walking up and down. Oh, God, there wasn't anybody to talk to. I tried to call someone. I tried to call Judy. I couldn't find her. All night long I couldn't find her. I didn't go to sleep with a bottle as I had sometimes during my lonely periods as a player. Then, I wasn't going through a love affair. I was just lonely. The drinking helped me fall asleep. It was just something to do.

I was powerless with her. I hated her for the control she had over me, yet at the same time, I just had to have her. I could make those 92,000 people in the Coliseum stand up and tap dance for me and I was powerless over one person. It became an obsession. I was going to win this. It stopped being so much Judy as control. I threw the same gusto into trying to reach her that I threw into being a player. It was not something I could walk away from or go to sleep on. It was a challenge.

It was hell.

And I had a game to do Monday. I wasn't into it. I had a good career going at NBC. They had big plans for me. They had even offered me a chance to work the World Series in the stands as a roving reporter. What a break for me! I didn't want to do it because I was looking for Judy. So I asked them for more money. They kind of laughed at me. They were giving me an opportunity to do the World Series. They were creating a spot for me, and I was asking for more money to do it. It was my way of telling them I didn't want to do it because I didn't want to be away from her again.

I once saw a cartoon on a wall in an NBC office. It showed two old bums sitting on a park bench. One bum was saying to the other: "I told him 42 years ago what to do with his job!"

That was me.

## Chapter 63: Judy gets a present

Judy had everything but big breasts, and now she wanted those, too. She came back to me in 1980 and talked me into paying for the surgery for her. In return, she gave me the reward of screwing me for a couple of months.

Before she went in for the surgery, I begged her, "Will you promise me you'll wear them with class and style, that you'll wear them but won't flaunt them?"

"I wouldn't think of doing such a thing," she said.

When she brought them home from the doctor's office, she was really in pain. I carried her upstairs and put her to bed. She stayed in bed for about a day and a half. When she got out of bed, she had me take her straight to Anaheim Stadium to see the Angels.

Now she's got the legs, the height, the beautiful face, the hair, the cheekbones. And the breasts. She put on these tight, tight pants that she wore with heels, California-style. And she put on a tank top with no bra.

I got good seats from the Angels, right in the front row of the loge level on the first-base side. They were excellent seats, but not good enough for her. She ended up going down and sitting behind the California Angels dugout. The guy she was seeing played for the Angels.

She had met this player the previous winter at a baseball banquet that I took her to. He and I were sitting side by side at the banquet table. Judy was sitting in the audience. She could look toward me but she was really looking at him. He even asked me what my girlfriend's name was. I told him Judy.

I was supposed to be one of the main speakers. But when they called on me to talk, they were out there whispering. I couldn't speak. My mind went blank. I was going to talk about things I knew so well I didn't need any notes. And I went blank so that I had to decline speaking.

So now it was the 1980 season. She had gotten her new breasts and now she's over at the Angels' dugout, but I didn't put it together. I didn't know why she was there. She was seeing her lover. She was seeing Don Baylor.

I do believe Don Baylor is a decent guy, but he was one of those guys who had his nose open. And she could hook anybody she put her mind to and she knew it. Plus she had the new tits that I bought for her. That's the ultimate in having control because that still didn't stop me from being hooked on her.

She had enough for everybody and I was trying to keep her from moonlighting. But somebody else was screwing her. I couldn't do anything about it anymore.

When I went up to manage the Seattle Mariners in 1980, she was living with Baylor. That's why I couldn't find her. The next year, we opened the season against the California Angels. She had been with him in Palm Springs and everybody knew she was seeing him. In spring training, everybody knows who's seeing whom because you can't hide in spring training. Everything is too open. It's not like the regular season when you have thousands of people in the stands and the games are at night. Everybody knew what was going on but me.

The Angels were kicking our butts in that first game and everybody on the Angels' bench was laughing. I thought they were laughing at our little racky-tack team, but they were laughing at this manager Maury Wills over there because Don Baylor was fucking his girlfriend.

I had walked right past him during infield practice before the game. He nodded to me and said, "How are you?"

When I found out about it later, I was going to go after him. I was going to find him and do him in, and he's a lot bigger than I am.

I finally talked to him in 1981. "She told me you guys weren't seeing each other anymore," he said.

"Why didn't you ask me?" I shot back.

He didn't want to ask me. He didn't want an answer.

It took me a long time to drop the idea of someday getting revenge, but I did. I dropped it long before I stopped resenting my own son. Isn't that something? The one I love the most, my son, I had the hardest time forgiving. Hell, I cut Judy more slack than I cut my own blood.

That's why sex is the strongest force on earth.

## Chapter 64: Manager Maury Wills

I thought getting the opportunity to manage was the break of my life, a dream come true, a blessing. But it didn't work out for me. It almost broke my back.

After my playing career ended, I did everything I could to stay in uniform. I wanted to manage in the big leagues, and once you're out of uniform, you're forgotten. I trained nine major league teams in spring training in the art of base running and base stealing. I drove down the winding and dangerous roads of Mexico managing in the winter Mexican League. I went to Japan four years to train teams there. All to stay in uniform.

I found myself pussyfooting around each major league camp—kissing ass, really—because the manager of the team didn't want me there. He knew I wanted a chance to manage, and he thought I was after his job. I did everything I could to let each manager know I didn't want his job. I just wanted my own. I did my best to train those clubs.

I wrote a book called *How to Steal a Pennant* about my theories of managing. I got a lot of press. A lot of players praised me in the papers. I did everything I could for a chance to manage in the big leagues.

Finally, in August of 1980, I got my call and it came at the same time that my romance was falling apart. If Judy had taken off in 1979, I would have had until August 1980 to build some scar tissue. The wounds would have healed. I would never be over it, but at least I would have had some kind of self-control, some kind of self-respect back. But she left me the same month that I got the job.

Dan O'Brien, who later moved to the California Angels, was president of the Seattle Mariners. He called to offer me the job. He took a big chance hiring me. Frank Robinson, the first black manager, was not managing after his stint with Cleveland and wouldn't manage again until 1981. Larry Doby had managed one year in Chicago. In 1980, I was the only black manager in the big leagues. It took guts for Dan O'Brien to hire me. He had to fire me, but he still believes in Maury Wills. And I still believe in Dan O'Brien.

Judy was with me on one of her visits the day Dan O'Brien called. She had come to stay for a week, to keep me on the string. I was relieved that I was able to see her at all. It was like how I felt when I came out of Buzzy Bavasi's office with a $20,000 raise after stealing 104 bases. I was just glad to still be on the ballclub. "Oh, it's going to be so beautiful," she said when she heard the news. "We're going to be together again." She was going to be my lady again.

I was so crazed over this girl, I was thinking that because I was a manager, that was going to bring her back because she liked status.

It was another one of her schemes. She said shc would take care of the house while I was gone, and said I had to make sure she had everything she needed to do that. So I left her money, a car, and credit cards. I told her she could have anything she wanted.

The Mariners were playing the California Angels when I took over in August with 58 games left in the 1980 season. The team was in seventh—and last—place. Dan O'Brien wanted me to stay in the hotel with the team, but I insisted on staying at my house because I wanted to be with Judy.

She came to the park, but didn't sit in the family section. Dan O'Brien knew about her and didn't make a big deal about his black manager having a white girlfriend, but I knew he would want me to be discreet.

And in bringing her to the park, I was putting her right where she wanted to be, because she had already taken up with Don Baylor.

We went to Oakland and she flew up there. After that, she flew back to Los Angeles. She said she'd join me in Seattle in a week or so. She told me not to worry.

She came up for one day. She did just what she wanted to do. She wasn't hardly there. She went shopping all day. She didn't come to the game. When I got back to the hotel, she wasn't there. She said she had gotten lost and couldn't find her way four blocks to the hotel. I believed it.

She had no need for me. She already had everything. In 1980, she and a girlfriend bought a house—I have to believe it involved my money.

I was paying all her bills and she had my credit cards. My daughter, Mikki, who had moved to Los Angeles, told me later that Judy went out and ran up $2,000 on my MasterCard. "So what if she did?" I said. I wasn't paying my own bills, and I didn't see where the money went. I didn't worry about it. And having her was more important than any amount of money she could be spending.

But I didn't have her. She had me.

She wasn't a good woman and Mikki tried to point it out to me. She used to come over to the house to see me and I saw her as someone who was trying to disrupt my life with Judy. But Mikki knew what was going on. She realized that Judy was manipulating and using me. She tried to tell me that, but I took offense to it. Then she joined Judy to further devastate me. Mikki did it out of contempt for me and Judy did it as a way of getting more power. They were running the game on one another and on me. It was a game everybody lost.

Meanwhile, I had already gotten off on the wrong foot with the Seattle media, specifically Tracy Ringolsby of the Seattle *Post-Intelligencer.* He was after me.

It started during my first series as manager against the Angels in Los Angeles. Roy Firestone, whom I had known in the Los Angeles area for some time, wanted to interview me for a local television special. Tracy wanted to interview me at the same time. I asked Tracy if he'd wait until after I did Roy Firestone. It was early in the afternoon, before anybody had come to the ballpark.

Tracy never forgave me for making him wait. He was the local beat writer and he felt he deserved the first shot at me. And if I had it all to do over again, he'd get it.

I made it through the rest of the season managing, finishing with a 20–38 record. The team was dead last. But the Mariners had shown some life. Sometime in September, we won something like seven in a row. I was happy over a pretty good two months. I felt good about the 1981 season. I had bought a new car, and I drove it down to Los Angeles to get back in touch with Judy.

And I couldn't find her.

## Chapter 65: The winter of my discontent

Judy was going to come up to Seattle at the end of the 1980 season and drive back with me to Los Angeles. She said she couldn't get away, though, and I drove down by myself, 1,500 miles, wide open all the way. I just wanted to get to Los Angeles to see her.

She wasn't there.

The house was cold and dark. I sat in that big, dark house looking out of the big bay window upstairs at the Pacific Ocean and Playa del Rey and the lights and the marina. I didn't want anybody to know I was home. Maybe Judy would come back. I was going crazy. Finally I decided I would get out of the house.

I went down to a restaurant and was just standing by the door when I saw this girl come in. That was the last thing I thought I would do, look at another girl. But I had never felt more desolate in my life. I stayed by the door and after a while she went back out.

They say that nothing's better for forgetting one woman than having another woman. But I didn't have the courage to say anything to her. I started talking to myself: "Maury Wills, you know you're a gutless little sucker. If you ever want to meet somebody, if you ever want to stop chasing this chick, now is the time."

I ran out of the door and stopped in the parking lot about 20 feet away from her.

"Excuse me, ma'am."

The parking lot was dark. She stopped and turned around and looked as if she'd been startled.

"I don't mean no harm," I said. I didn't come any closer, but kept talking. "Are you a baseball fan?" I asked her.

"A little," she said cautiously.

I told her my name and said that I had played for the Dodgers. She didn't believe me, but while we were talking, I got close enough to where I was standing next to her. I asked her if she wanted to go in and have a drink with me. She still didn't believe me, though.

Just then the band inside took a break and the drummer, who had seen me inside, ran out into the parking lot to see me. I told him I was talking to this lady to see if she would have a drink with me.

"Doesn't she know who you are?" the drummer asked.

"No," I said. "Why don't you tell her?"

So he did and she decided she wouldn't mind having a drink with me. Before you knew it, she was sitting on my lap. Next thing you know she liked me well enough to go up to my house with me. She was really a nice girl, young and beautiful. She found me interesting and liked me. I was feeling better. My original reason for stopping her was to see whether I could have sex with her, but that reason went out the window because this time, somebody liked me. We were talking and having a good time for a while when she pulled a little bit of cocaine out of her purse. She said you whiffed this stuff up your nose and it would make you feel good.

This was my first contact with cocaine. A girl introduced me to it. They say that behind every skirt there's a slip. Every woman in the world's going to be all over my butt over that statement, but that's what they say. That's how it was with me. I hadn't even heard much about cocaine. Now that I look back, though, I realize some of my players might have been using it. At that time it was really in to be using it. As the manager, I used to sit in the front of the plane where Walter Alston used to sit. That way the players were behind me where I couldn't see them. That let them relax from the pressures of the game. I swear, it was amazing how the same players went to that restroom in the front of the plane so many times during a flight. As I learned more about cocaine and became involved in it, I found myself in situations where I was going to the bathroom with great regularity, too. My players were doing the same thing.

When she pulled the stuff out, though, I wasn't up on all that. She had it in a little cellophane package. She laid it on a mirror and chopped it up into lines. She got a straw and cut it down to less than half its full length, beveling one end. I couldn't tell her I'd never done it before, so I let her do a couple lines to see how she did it before I did a line.

The first whiff didn't do much to me. I was just going along to stay in concert with her. I was being cool. "Yeah, that's all right," I said.

She didn't have very much stuff, but it was enough. I didn't get any great high from it, but it gave me a feeling of false self-esteem.

Just then, she said she had to go. I didn't want her to. I asked if she'd come back for lunch the next day. She said she would and she did. Finally, I had found someone I could depend on.

I took her to a nice restaurant on the pier. We came back to the house and had sex. She asked me if I wanted some more of that stuff she had the night before. "Yeah," I said, being cool, "did you bring some?"

"No," she said, "but I know where we can get some if we had some money."

I had a ton of money. "Let's go," I said.

We jumped in the car and went over to a house where she knew the people had cocaine to sell. We were going to get some and go back to my place. While we were there, some people were in the bathroom freebasing. I didn't know what that was, but when they invited me in, I joined them.

I got one whiff of that freebase and WOW! My lights went out. Oh, what a rush! I had found a friend.

I stayed in that house for a week. The girl was there with me but I forgot about her. I spent $2,000 keeping everybody happy with cocaine before I left.

"Are you sure you want to do this?" they kept asking. "Can you afford this?"

"DON'T WORRY ABOUT THE MONEY!" I roared. "Just fix some more of that stuff!"

A couple lived in the house. They knew who I was. They showed me how to cook the powdered cocaine with baking soda into a rock and how to smoke it.

When I finally left the house, I went straight to somebody else's house where I could buy some and bought an ounce. It was the damnedest thing I ever had in my life. And it was just what the doctor ordered. It made me feel that everything was all right.

But the girl who had introduced me to cocaine was gone. My attention turned back to Judy again. Where was she? She was still stronger than the power of the shit—the cocaine. I just had to find her.

I looked all over for her. I finally tracked her down and talked to her on the phone. She wouldn't see. "You're acting crazy," she told me. "I don't know if I want to come back."

She was driving a little MG Midget. She told me if she had a new car she could get around better. She'd feel better towards me and we could get along better. So I gave her my new Audi 5000 and took her Midget.

Now I'm driving around in this little car, going back and forth. Her house was in Lakewood, down by Long Beach. It took me 22 minutes to drive there on the freeway. I'd drive there in the Midget and stay in her driveway all night waiting for her to show up. It was rainy. It was foggy The house was pitch black. I didn't know where she was.

She saw me when she wanted to, which was very seldom. But she never stayed away long enough to give me enough time to start to get over her. I don't know how long that would have been.

Meanwhile, I had to go back up to Seattle. The Mariners had a new owner, George Argyros, who bought the team in January. I had to meet him. During the winter, I had to go around the Inland Empire with Dan O'Brien plugging the team, going east from Seattle over the Cascades to Spokane and Yakima, down to Portland and Tacoma, north to Canada. It was a bummer for me. My behavior had changed. I wasn't using drugs while I was doing my job, but I was just miserable.

I think Dan O'Brien noticed. I was barely there. I didn't have any spirit or anything.

"You're sure intense," Dan would always say.

I wasn't intense. I was pissed. I was getting mad because I was depressed. I told the press that Seattle could win it all, and they thought I was nuts. I don't know if I believed it myself. I was a disturbed man. My life was crumbling underneath me.

The cocaine I used that winter cemented some of my anger and hostility. That stuff will take you anywhere you're going. If you're happy, it will take you into a happy mode. If you're depressed, it will make you more so. And now the anger was locked in. The resentment was locked in. The things I was going through were making me bitter and more bitter. My self-esteem was going down the toilet.

## Chapter 66: Cananea Reyes

When I was managing in Mexico, traveling around and trying to stay in uniform, I had a coach named Cananea Reyes. Cananea was a manager in the Mexican summer leagues, and in the winter, he coached for me. We used to sit around and talk baseball all the time. I liked him so much I told him that if I ever got a chance to manage in the big leagues, I'd take him with me.

I had finished the 1980 season with the coaches I inherited from Darrell Johnson, the previous Mariners manager. When it came time to pick my coaching staff for the 1981 season, I told Dan O'Brien that Cananea Reyes was going to be my third base coach.

*"Cananea Reyes?"* O'Brien said. "Who the hell is Cananea Reyes?"

O'Brien was thinking along the lines of Bobby Valentine, Bobby Bonds or Rene Lachemann to coach third.

"No," I said firmly, explaining who Cananea was. "Cananea Reyes is going to be my third base coach."

"Maury," O'Brien asked, "what do you think these people are going to say when I tell them your third base coach is going to be Cananea Reyes, who can't speak much English and is from the Mexican League?"

"The man is good," I insisted. My players thought I was nuts, too, but Cananea Reyes it was. I took Tommy Davis as my batting coach and Frank Funk as my pitching coach. Dan made me keep Wes Stock, a holdover from the previous administration, as my other coach. I guess Wes was the grapevine that every president and general manager likes to have.

When we started the season, Tommy Davis was selling boots to the players. Cananea Reyes was selling teakwood statues from Mexico. And the manager wasn't getting to the park until batting practice had started. It had to be a funny scene in that clubhouse. It was terrible.

If I had it to do all over again, Cananea Reyes would still be my third base coach. He's a damn good baseball man. Besides, I had made the commitment to him and to myself to hire him if I ever got the chance. When I gave him the job, I went all the way down to Hermosillo to make it official. We had a big press conference in the best seafood restaurant in town. All his family and every photographer in the province and the president of the league came. The newspapers plastered the news all over Mexico. I wasn't going to go back on that.

It was such a delight to call him and tell him, "Cananea, you're going to come to the big leagues." Other managers get to bring their men with them when they take over a team. Billy Martin never went anywhere without Art Fowler and no one complained.

I didn't get away with it as easily, but I did get him. And when I was suspended for three days for moving the batter's box, I gave the line up card to Cananea and had him manage. And when I got fired, he finished the season with the Mariners.

Cananea went back to Mexico and told his kids and his grandkids and all his friends that he was in the big leagues—*las ligas grandes.* A guy from this little Mexican town managed in the big leagues.

I'd have done a lot of things differently if I had another shot, but I'd still have Cananea Reyes coaching third.

# Chapter 67: Japan

My real problems in 1981 started before spring training even began when I went to Japan for the month of February. I was totally wrong to go. Spring training starts March 1, but pitchers and catchers report to camp in the middle of February, and the manager is supposed to be there when they arrive. But I had been to Japan three straight years to train teams in the Japanese leagues and had made the commitment the year before to go again. It wasn't important to me to be in camp with the pitchers and catchers. Plus, I was in love with going to Japan.

Japan was the one area where it seemed I was really appreciated. I played their kind of baseball—scratching out hits, bunting, stealing and generating one-run rallies. They called me "Mr. Perfect" over there. I was hurting in the self-worth department and that was a country where I could find it. I was even tall in Japan.

I worked with the Japanese in all areas of the game. They put the information I gave them into computers and had tremendous success with it. I told them what catchers could do to help stop base stealers. I helped their pitchers learn to hold runners on.

The Japanese are willing to listen where Americans aren't always willing. Technically, the Japanese might be sounder than we are. They work hard—maybe too hard. They really believe in long hours, but I don't know if they engage in perfect practice. You can't equate longer with better.

As much as they practice, the Japanese can't beat American major league teams. They never will. The two things that make a great athlete are speed and strength. The Japanese don't have either. They've got some guys who throw the ball hard, but they don't put emphasis on velocity. They throw breaking balls and a lot of pitchers throw from down under. It's a breaking-ball league.

One guy who could have hit in any league is Sadaharu Oh, the Yomiuri Giant great who hit more home runs than anyone in the history of baseball. I doubt he would have hit as many home runs in the major leagues as he did in Japan because the Japanese parks are smaller. But I saw him hit balls in Japan that were still rising when they cleared the wall.

Going to Japan had always been something that Judy and I looked forward to. So that year, when I confirmed with the Japanese that I was coming, I tracked down Judy, hoping to buy her off with this beautiful trip. She said she couldn't come with me. She had to work to support her child. She had a job as a waitress, and I offered to pay her the money she would lose by not working. Finally, she agreed to come for a week if I would make up the lost pay, which she said was $1,000. Whatever she told me was all right even if it was like buying a hooker. She didn't fly over with me, but came out later.

When she got to Japan, Judy was very arrogant and distant. She said she belonged to herself, not to me. It was a rough time for me. I was doing my job, but for the first time I didn't enjoy my Japanese stay.

And I was going to be late for work back in the States.

## Chapter 68: Spring training

When I got to spring training March 1, I was already in trouble with Dan O'Brien. The emotional problems with Judy were distracting me, but I felt I was still good enough to get the job done.

I couldn't be angry at Judy. I didn't want to be. So I took out my anger on my players by being impatient, by working them hard. I was still in the ballgame, but I couldn't find any happy moments. I couldn't relax. Ultimately, I was punishing myself.

She wouldn't come to spring training with me. I didn't know it at the time, but she went to Palm Springs where the Angels—and

Don Baylor—trained. Then she came to see me for a couple of days and that only disturbed me more.

I worked the guys hard. One of my players was quoted in the newspapers as saying about me: "All he talks about is winning, winning, winning. Why doesn't he leave us alone and let us play." What a statement. It reminded me of what John McNamara told me one time when I was with NBC and he was managing San Diego. The Padres were deep in last place. McNamara told me, "There are no problems on this team, Maury. These guys get along just great."

"Yeah, John," I said. "They're buried in last place."

I had a kid, a shortstop, named Jimmy Anderson. He was really eager to please and willing to work. He just didn't always do the right thing. Soon after I took over the team in 1980 we were in Boston and I got permission to use the field early to work on base stealing with my speed guys. Jimmy, who wasn't a speed guy, volunteered to come to the workout. He was doing pretty well, too.

That night against Boston we stole three or four bases early. Then Jimmy got on first base and took off for second. He got thrown out by 20 feet. It took us out of the inning.

When he got to the dugout, I asked him, "Did you get the steal sign?"

"No," Jimmy said.

"So why are you running?"

"I thought I could make it," he said.

"You *thought* you could make it! What is this, Jimmy?"

I called for my backup shortstop and pulled Jimmy from the game. Jimmy slumped. He picked up his glove and headed back to the clubhouse.

"Where're you going?" I demanded.

"I'm going inside," he said.

"Go to the bullpen and help warm up the pitchers," I ordered.

That was terrible. It's humiliating to do that to a player in the middle of the game. If a manager thinks he has to take the guy out of the lineup to discipline him, there are ways to do it delicately, but I made a big fuss over it. It had to be awful for him.

In spring training the next year, Jimmy made a bad play on a relay from the outfield with two outs. Instead of getting the runner going to third, who was 30 or 40 feet from the bag, Jimmy tried to get the guy going home, who was only 10 feet from the plate. The whole play was in front of Jimmy, and not only did he throw to the wrong base, he was so eager to get the runner at the plate, he fired the ball into the backstop and let in another run.

I was so disgusted I took him out of the game in the middle of the inning. I ran him off the field and, instead of letting him go back to the clubhouse, I made him sit on the bench and watch the rest of the game.

I liked Jimmy Anderson. He was my starting shortstop. It was my impatience that made me treat him that way. Once I left Seattle, I didn't see Jimmy again until Nov. 17, 1989, when I ran into him on business. Almost nine years too late I told him why I had acted that way. I told him how I was going through the broken romance with Judy and couldn't think. I made amends with Jimmy. "That's all right," he told me.

"No, it's not all right," I said. You just don't do that.

New managers are supposed to get a honeymoon with the press. Mine lasted until the final game of spring training. Normally, in the last spring training game, you want to give your starters the day off so they can take an earlier flight to your home city and get settled with their families before the season starts. So I excused a bunch of the guys and was going to take the scrubs to the last game against the Brewers in Sun City, Ariz.

But Dan O'Brien told me we owed it to the Brewers and to the fans who had bought tickets to play our front-line players. So I had to tell some of my starters they couldn't go early. They ended up getting hold of Tracy Ringolsby and bitching about it. It ended up in the newspapers. Now I was getting bad press and the players were mad at me. It just got worse.

# Chapter 69: 6 — 18 = Goodbye

I had gotten hold of Judy and asked her to come up to Seattle with me.

"If I had a new car," she whined, "I could come up and see you. My car is always breaking down."

I bought her a brand-new Audi coupe.

"And I gotta work two jobs because now I don't have your support," she whimpered.

She probably didn't even have one job, but I paid her a full year's wages so she could come up to see me. Then she didn't come and I was going berserk.

My managing the Mariners was a big deal. The whole world was watching. Black people were saying, "We got a manager now. Maury Wills will show them how to manage. I saw him play. I saw him on NBC. He really knows his baseball." The white people were on my side, too.

But my behavior was really changing. I had used cocaine that winter, but I had stopped before I went to Japan. I wasn't addicted, but I had an addict's brain. I was drinking, but not more than anybody else so it didn't seem as if I was an alcoholic. It wasn't the amount I was consuming. I was at the point where any amount threw me. My mind was changing. I was crying myself to sleep at night.

I had always wanted two things—to have a real relationship with a woman and to manage in the big leagues. These were my adulthood dreams. The two things that were going to make me a complete person and fulfill my life turned out to be my demise.

I was a major league manager. Why couldn't I welcome the fact that Judy was gone? That would have been addition by subtraction. But it was as if I couldn't survive without her.

It's amazing how, after 10 years of staying ready and praying for a chance to manage in the major leagues, the opportunity couldn't have come at a worse time. My situation with Judy was toxic. If she had met Don Baylor a year and a half earlier, maybe managing would have been a good way for me to get away from it all. But it all had to happen at the same time.

The one time Judy came up was during the Angels' series. I hardly saw her. I was supposed to meet her at the hotel after the game, but she got lost. She got lost going shopping before the game. She couldn't find her way back. And it always seemed she had to go shopping at about the same time Don Baylor would be getting lunch before the game. She got lost at about the time Don Baylor was getting back to his hotel after the game. I still didn't know what was going on. It seemed I was always a month behind figuring things out. When the Angels left, so did she.

A friend told me some guys would have jumped out a window by then. I'm trying to figure out why I didn't.

On top of Judy being gone, we started losing games. As I look back, the only friends I can really say I had then were Tommy Davis, Frank Funk and Cananea Reyes. They saw me hurting and pressing and they did so much to try to help me think properly. Frank did his best to get the lineup out as soon as possible. He'd come to me and offer two or three different lineups. I'd pick one.

The players wanted the lineup for the next day posted after each game. I didn't see any reason to do that. I didn't see why I had to have a lineup out before batting practice. Sometimes, Frank would tell me, "I have to have the lineup pretty soon. The guys want to know who's playing."

"Screw 'em if they can't play until they see the lineup," I'd say.

I lost my patience with my team. I had thought I could do things with them, but it wasn't my kind of team. We had no speed. We were weak on fundamentals. It was a lousy team. It was the Mariners.

I was talking to them as if they were a bunch of bums who couldn't play ball. A manager just can't do that. I knew I had a young expansion team. A lot of the guys weren't major league caliber. But I wasn't thinking clearly enough to treat them accordingly. I was just hard on them.

When the media started asking pertinent questions, I brushed them off. "I don't know," I'd growl. "I don't remember."

Dan O'Brien told me, "Maury, you've got to answer these guys."

"Screw 'em," I said.

I had Dave Henderson, who won a World Series ring with Oakland in 1989, on that team. I didn't like him and I didn't play him. The press got on me about that.

When I took over, I had short meetings after the games to review what we had done well and where we had screwed up. One night after a loss, I told them they had played a great game. They had, too. They had played up to their potential. They just got beat because the other team kept going to their bench and overpowered us. The players went to the press with that and said, "How the hell can he tell us we played a great game? We lost."

All the blame fell to the manager and I didn't make it any better. I'd go back to the sportswriters' luncheon and start raising hell: "I'm not going to answer that question!" "Weren't you there? Didn't you see it?" Stuff like that.

We were in a game that we were losing by four runs in the ninth inning. Lenny Randle was on first base with one out and looked at me to see if I wanted him to run. I gave him a sign that said, "If you get a good jump, go. Suit yourself." He went and they nailed him by a mile.

After the game, Randle told the writers I gave him the steal sign. The writers came back at me: "You're down four runs in the ninth and you gave him the steal sign?!"

"Yeah," I said, "I gave him the steal sign." I wasn't even going to explain.

"How the hell can you give him the steal sign?" they asked.

"Because I wanted to. That's why," I said.

"Didn't you know what the score was?"

"No," I said, dripping sarcasm. "I forgot the score."

That became part of the story, too. Maury Wills forgot the score.

As I was sinking, Tracy Ringolsby was going around to the players collecting stories. A writer can go up to a player and tell him everything the player wants to hear to make him put the blame somewhere else—on me. There's a network of writers around the country. One guy writes a story and everybody picks it up and repeats it around the country. It doesn't always matter whether it's true. Tracy was the catalyst. And it got worse as it went on. He was after me and I developed a dislike for the way he was treating me that developed into a dislike for him personally. The feeling was mutual. And all you have to do is be shitty with one writer and the other writers take offense. I turned the media in Seattle against me.

Contrary to what I thought, I really needed managing experience below the major league level, to learn how to organize, how to delegate responsibility and how to deal with the press. Buzzy Bavasi had told me I should manage in the minor leagues. I said I didn't have any reason to go to the minors, but I really should have. They said managing in Mexico didn't count. I laughed at that, but maybe they had a point. I didn't have any problem with the press in Mexico because I didn't have any dealings with them.

I figured there was no way in the world that one sportswriter was going to ruin my career as a major league manager so I wasn't going to give in to the asshole. And Tracy was saying, "I will get him." And that's the way it was. He had more tools to work with than I did.

You don't get in a pissing match with a skunk and you don't get into a war of words with people who buy their ink by the barrel.

Everything that happened with Tracy comes with the territory.

Now, here comes Ross Newhan from the L.A. *Times* up to Seattle to write a profile on manager Maury Wills. He came up with a big smile. I tried to avoid him because I didn't know what kind of story he was going to do. But finally I talked to him and he ripped me to pieces in my hometown paper, where everybody thought I was so great and thought I'd be a hell of a manager.

I was losing control of the team. I was acting erratically. I could see the writing on the wall. I was screwed up over this girl. All I wanted to do was get out of there.

I started losing interest in coming to the ballpark. I was there only a little over three weeks—24 games, 18 of them losses. The ballpark had always been my refuge, the place where I felt whole. But that was when I was a player and I was in control of how well I played. Now I'm calling the shots, but I'm not in control. I was powerless over the morale of my ballclub. I lost the guys. The players didn't want me there anymore. They didn't like me anymore. I didn't like them. I wasn't going to quit, but in essence I had quit.

I didn't think I was throwing something away, either. I thought it was probably the best thing. Being in the ballpark was like being in hell. It was hell in heaven. That's what it was.

One night in Minneapolis I was alone in this big, damn manager's suite and I couldn't find Judy. I was supposed to stay in the suite because Dan O'Brien said he was going to call me. My players were downstairs in the disco having a ball and I had to stay in the damned suite.

Finally, I went down to the lobby just to get out of the room, just to go downstairs, take a look, and go back up. I left word with the operator that I would be in the lobby and if a call came for me to switch it down there. Would you believe Dan called in that short time and, of course, the operator didn't switch the call.

When I got back to the room, the message light was flashing. I returned Dan's call and he chewed my ass out. So now I had him on me.

I was just waiting to be fired.

Late on the morning after my 24th game of the season, Danny called me at my new apartment. "I'd like you to stop in the office, Maury," he said.

It was obvious what was coming next.

"You're going to make a change, huh?" I said.

"Yeah."

"I don't have to come down," I said. "It's all right."

I didn't blame Danny at all. I finally saw him again at the 1989 major league baseball winter meetings in Nashville. I didn't know what to expect, but he made it easy.

When Danny gave me the word that I was through, it was as if 4,000 pounds had been lifted off my shoulders. But if I were the general manager, I wouldn't have fired Maury Wills after three weeks. I don't believe I was driving fans away from the park. There weren't any fans to drive away. Maybe if the writers didn't have me to write about there wouldn't have been any news about the club in the papers at all.

I didn't feel I lost the job because I was incompetent. I didn't feel it was the real Maury Wills out there doing the job the way I know how. It was mainly the distraction of a broken romance and then getting off to a bad start with the players in spring training. Getting fired hit me harder because I felt I never had a chance.

Maybe if I had just held the players' hands, said all the right things to the press, talked nicely to the owners and their families, smiled and collected my check, I might have lasted longer. I didn't have the ability to do that.

I went down to the Kingdome and cleaned out my office. The writers couldn't find me. I hadn't given any of them my phone number. I gave only one interview on the way out, to a woman sportscaster for a Seattle television station. She was nice to me, so I did it for her.

It was over.

## Chapter 70: Devastation

I had just lost my job but I was still in Seattle, and of course I listened to the ballgame on the goddamned radio the night I got fired. Under new manager Rene Lachemann, the Mariners were kicking the Yankees' ass. The Mariners' broadcasters are saying things about Lachemann like, "Where has this man been?" They were saying how the players were relaxed now, they were comfortable, they were out from under the pressure and now they were playing well. They kicked butt, all right—for about two days. Then they were right back where they were when I was there.

I stayed in my apartment four days. Then I just left. All the furniture was rented, and I called the secretary for the Mariners and asked her to tell the rental company to come and pick it up. I went back to Los Angeles to try to find Judy.

I had bought her a new car. I had paid her salary for a year. She was going to come up to Seattle and everything was going to be fine. And she had disappeared. I was going crazy.

I was whipped psychologically. I was scared and deflated. I

called her mother, her husband, her girlfriends trying to find her. They said they didn't know where she was. I drove to her house at night and sat in her driveway waiting for her to come home. It turned out her friends weren't lying. She really wasn't around. That's when I found out she was with Don Baylor.

I didn't give up. I still thought that I could figure out a way to fix it, just as I had on the ballfield.

But I was beginning to see that I never really had control. I had believed I had control when everything was going fine. Whatever I saw became what I wanted to see rather than what I was actually seeing.

I started trying to find her on her job. I was drinking now and staying up around the clock because I was in all the bars, all the nightclubs that we'd gone to. I talked to her on the phone once in a while and she would tell me to meet her at the restaurant where she worked. I'd get there and she wouldn't be there. I finally realized that I should go to the restaurant not when she said she was working but when she said she was off. I did and I found her.

When I found her, I got in trouble with the management of the restaurant and with the cops. She said I was harassing her.

Legally, I probably was harassing her. I could have gotten into big trouble, because she worked in a place called Charlie Brown's down in Signal Hill, a little area halfway between Los Angeles and Long Beach. Around that time there was a highly publicized case in which a black football player supposedly hanged himself in his cell in Signal Hill, but it was widely believed that somebody murdered him. It was the kind of police department where if you were black, you didn't want to be down there.

Judy got those cops on my ass. I'd be in the parking lot and I'd see those black-and-whites charging in. I'd pull out just ahead of them. Between looking for her ahead of me and watching out for the cops behind me I was playing a dangerous game.

This went on for about a month before I just went back to my house, locked the door, and stayed there.

For the first time in my life, I was faced with absolute emptiness. I had always had something. First there was baseball. Then I had the NBC job, the managing in the winter league, the spring training jobs in Japan and the States, Judy, and finally Seattle.

Now, the last two things that I had in life were gone. I had nothing to look forward to, no place to go. I had no reason to go to bed at night and no reason to get up.

I was defeated. It wasn't just a loss. It was a devastating defeat.

## Chapter 71: Addicted

I remembered the coke as a thing that could help me feel better. Since first using it the previous winter, I hadn't used cocaine. Now I went looking for some.

Some people might be weekend users of drugs, not abusers. They say drug abuse is bad, but use is all right. But drug use is setting yourself up so that if you have a devastating experience and become depressed, you're going to reach back for the drug, and use will become abuse. That's how it started for me.

I had to hunt around for the coke. I remembered one place I had gone with the girl who introduced me to it. I found those people and they got me a whole ounce. The next night I was back at their house to get another half ounce. They were giving me dirt —stuff that was all mixed and cut with other things—but I didn't know the difference. When they cut it, they use all kinds of adulterants, and that stuff makes you even more goony. It can kill you.

The coke just made me madder and more angry, but I got to liking it so much that I finally called Judy again and talked her into meeting me. She was getting off at 11 p.m. I called about a quarter to 11. She said, "Okay. I get off in 15 minutes. I'll wait here for you."

I thanked her profusely and hung up. I got as far as the front door, then I turned around and went upstairs to my bedroom. I picked up the phone and called her back. "I'm not coming," I told her.

I was finally free of her, but coke had replaced her. Now, with that same goddamned obsession I had gone after her, I went after the coke.

The coke made me think I didn't do a single thing wrong in Seattle. They didn't know how to play ball. Those guys were picking on me. Judy was the scum of the earth to leave me at a time like that. But fuck her. Who needs her?

When Judy got wind that I was all screwed up, she started to worry. But she was worried more about losing my money than she was about losing me. She came back a few times before it finally ended.

The last time I saw her was a couple of years later when she came back to the house for something. She brought a cop friend of mine with her. When she left that day, she was gone. I never saw her again.

## Chapter 72: Jonesing

The stories about all the things I was supposed to have done in Seattle didn't hit the papers until after I was fired. Then Tracy Ringolsby wrote a big story that got picked up by all the other papers. It wasn't enough for them to get me fired or to help get me fired or even to attempt to get me fired. They had to railroad me out of town and vilify me with those articles. And since I was gone, everybody could embroider all their stories.

The articles about my experience in Seattle went even to Japan. When the Japanese saw it, they didn't want me back there either.

People sent me the articles. One came from a Texas paper. Some came from New York. They came from all over. And there was only one person who said anything nice about me. That was Bobby Bragan. He said he was proud of me because I didn't resort to sour grapes. I didn't strikc back. I took it like a man.

The articles sent me deeper into the drug. For 3½ years I hardly left the house. I spent most of one year in just my bedroom. I remember staying up there with my pipe for months on end, just running downstairs to the refrigerator and right back up, or to the door to pick up the liquor and groceries I had ordered. I felt that nothing was my fault. They just screwed me. Everybody was an asshole. The whole world was fucked up—everyone but me.

Initially, cocaine makes you feel great. But it also consumes the neurotransmitters—the brain chemicals—that make you feel good. Coming down from the high drives you deeper into depression. It disrupts the brain's pleasure center. It robs you of your ability to feel normal.

When that happens, you really crave it. "Jonesing" is the word in drug circles. When you're jonesing, you really need a fix.

I stayed up as long as 10 days at a time, using constantly. I had to keep using to keep myself up and to keep my false sense of security. I used to be very interested in current events, and kept up with everything happening in the world. Now, I didn't even know who was playing in the World Series. I was living in a chemical world, freebasing constantly. The only time I wasn't using was when I was sleeping. It's a wonder I didn't die.

I kept four ounces at all times as my personal stash. I always kept $70,000 cash in my safe. When my supply of the drug got low, I'd just give somebody money and send out for more.

I haven't told anyone this: In 3½ years, I spent more than $1,000,000 of my own money on cocaine. That's about $1,000 a day. I put most of that through my own system and I'm still alive. I must have a mission in life.

The money came from all over. There were accounts I didn't even realize I had—$20,000 here, $40,000 there, $15,000 somewhere else. I had $30,000 cold cash in a vault in Las Vegas. The Mariners continued to pay me my $80,000 salary the first year. Then I started mortgaging the house. I had bought the house for $120,000 eight years earlier. By then, I owed only $30,000 on it, but it was worth $650,000. I smoked that. The Hickok Belt I won in 1962 was 2.5 pounds of solid gold studded with rubies, diamonds and sapphires. I gave that to my friend to display on the wall of his Las Vegas hotel and somebody stole it. My friend had insured the belt for $50,000, and when it was stolen I got that money and went through it in no time. It didn't seem as if having the belt stolen was a loss. It was a great gain.

I figured everybody was waiting for me to kill myself and they could hardly wait until the body was cold to see what was left. I was determined that there wasn't going to be anything left. All of it went up in smoke.

I didn't care if I died. I didn't have any plans. I lived one day at a time in my misery. All I cared about was that I staying altered.

I didn't use any drug but cocaine. I stopped drinking because I didn't have the time to drink and smoke. I couldn't put the coke pipe down. I'd go through at least 14 grams a day. That's a half ounce. I might go through an ounce some days. One time I went through five ounces in five days.

I was in the home I had lived in for years and I didn't know what room I was in. I ended up hallucinating, seeing all kinds of strange things so often they became normal to me.

I never fell asleep; I just passed out. I might wake up days later in any part of the house and, when I did, I wouldn't know where I was. I didn't know what day of the week it was. It didn't matter. I'd be closer to being civil before I took that first hit again. That was when I'd go outside and cut my little lawn, which regularly grew knee-high between mowings.

Before that first hit, when I wanted to feel better, I'd look at my plaques and trophies in my den and go through some old photographs of me in my playing days. I'd look at them and I could just about hear the crowd in Dodger Stadium chanting, "GO! GO! GO!" I'd start thinking, "Shit, I got to get out of this." I'd get a good feeling. But I was afraid to go outside and I couldn't accept the agony of thinking about all that, so I'd get the pipe again and it would put me back in the other world.

There were times when I said, "I'm going to quit this," and I'd smash the pipe in the fireplace. But I always had a couple more pipes. I knew that when I threw it in the fireplace.

Once I got going, I couldn't just quit and go to sleep. I learned to program myself so that at a certain time, after smoking a certain amount, I'd lie back and I'd just pass out.

I had nothing to drive me or motivate me, nothing to wrap myself up in while I was doing the drug. I started playing games with it. I figured out ways that I could save my own life if I took an overdose. I found ways to cook it to make it better and more efficient. I spent endless hours on my feet doing that cooking and smoking and trying something different until my feet were swollen and sore. It was no fun.

I would become paranoid and thought that everybody was looking in my windows. I used to sit in my bedroom upstairs at night and stare out the bay window at the ocean until one night I saw all kinds of people—people who weren't really there—looking in at me. I went around the house and put blankets over all the windows.

I'd give somebody $10,000 to buy four ounces. It was $2,300 an ounce, and they'd bring back $400 change. I went through $12,000 worth—five ounces—in 10 days once. That's twice what I made in my rookie season, and it didn't mean anything to me.

Not all of it went through my body. I'd have other people there, too, sometimes. When you have people over, you have to show off, and they consume a ton because they're not paying for it. They're also taking as much home with them as they can sneak in their pockets. They think you don't see them, so they take it. They call that stealing, but it comes with the territory. You don't want to call them on it because you don't want them to stop coming to your house. You want to be nice all the time and part of being nice is letting them steal from you.

I later came to enjoy spending money on wholesome things. Like going down to Dodger Stadium and spending $150 or $200 on jackets, T-shirts, World Series pins and little souvenirs to give people. When I was using, that would have been enough money to pay for less than two hours of killing myself with drugs. I wasted so much money in my life, I later got such pleasure from buying something you can put your hands on and wear, something that you can look at and enjoy.

I spent three Thanksgivings in the darkness of my home when I had the local butcher bring me a roasted chicken. I had a long, antique table, and I would put the chicken on it and sit down. Maybe I lit a candle, and maybe I was in darkness. I sat there and looked at the chicken and said a prayer. It wasn't a prayer of thanksgiving. It was a prayer of "God, help me." Then I got up and went back upstairs to my room and started smoking my pipe again.

Days like Thanksgiving and Christmas were the things that kept me alive. Those had been the only days of the year when I was a kid when all 13 kids came together with my mother and father. Birthdays don't mean anything to me. When I was a boy, I remember telling my mother once that it was my birthday. "It is?" she said. "Well, congratulations, son." But Thanksgiving and Christmas mean a lot.

I met another woman, Angela, who would become my wife—my drug wife. For the next two Thanksgivings with Angela, I went to a store that had all organically grown products. I bought more than $125 worth of food—a turkey, sweet potatoes, corn, fruit, peas, cranberries, everything. The first year I did that I put it in the trunk of the car. On the way home I picked up just an eighth of an ounce of cocaine. I drove into the garage, closed the garage door, left the turkey and all the trimmings in the trunk, went in the house and got high for four days before I came back and took the rotted stuff out of the car.

The second year, I got everything into the house and fixed that turkey dinner. I love to fix turkeys. When it was done, I put it on the table and dressed it up with peas, cranberries, mashed potatoes and gravy, corn on the cob, sliced tomatoes, beets and everything else you can think of. I set the table for four with cloth napkins. I lit two candles. Then I went into the kitchen and cooked my cocaine. I never touched the meal. It stayed on the table for four or five days until it was spoiled. People who came through picked at the carcass. It was crazy.

I'd always tried to be the best at anything I did. Even when it was bad for me, I was the best I could be. I was the best drug addict going. I took great pride in doing it right.

We had our role models among users, too. You always sought people who knew how to do it right, how to get the most out of it. That means getting the biggest high, the most euphoric feeling out of a fix. That's the feeling that stops just short of making your heart stop forever. That's what you were trying for.

I knew I was an addict, but at least I was an addict with class. At least I did it right. At least I wasn't sloppy about it. There are levels in the drug scene, all the way from the ones you emulate down to the slobs.

At times I wanted to be a part of the crowd, but I never had any fun that way. They never wanted me participating with them. They just wanted to use my stuff to get high.

The person who was sharp enough to read me and tell me all

the things I wanted to hear got all the things they wanted from me. They could even screw my wife if they told me the things I wanted to hear.

## Chapter 73: Dropping in on the hereafter

I've been to Heaven and I've been to Hell.

Literally.

It was Thanksgiving, the day I went to Hell. I had been at a guy's house for about three days, going nonstop on my pipe. I had been there because I was tired of being in my house alone. On Thanksgiving Day, I left to go home, which was only about 10 minutes away. Just before I left, I took a Valium, figuring it would kick in just after I got home and I would be able to pass out.

I left the guy's apartment in a nice part of town and started driving down the street. It was about 4:30 in the afternoon, just near twilight.

The area I was driving through is populated with rows of stores and parked cars lining both sides of the street. But I didn't see a soul. I didn't see any cars, either, moving or parked. It was like a scene from a science fiction movie depicting the aftermath of a nuclear war. I can't even remember seeing street lights.

I was driving down this deserted street when, all of a sudden, I was in a dark tunnel. I drove to the end of it. At the end of the tunnel, over in the corner, I swear to God, I saw a figure about 12 feet high with shoulders four or five feet wide. I saw two god-damned ears coming up like horns and I saw the pitchfork with three blades on it sticking up with a hand on it. The figure was standing motionless. He was standing with his feet apart. The scene got bleary near the ground, but I could see it. He was all gray and standing behind a fire that was coming out of a hole about five feet across. The flames were coming about two feet out of the hole. The hole was deep. I could see that. He was standing there behind it and just to the left. Waiting for me.

All I had to do was take one more step, just one more step, and he would have me. I saw that and stopped. I froze. And I looked at him, looked at his face. I didn't see his features. I saw him as a shadow.

I knew it was the Devil. I saw that sonuvabitch and I just stood there. I figured if I stood motionless as he was, there was nothing he could do. He couldn't do shit.

I had to take that step. He couldn't reach over and grab me or get me with the pitchfork. He was helpless, useless. As long as I didn't move, didn't go any farther, he was harmless.

I turned around and walked away from him. I found myself walking out of what looked like a big tunnel of intestines. I think I saw a picture once of Jonah and the Whale. It looked like that, all gray and slimy like the bottom of the Anacostia River where I saved that kid when I was little. The footing was slimy like that river. Every time I go through a tunnel now I think of that.

I remember taking about four steps away from that pit. I remember saying to myself, "That's Satan himself. Goddam, that sonuvabitch is big. That's what he looks like—a big sonuvabitch with a big head on him and big ears coming out in points."

I walked out of the tunnel and the next thing I knew I was back in my car, stopped at a traffic light. I drove the rest of the way home, following the curb on the right side of the street. I never saw anybody the whole way. At one spot in the road, the curb cuts in for a bus stop. I thought it was a turn and pulled in. I ripped my front tire apart hitting the curb and drove the rest of the way home on the rim.

This wasn't a dream. This actually happened.

It was scary enough to make me put my pipe down and go home and lie down. I slept for four days.

I went to Heaven a different time. I remember that as if it happened yesterday.

I was alone, high and locked up in my house. I was sitting on the edge of my bed when I came out of my skin like a snake would peel. I actually peeled out of my skin. I was trembling and sweating. It took about five minutes to totally get out of my skin. I could feel my body coming out of the skin methodically. As the skin fell down, I was rising to my feet and emerging. I rose right up through the sky.

The next thing I remember was up on a big, white, fluffy cumulus cloud. I was in the prone position, looking down at the earth. A chubby little guy with a bulbous nose—he looked Irish—was lying beside me. He was wearing a little white robe that came just below his knees. That was all he had on. We were lying side by side looking down.

I looked back over my left shoulder and saw the Pearly Gates. The Pearly Gates were just a little set of gates in a white picket fence, about three feet high. The fence was lopsided, and the hinges on the gates were halfway broken so they were lopsided, too.

Everything was pure white. There was no discoloring at all, no off-white here, egg-white there, and white-on-white over there. Everything was white-white.

I didn't see any grass. The ground was covered with a fluffy, white mist. I didn't see any movement at all. I didn't see anybody go by.

I was looking down, and it was like those pictures from the space shuttle you see on TV. That's how high I was. And yet I could see everybody moving around and all the cars and everything.

The people looked like ants, scurrying all over the place. I said to the little man next to me, "Gee, is that what I look like down there? Is that what it's like? Look at them! They're all over the place, running into one another."

"Yep, that's what it's like," he said.

It was so peaceful up there. I was looking forward to going on over to the gates and going in when he said, "Okay, Maury, it's time to go back."

"Go back?" I said with alarm. "I gotta go back there? No! I don't want to go back!"

"Oh, yeah, you gotta go back," he said placidly. "And you gotta hurry, too. Your time is up."

"Oh, no," I begged. "I don't want to go. Not now, anyhow. I don't want to go."

"C'mon, Maury, you gotta go," he insisted. "You gotta hurry up." It was as if there was a timer running.

"I don't want to go."

"You got to go."

Before I knew it, I was sitting on the side of my bed again. I felt kind of refreshed, replenished. I wasn't sweaty anymore. I was back in my skin. I hadn't felt myself going back into it. I was just there.

Alone.

## Chapter 74: Bringing 'em back alive

It's hell seeing somebody almost die right in front of you. It happened four or five times in my house. People OD'ed—overdosed. I brought them all back.

There is no warning. All of a sudden, the head goes back, they're gasping for air. The mouth's open and they want to swallow their tongue. You've got to reach in there and grab that tongue and pull it out. You can get your hand bitten, but you have to do it. You have to have something to press inside the mouth to hold the tongue out. You give them mouth-to-mouth resuscitation. You push on their stomach and lungs to pump the heart. When they come to, you slap them to keep them awake because they want to pass out. You can't let them do that. You have to keep them awake. Put cold packs on their necks. I always kept a towel in my freezer just for that purpose.

The hell of it is that when a person comes out of it, he doesn't remember anything. He doesn't even realize how long he's been out, how severe it was and how close to death he was. The first thing he wants to do is take another hit.

One time it happened was four in the morning. It always seemed to be four in the morning. These two big, rough white boys showed up. I know for sure one of them didn't like niggers. That was the one I didn't know. I knew the other guy. I do believe they came around to hurt me.

The redneck was after my drug wife, Angela. She had been

shaking her hips at the guy—cockteasing. So they came around hoping to see her, and I let them in and let them use my stuff.

They laid out some lines a foot long and about a half inch wide. Then they got out a machine that sucks the stuff up and pumps it into your nose. I left the room.

Next thing I knew, I heard yelling in the living room. I went in and the redneck had OD'ed and was dying right there on the floor. His eyes were rolled back in the top of his head. His buddy, a big body-builder who turned out to be a little punk—was standing there screaming, "HE'S DEAD!!!"

I grabbed the guy on the floor and slapped him. I opened his mouth and blew into it as hard as I could. I pumped his chest, screaming as I was working on him for somebody to bring me the towel out of the freezer. They brought the towel and I put it behind his neck. I blew into him a little more, slapped him some more, breathed some more. Before you know it, he started to come around.

When he regained his senses, such as they were, he came back like an animal. He came back in the frame of mind I thought he was in when he came through the door. He had disguised it then with a smile, but now he was screaming at me.

"I'm going to kill you!" he yelled.

I was face to face with him when he said that. Before he could do anything, I moved with all the speed and precision I used when I took a lead off first base against Juan Marichal and stole second. I slipped behind him and grabbed him in a full nelson. The guy looked strong enough to move a house, but with the fear I had of his getting loose, I held him so tight he couldn't budge.

"I'm gonna get you," he hissed and growled.

"Throw a little more water on this guy," I told his buddy. "Slap him in the face. Wake him up!"

They took my advice and the more they did that the more the redneck hissed at me: "I'm gonna kill you."

"You ain't gonna kill nobody, buddy," I hissed back.

He was gradually coming down. When I felt it was safe enough, I let go of him and moved quickly to the far side of the room. He stood there staring at me.

"What are you staring at him like that for?" his buddy said to him. "Maury just saved your life, asshole."

"Whaddya mean, he saved my life?" the guy asked.

"Yeah," he said. "You OD'ed. He saved you."

"That's right," I said with a smile. Then, biting the words off and throwing them in his face, I added: "And I gave you mouth-to-mouth resuscitation, too!"

When he heard that he spat. He couldn't handle that. He and his buddy left.

This was the second person I saved. I saved three women that I can remember after that.

Eventually I got tired of those kind of low-life people hanging around me. I decided I wanted to do the drug by myself.

During some of those periods of doing it alone, I was doing so much that I knew that if I OD'ed, nobody was going to save me. It hits you so fast, you're paralyzed. So I trained myself to get out of that pickle just as I trained myself to get interference by running into the first baseman. I applied perfect practice to saving my own life.

I figured I had about three-tenths of a second to feel it coming and react. I knew that from watching other people who OD'ed. With that little time, I couldn't smoke it in the bedroom or the garage or the living room. I had to smoke in the kitchen or the bathroom. I actually drilled myself on getting the cold towel out of the freezer in the kitchen and getting into a cold shower in the bathroom in three-tenths of a second.

I never had to do it. But I felt if I had to I could.

## Chapter 75: Sex and the single addict

Judy was long gone. I had more strangers come through my house than I could count. Girls would stop for a while and stay. I can't even remember most of their names. Some stayed a while. Others were in and out.

I had locked myself in and the only people who came were dope people. With sex, it seemed everybody was getting it but me. And they were using my stuff. Guys would bring their dates and people would disappear from time to time and then come back.

It never was glamorous, not like the cases you hear about with orgies and wild times. It's not like that. There's never any real fun involved in drugs.

I had two girls who had been living in their car come stay with me for a while. Another girl came for a party. She had a date and so did I. During the party, my date left and the guy she came with left. The party started on a Tuesday. Fifteen Tuesdays later, she was still there. She was good to me and she cleaned the house. It was an ideal situation. I had no feeling for her, which made it better. I had my love. It was the drug. It just happened that the drug was her love, too. When she left, it was no big deal.

One time I had five girls, all good-looking, and five o.z.'s—that's ounces—of cocaine in the kitchen with me. It might even have been six girls.

We stayed in the kitchen for eight or nine days until all the stuff was gone. Some of the girls were naked, some were half-naked, and some were getting ready to get naked. For some reason, the women were much more uninhibited around one another than they were when a bunch of guys were around. Then they're hesitant to disrobe. Without any other men around, they weren't hesitant at all. All we did was fuck around and do coke in the kitchen. That was my favorite room because you had to cook the stuff in the kitchen and smoke it over the gas stove. We were screwing on the kitchen table, the sink, in the refrigerator, on the floor, in the window with the curtain up. It didn't matter.

Most guys think that's heaven. It wasn't heaven. But it was fun.

Those were the only times that I really enjoyed my addiction, when there weren't a lot of guys around and I was in control. When I tried to have some semblance of normalcy, like at a party with some guys and some women, it always got all screwed up and I lost control. As long as I was just there with a couple girls by myself, I had all the control because I had the money and the stuff and the only dick there.

During those eight or nine days, it got to the point where a lot of times the dick wasn't important anymore. I wasn't King Tut all the time. There was a Queen Bee in there, too. The girls had a lot of fun without me. Sometimes the girls got so interested in one another, I took my stuff and went upstairs. Then they'd come up and apologize and ask me to come back down with the stuff. That's when I still had the power.

One time during that period I wanted to find something to do to get away from using the goddamned stuff and to get away from those girls. I started working on a clock-radio that was broken. I was standing against the sink with a screwdriver and a pair of pliers and the radio halfway taken apart when I fell asleep for two hours. I just stood there passed out. A whole ounce of cocaine was on the counter and the women were having a ball. When I came back to my senses, they were arguing over who was in charge of the stuff while I was asleep and who had had more hits.

When the coke was gone and I wasn't in the mood to go get another bag, they decided it was time to leave. I was pissed off because I thought the stuff was really disappearing fast, so before they left I dumped their purses on the table. They were crying and complaining about my not trusting them, but when I dumped the purses, big rocks of cocaine fell all over the place. I kept the coke and threw them out.

There's nothing worse than a bad blow job. I know people who say there's no such thing as a bad blow job, but there are a lot of bad ones in the drug scene. People are so concerned about getting back to the drug that you get a lot of teasing. A woman will just go through the motions and make you feel you're going to get what you want and then she'll stop to get another fix. Then you have a fix, too, and before you know it getting fucked up takes the place of getting fucked.

After a while, the drug takes away a man's ability to have sex. After years of use, that's what happened to me. I'd be offered sex, but I couldn't do anything about it.

Then, after sleeping two or three days and depleting the cocaine and alcohol from my body, my system would start to get back to normal. Suddenly, I'd find myself with an erection like I hadn't seen for months. I'm saying to myself, "Where'd that come from? Oh, man! Where is she now?

I'd call a woman. Boy, I'm going to raise hell. Yessirree, I'm hot now. I'm ready and even the stuff ain't going to stop me now because I'm never going to lose this hard-on. This might never go down.

Now she's here. She's at the door. She's in the apartment. "Hey! Let's have a little coke first!" I take a hit and WHOOMP! I look down and my hard-on's gone. It died the instant the coke hit my system.

That's why all the bizarre scenes and all the abnormal sex take place. That's why I had five girls in the kitchen with me, to find some excitement strong enough to break through the drug and get an erection. Once you needed one girl to get it up, and now you need five. Then even five aren't enough and you have to call in six or seven because maybe that will do it.

You get to a point where nothing does it. Then, two or three hours later, when all the stuff is gone, the body goes through some kind of mysterious change and here it comes again. WHANG! But by this time the girls are gone because there isn't any more dope. You call one up: "Hey, c'mon over! I got some more stuff!" She comes over. You order some more stuff. And as soon as the drug man knocks on the door to deliver the stuff—WHOOMP!—Mr. Erection's gone. It's a Catch-22.

So I'm sitting there with this brilliant mind of mine. Just as I figured out how to get out of a baseball rundown, I'm going to figure out how to make this work. The light bulb goes on in my head. I got it! I'm not going to use it! I'm going to get some stuff and let her use it, but I won't. Hot damn!

I called a girl and got what they call an eighth—that's 3½ grams or an eighth of an ounce of cocaine. She came over and I fixed some up for her.

"You want some?" she says.

"No, honey! You go ahead and take the first one."

I figure the first hit is going to make her take her clothes off right away.

"You want some?" she asks again.

"No! I'll take mine later. I'm all right." I start getting out of my clothes. "How is it?" I ask her. "Is it all right?"

"Oh, I missed that," she says. She didn't get all the way off on the fix. "I want another one."

No problem. I fix her a big one and give it to her. I figure she's going to come out of her clothes when this hits her.

"S'more! S'more!" she says. I fix her more. "Oh, my god! That's so great!" She's got that big rush.

Now's the time! I'm ready for action.

"Wait a minute," she says. "Not right now. I've got claustrophobia. Let me get myself together."

She has to go outside to air out a little. Ten minutes later, she comes back in.

ME: "Here I come! Are you ready, baby?"

SHE: "Wait a minute. You got any more? I didn't have enough."

ME: "You just had it!"

SHE: "But that's gone now."

ME: "I know it's gone. I thought you were up there where you wanted to be."

SHE: "That was too much."

I fix her another charge. I give her half what I gave her before.

ME (Pleading): "All right? C'mon. C'mon!"

SHE: "I missed that. That's not enough. You gotta give me a bigger charge."

This went on for two hours until three whole grams were gone and I still hadn't gotten to her. She was holding out because the whole idea for the woman is to get all the stuff without giving up anything. But I had saved the last half gram at the end. I took that out and fixed it for myself.

"Can I have some of that?" she said.

"NO! This is mine!"

Then she had the audacity to act as if she were being mistreated because I wouldn't give her any of that last half gram. I was a jerk. I was a rat. They call those kind of women coke whores. To me, that's a woman who manipulates you until all your stuff is gone and then leaves you. There are men who are coke whores to women, too. Those people find out where your Achilles' heel is and then they go for it. It's easier for a woman to do that than it is for a man. It's also easier for a woman to get into a really bad situation in which she's utterly dependent on somebody. And a lot of these guys are real jerks who will beat a woman up if she doesn't come through.

I was a soft touch. I didn't get hard on them. I was very popular for that reason. But I wasn't respected at all.

When this girl didn't come through, I just got rid of her, got some more stuff and called another girl. But now I'm using and I can't get an erection. I'm right back where I started. My brilliant plan didn't work.

## Chapter 76: Stupid drug tricks

I had quit hunting long ago, but I still had my guns. I kept them in the house just for show and for the memories. When I got bad and was locked up in my house, I sawed off my shotguns for protection. That's how paranoid I got. I sawed off my Browning 12-gauge and took the plug out of the magazine so that it could hold seven shots instead of three.

Another thing I did in my stupor was stand in the kitchen and throw heavy kitchen knives, bayonets and hunting knives right through the door. You're always doing things like that when you're doing drugs and trying to get on top of everybody. Everybody wants to be the baddest dude around. Everybody was trying to take things. They especially wanted to take my woman. I wanted everyone to know the baddest dude in the house was me. Then they'd be smooth enough to pacify me, tell me what I wanted to hear so they could get what they wanted.

I eventually lost the guns. I gave them up as collateral for drugs.

When I was using and abusing, any time somebody got in my way, I got volatile. I ran into some big guys and I got rid of them. I was a warrior. I kicked ass like you wouldn't believe. I didn't care if it was Godzilla. I guess I was making up for all the things that happened to me during my life, every slight.

I liked to go into my garage and make weapons. I had hoses. I had big chains like you'd use to lock up a motorcycle. I'd put a dog leash on the end of them and then they were legal. Otherwise, it was clearly a weapon and it would be a felony to be caught with it.

I whipped some big guys with those things. I wrapped that chain around one guy's head and drew blood that hit the beams in a cathedral ceiling. I had as many as seven policemen with dogs and shotguns come to my house just for me. They jacked me up pretty good because one of the guys I whipped ran two miles all the way to the police station screaming that Maury Wills was up there and had tried to kill him. Nothing came of it. The guy was an addict and wasn't about to press charges.

One time, I got down to my last two grams. It was about three in the morning. I figured I'd smoke those two grams then pass out. When I woke up, I'd have another seven grams sent to me. I started cooking the last of the stuff. You do that by putting it in a closed vial with baking soda and heating it. First it foams, then it turns into an oil, and then it rocks up into a solid. That's what you smoke. The process removes the impurities. They didn't sell crack back then. Crack is cocaine that somebody has already rocked up, but they do it with all kinds of adulterants. Crack's not clean like the rocks you make yourself and it's vicious.

Anyway, I got careless. I could hardly wait to get it cooked up and forgot to release the pressure cap on the vial. The vial burst, and bam! It was gone. That was severe. I was programmed to have those two grams. They were going to last about an hour and a half and then I was going to pass out. I wasn't programmed to stop before smoking them. When the vial broke, I could have hanged myself, that's how bad it was. I started laughing hysterically, just as I did when I found Bump and Judy together. I was all alone in that big house laughing like a mad scientist in a horror movie. If I didn't laugh, I wouldn't have been able to handle it.

I had to get some more. I got in my car and started driving to my connection. I was going 80 mph in a 40 mph zone on Vista del Mar highway. On the wrong side of the street. I went a couple of miles. Fortunately, no one else was on the road. At least I didn't see anybody. I don't know how many cars I may have forced off the road.

The road runs along the ocean from Playa del Rey to El Segundo. Coming into El Segundo, there's a double curve where the road goes past the Scattergood Generating Station. I had to slow down through the turn. Then the area gets more developed as you go through El Porto and finally into Manhattan Beach. It was in Manhattan Beach, right in front of Pancho's restaurant, that two cops caught up with me and pulled me over at almost four in the morning.

The cops approached the car with their holsters unsnapped. One came to the driver's window while the other stood back in case this lunatic tried something. The cop at the window was ready to snatch me out of the car and put me in jail when he saw who it was.

"Maury!" he exclaimed. "Oh, my God, what are you doing?"

"Was I on the wrong side of the street back there?" I asked innocently. "It seems like I might have been."

"Yes, you were," the cop said. "Do you know how fast you were going?"

"No," I said, playing dumb. "I think I was speeding a little bit, wasn't I?"

"Maury, we had trouble catching you," the cop said. "Where are you going?"

I couldn't tell him I was going down to my connection. "I'm going to see a friend," I said. "I was lonely. I live alone and I was lonely."

"Why don't you call your friend and have him come and pick you up?" he suggested. He was really concerned for my safety.

"I can't do that," I said.

"Well, call a cab," he suggested. "We'll call one for you."

"I can't do that, either," I said.

"Tell you what," the cop said, still being helpful. "One of us will drive you down there in the cruiser and the other one will follow in your car."

Now I really didn't want that. "Aw, I don't want to put you out," I said, acting just as concerned about the cops' comfort as they were about mine.

They had me stand outside the car and shined a light in my eyes. They decided I wasn't that bad off. "If you don't have far to go, you can drive down there," they said. "But, please, be careful."

They let me go.

That was in 1982 and the California Angels made the playoffs that year. I called around and got the names of the two cops who had let me go. I bought them tickets for the World Series without their knowing it. I was all set to send them the tickets when the Angels lost the damned playoffs to the Brewers.

## Chapter 77: Angela

I met Angela after the 1980 season, when I first got involved in drugs. The girl who introduced me to cocaine took me to a house where we could get some more. I ended up staying there a week. The guy who lived there had a girlfriend, a skinny blonde. She looked sweet and innocent, but I didn't pay attention to her.

The guy knocked her around the whole time I was there. He'd grab her by the collar and slam her around because she wasn't doing things right. He sent her out on a run to take some stuff to somebody and to go buy some more from somebody else. She stayed a half hour too long and he accused her of messing around with the guy she was supposed to get the drug from and jacked her up for that. She just took it. That was the first time I saw that there's no trust in the drug scene. I found it all amusing, because I was learning that other people have problems, too.

That woman was Angela and after I left that house, I didn't see her again until 1983 when some girls stopped by and one of them knew Angela. When the girl said that Angela had some of the best stuff you ever saw, I asked her to arrange for me to buy some from her. She did. I bought the stuff and then I didn't see her for about two weeks.

The next thing I knew, Angela called to ask if she could stay at my place for a few days. She had been up to Seattle to see her mother, and she'd asked a girlfriend to watch her apartment while she was gone. The girlfriend had a party and the apartment got ravaged. They broke everything, took her TV and raised so much hell the landlord told her to get out.

Angela was still running from the guy who was beating her. She just wanted to stay a few days while she found another apartment, but she said while she stayed with me, there'd be no hanky-panky.

"You got a lot of nerve. What makes you think I'd want to go to bed with you?" I told her when she came over. "You're going to stay here for three days and you're going to make the rules? Forget it. You can leave now or you can stay. It doesn't make any difference to me. I got enough women coming around as it is."

Within about six hours, Angela and I were at it. She came for three days and we ended up getting married. Our relationship was all drugs and sex, but the drugs were more important. Sex was supposed to be the result of doing the drugs. It got bizarre and it got heavy. It's just unbelievable as I think back that the drug affects your brain that way. She was a sweet, nice girl, but we were both bad.

Angela came from a good family. She had been born in California and raised in Seattle. She was 28 when we got together. She didn't have a job. She said she was a poet and an artist. I even enrolled her in some art classes at a school recommended to me by an art gallery. She went to one class and didn't make it to the second. She said the teacher didn't know what he was talking about.

She drank 151-proof rum straight. She had to have Valium all the time and she did coke—all at once. She was a sloppy drunk. She'd get all dressed to go out and a half hour later she was falling in the bushes, her hat was cockeyed, her make up was smeared and her nylons were snagged.

The thing that Angela loved me for in the beginning was my strength. She didn't realize that nothing could affect me because I had only one obsession. That was to get high. Nothing else was important to me. It wasn't a strength. It was a weakness.

That same attitude destroyed our relationship. She did things to damage herself in an effort to get a reaction out of me. She thought I was strong because nothing she did bothered me, but I was just concerned with getting high.

## Chapter 78: The Care Unit

There are very few people who realize they have a drug or alcohol problem, go in for help and succeed on their first attempt. For most of us, recovery starts with only a hope, a thought of wanting to do something. It takes a while to admit you're powerless. Even after you admit that, it takes longer to believe that there is a power greater than any on earth that can bring you to sobriety.

My recovery began in 1983, five years before I finally stopped using. Fred Claire, who was then the Dodgers' vice president in charge of operations, had heard rumors that I was dead. He decided he had to try to find me and get help for me. He and Don Newcombe, who works in the Dodgers' substance abuse program, decided to try to help me.

"There was a rumor that swept through the press box that Maury Wills had died," Fred said in explaining how it happened. "I thought to myself, 'What a tragedy.' I wondered if there was anything that I or anyone could have done to have helped him."

Claire and Newcombe came to my house to try to see me, but I had two Dobermans chained up outside. You had to go through the dogs to get to the door, and once you saw the dogs, you lost your desire to get to the door.

So Fred started calling me, urging me to commit myself to a program. At the same time, Angela said to me, "Maury, if you go and clean up, I will, too."

I wasn't ready to be rescued when Fred called. If I had been ready, I would have stuck to the program. But I went with Fred and Don because I had no choice. They set up a day and a time when they were coming and I made the commitment to Fred to be there. I loved Fred Claire. Once I made the commitment to him, I had to go through with it. I wasn't as crazy about Don Newcombe. He came off as one of those hardcore AA guys. He cleaned himself up so everybody else should, too. He said things from time to time over the years that just created embarrassment, guilt and resentment.

Fred and Don came to pick me up on the appointed day. I wasn't ready. I invited them in, then went upstairs and piddled around getting my things ready and going through all kinds of changes for about two hours. I wasn't firing up, but it was a tempting thought. I had programmed myself to stop using when they got there.

They were so patient. They didn't say anything while I was up there. Finally, I came down the stairs and said, "Okay, I'm ready."

God, that was tough. I felt I wanted to go out the door upstairs, jump over the balcony and escape. I wanted to say, "I'm not going."

But I went. Fred sat in the front while we drove to The Care Unit, a drug and alcohol rehab center. I sat in the back. Don drove.

I was thinking, "I can't go in there. The press will get hold of it. It will be in the papers. Everybody's going to know." So we thought of using an assumed name. I decided to use Don's and Fred's names and enter the center as Donald Claire.

They dropped me off and I was put in the admissions section. It's like a hospital room with hospital beds. Normally, you spend about two days in admissions before going to the other side of the center where you start attending classes and therapy sessions.

The longest I had gone without the drug—other than when I passed out—before I entered The Care Unit was maybe half a day. That was when I first started to dream about trying to get sober. Other than those rare occasions, I was constantly high. There was enough drug in my system to keep me stoned for two days without having any.

In admissions, they just let me sleep. It wasn't like in the movies where you're shaking and grinding your teeth during withdrawal. I was so tired anyway from being up for about five straight days before I went in.

I was supposed to stay in admissions only a couple of days, but I stayed for a week. I was going through a lot of anger and resentment. I didn't want to be there.

They were trying to get me to go over to the other side of the hospital.

"What's there?" I asked.

"Classes," they said.

"Classes! I don't want to do all that stuff!"

Finally, they sent another major leaguer who was in the program to talk to me. This was in 1983, when drugs were rampant in the big leagues.

The player was Vida Blue. His rehabilitation had been highly publicized, but I hadn't known anything about it. He told me how great it was on the other side, that we would be roommates, that I could play ping-pong, that I should come over. He talked me into going.

I started going to the classes and group therapy sessions, but I didn't say anything. Ten days into the program, the guy who was leading the group realized that I was never going to put my hand up and share. So he had everybody share in rotation around the room. When he got to me, I was feeling bad.

"The first thing I want you to know is my name isn't Donald Claire," I said when I finally stood up.

"No shit, Maury!" the group replied in chorus.

From that day on, I started to improve.

The improvement wasn't dramatic or even steady. It was more like a seed that had been planted but still needed to be watered and nourished. It hadn't even sprouted. It was still just a seed.

The rehab program is 28 days. I didn't really apply myself. I didn't understand it. I thought I went there to quit drinking and using. And I did stop because I didn't have anything to drink or use. After being in there for a while, I didn't even want any.

But it's more than quitting the drug. It's learning how to live again. It's getting all the tools that you need to work with to keep from going back to using. I didn't realize that part. I figured as long as I wasn't drinking and wasn't using drugs I was doing the program. I didn't apply myself in classes. I wasn't listening. I didn't use the tools they were giving me. I was doing the same thing I had done as a kid in school. I was skating through.

After two weeks, Angela came to visit me. She was stoned.

Then I got a pass to go home accompanied by a volunteer worker. I had called Angela and told her I was coming. She said she'd be expecting me. Everything would be clean and in order, she promised.

I went in the house and they had had a wild party the night before I got there. Angela was on the bed. She hadn't gone to sleep; she had passed out. I tried to wake her and couldn't, so I went and got a scrub bucket and filled it to the brim with cold water and ice cubes. I stood right up on the bed and poured it on her. That woke her up—for about five minutes. Then she passed out again.

I went back to the hospital with the trustee. I was really torn. Now I really couldn't concentrate on my program.

The next week, I got another pass. This time I was allowed to go home alone and stay for about five hours. I had to be back by seven o'clock.

When I got to the house, I didn't want to leave Angela. I didn't like what was going on. I thought I was losing her to the drug scene.

"I'll be all right," she said. "Why don't you go back."

I got to feeling that she wanted to get rid of me so the parties could continue. The phone was ringing and I could tell the people calling were finding out that Maury was still there.

I stayed past seven o'clock. I kept calling the nurses at the hospital, telling them I'd be back. I wasn't using and I wasn't doing anything wrong. I figured I was okay. But part of the program is learning to be accountable and I wasn't doing that. The whole hospital was worried about me. When I got back at midnight everybody was awake even though lights were supposed to be out at 11 p.m. There's a real closeness at the hospital. If one patient goes out and messes up, it affects everybody. I didn't realize that. I thought it was just me.

They were glad to see me, but the first thing the nurses did when I got back was take a urine sample. Then they took away all of my liberties.

"What's all the fuss about?" I asked. "I'm here, aren't I?"

"You don't understand," they said. "Sobriety is keeping your word about things, keeping your commitments, keeping your promises, showing up on time."

"Huh?"

"You're in here to learn to be a responsible person, not just to stop using," they explained.

They called Don Newcombe in to talk to me and meet with the therapist. I was defiant and rude. Newk didn't say anything I wanted to hear. He told me to stop the bullshit and get down to business. He was absolutely right, but I told him in front of everybody to mind his own business.

The doctor said something about my manipulating people. I didn't like that word. He said I was full of shit. I didn't like that, either. Newk finally gave up and left.

In the meantime, I was calling home. The line was busy. They were partying and partying—on my money. Finally, I got through to Angela. I could hear the party in the background, men in my house.

It was a 28-day program, but after 25 days I packed my bags and went home.

It took about 35 minutes to drive home. I was mad, bitter and depressed. I was coming back to my own house and all these people were there. The place was riddled with drugs and alcohol. They didn't even say hi when I walked in. It was like, "Who is he?"

Angela was shocked when I showed up, but she didn't show any guilt about all the partying. She tried to pretend she was glad to see me. She wanted to make me a celebrity because I had been in The Care Unit. I didn't want anything to do with that or with the people. I wanted to get back to the drug. I had to buy the drug—my own drugs—from the people who were there. I took the stuff and went upstairs.

There's no telling how long that binge lasted. I locked myself up in the house again. I knew that the Dodgers were going to find out. I knew this time I was going to get in trouble with the law if I went out, so I stayed inside. I couldn't get in trouble there. I had one obsession and that was to get high.

I had a telephone answering machine. I remember sitting in my house and listening to my mother's voice begging me to pick up the phone. "Maury, if you're there, please talk to me," she cried. My kids called. My son Bump called again and again. He found every phone number I ever had and called. I sat there and listened to their voices, but I couldn't pick up the phone. I couldn't talk to them.

During my first session at The Care Unit, somebody got up to speak who was there for the third time. He said that more than likely the majority of us in that room were not going to make it. I had taken great offense to that. I gave the guy hell for challenging my ability to stop. I'd never be back, I said. I was right. I didn't go back. But I didn't stop, either.

You have to learn to live again. The drug was not my problem. The drug was my solution. I didn't know what my problem was yet.

## Chapter 79: Caught stealing

Just after Christmas, 1983 I was arrested for stealing a car. The cops found my pipe in the car and the news hit the papers that Maury Wills had been arrested for auto theft and cocaine possession.

It shouldn't have happened. The car I was charged with stealing was my car. It was the Audi I'd bought for Judy in 1981.

Angela had gone to Oregon to see her grandmother for the holidays. I still couldn't find Judy. So I went to her house one night while she was sleeping and took my car back. I had a set of keys and just drove it away.

She called and asked if I had taken the car. I told her no. She didn't believe me. She begged, pleaded, and bargained with me. I stonewalled her. "I haven't seen the car," I insisted.

So she reported it to the police as a stolen car. That might have been the end of it, but I drove it out on the freeway late one night. The side window was broken where someone had got in to steal the radio. The police would report that they stopped me because they saw a car driving down the freeway with the window open in the rain.

It wasn't raining, though. It was just drizzling a little off and on. The truth is the cops stop certain types of cars at certain hours with a certain type of person driving. I was a black man driving an expensive coupe in the wee hours. That was enough.

I also drew attention because I was lost and going slowly. I was looking for an exit ramp and driving only 20 mph. I changed lanes when I thought I saw a ramp, but the ramp was closed and I had to go on. Nobody else was on the road.

The cops—a man and a woman—came up behind me and it was just my luck they had a new computer in the car that gave them instant look-ups on stolen cars. They punched the license plate in and the car came up stolen.

They had a ball. They jumped on my ass and jacked me up something terrible. When the male partner found out who I was, he got on the radio.

"Hey, guys!" he's yelling into the radio. "Guess who we got? Maury Wills! Yeah! That's right! I got Maury Wills!" He was really pleased with himself.

He tightened the handcuffs on me and pushed my wrists up into my shoulder blades.

"Do you have to make them so tight?" I complained.

He didn't say anything. He just tightened those suckers up some more.

They took me to the station house and threw me in a cell. I was in there about five minutes when the watch commander came out and gave them hell for treating me that way. He took me into his office and let me sit in there while they decided what they were going to do with me.

The arresting officers had gone through my car. I had a bag in there with some clothes. I had gotten tired of sitting in my house alone and was going to visit somebody. They found my coke pipe in there. They scraped it out and came up with .06 grams of cocaine residue—not even enough to smoke.

They ended up dismissing the case. My lawyer advised me not to worry about the car. I left it in the impoundment lot. I never found out whether Judy recovered it. I never even found out whose name it was in. I only knew I paid for it with cash and I never saw it again.

By the time they dismissed the case, the damage had been done. There was no real evidence that I was using or was an addict, but the damage to my life and image had been done. Don Newcombe made it worse by reporting that I was an addict and had been in rehab but hadn't recovered.

I'm not saying the cops were wrong. They got lucky and I got unlucky. Yes, I was addicted at the time, but until that incident, at least the public didn't know.

When I got home, I called Angela in Oregon and told her I really needed her. She said, "Fuck you! You got in trouble. I can't babysit you." And she hung up.

## Chapter 80: The wedding from hell

My 25 days in 1983 in The Care Unit had been my one brush with recovery since I left Seattle. By 1985, I started the real struggle to recovery. *That's when Angela asked me to marry her.*

Angela wanted to be married Oct. 23, the anniversary of her father's death. I had married my first wife, Gertrude, in October, also—Oct. 20.

Angela had wanted me to get cleaned up so she could, too. I realized some time ago that my problem with my addiction stems from my trying to do what somebody else wants me to do to make things better. I thought it was neat that Angela wanted me to get cleaned up. I thought we might be able to have a decent life together. She might have been sincere, but she wasn't strong enough to do it. It's a powerful disease.

When the wedding was set, I stopped using. Before we could get married, I had one thing to clear up. I was still married to Gertrude. I had to go to Spokane to finalize my divorce.

I rested for a few days before I went up to see her. I went to an attorney who had drawn up divorce papers years before. We had never finalized the papers because there was some land that was sold and she wouldn't release the money. I went up there and said I'd sign the papers. Just give me a couple of bucks. The money had been in a savings account for something like 10 years and had grown to $115,000. I asked her if she would give me $20,000, but she wouldn't. She gave me $13,000.

She let me stay at the house while I was there. I slept in the basement. She stayed upstairs in her bedroom. I could hear her crying the whole night. I didn't feel anything for her. I didn't want anything to do with trying to be tender.

We signed the papers and I left the next day with the $13,000. That was the last time I saw Gertrude.

I went down to Ashland, Ore., a little lumber town with a population of about 14,000 in the southwest part of the state. Angela's grandmother lived there and that's where we were going to get married. I gave Angela a couple of thousand dollars to prepare for the wedding, then I went back to Los Angeles where I blew about $8,000 right away on drugs. Then I went back to Ashland to get married.

My best friend, Mel Exber, couldn't make it from Las Vegas to be my best man so he sent his son, Brady, to stand in for him. He also sent $3,000 as a wedding gift.

The first night there we had the rehearsal dinner. I didn't know anything about such things. I got up and told a few tales about Angela and everybody laughed. I was still a pretty big deal. But then her brother came in from Portland with all his buddies. They didn't have much to say to me. I extended my hand to him, but he ignored it.

"I sure want to be your friend," I told him.

"That depends on how you treat my sister," he said. It was clear he didn't know what his sister was all about.

We were in the biggest hotel in town, a brand-new, modern place. Angela rented out just about the whole place and gave everybody who came for the wedding the authority to sign for their expenses. We had about 150 people coming in. We were going to get married in the hotel, and the hotel was catering the meal. We're talking expensive.

The rehearsal was the night before the wedding, and she told me I wasn't supposed to see the bride that night. That sounded ridiculous to me. After all, we had been living together. We'd been through the drug scene together, and I'm not supposed to see her?

She had rented a big suite for herself and she gave me a little room off the main room. She was in the big room getting loaded with her bridesmaids and some of her brothers' friends and they're having a ball. I stayed in my little room, but after a while, I couldn't stand it anymore. I went out to see what was going on and they got offended and went down to another room to continue the party. I slept.

The next day—my wedding day—arrived. And I realized we didn't have any tuxedos. Her uncle Bill knew about a tuxedo place and we rushed down there and got everybody fixed up. I'm paying for everyone. Her two brothers are there and they don't have squat to say to me. It was like *Guess Who's Coming to Dinner?*—and he's marrying her. I had nowhere to hide.

I had forgotten to get a ring before I came to town. I managed to get one after the rehearsal dinner from a jewelry store in town. The store was closed when I got there, but the owner was inside. I tapped on the door and he recognized me.

"MAURY WILLS!" he said.

I told him my problem and he brought out the wedding rings. I reached in my pocket and realized I had given almost all my money—what was left of it—to Angela. I had maybe $50. I bought a ring that cost $39. It was just a little band. But it was good enough. I figured it was only a rain check.

So now it was time for the wedding. I didn't need to use before my wedding. I was hoping this would be the turning point and I wouldn't need any more drugs.

I came out and stood in the front of the ballroom with Brady and the groomsmen. Then Angela came into the room with this long, white dress on. She hadn't slept all night. She was plowed when she came up, plowed when she went back and plowed the whole time she was in Ashland. But at that moment she was the most beautiful sight I had ever seen in my life.

The aisle was about 40 feet long, and as she walked down it, the singer we had hired sang a great song in a beautiful voice.

I had gotten married when I was 17, but I could hardly remember it. It took maybe 15 minutes and then we walked out. I might have been wearing sneakers.

But this was a *wedding!* I mean, I'm getting married. And I start crying. I mean I'm boo-hooing and sobbing. Snot is coming out of my nose. Poor Brady looked over and saw that I didn't have a tissue or handkerchief. Brady had a handkerchief, though. He dabbed at my nose, but it just kept pouring out of me. You know how your nose runs and it doesn't stop? Well, I took the handkerchief and blew, but I was afraid to blow too hard because a pound might come out of there.

The preacher started going through the ceremony and I'm still crying. It came time to put the ring on, and I'm still crying. I pulled out my little $39 ring and put it on Angela's finger, and she looked at me with utter disgust. She was totally embarrassed. She's marrying Maury Wills, and this is the ring he buys? But what did she expect? She rented the entire hotel. We had drugs. We had a band. We had food for 150. We had tuxedos. We had a singer. It cost more than $10,000. What does she want, a ring, too?

The preacher pronounced us husband and wife. I'm boo-hooing. And now all I want to do is just hold her and hold her and hug her. But Angela was putting on a big show for everyone. She always said she was going to come home and do something crazy that was going to shock everyone. And this was it. She's bringing Maury Wills, the baseball star, home to marry. And Maury Wills is black. She's really having a swell time over this. And to top it off, instead of a hug and a nice little kiss, she throws this big, passionate, movie-star kiss on me in front of everybody. It was the worst kiss I ever had in my life. And the snot was all over my face.

We walked out together and headed upstairs to the suite, just the two of us. Before we got to the elevator, here came her girlfriends.

"You go on," Angela told me. "I'll be right up."

Two hours later, I was still alone in that big suite. She was downstairs in another room partying with her friends, including three of her old boyfriends that I knew about and one that I didn't.

Finally, I got one of her bridesmaids on the phone. Some of her bridesmaids were among the girls who had spent eight or nine days in my kitchen. Angela had made them her friends to take them away from me.

"Come up here and bring something with you!" I ordered the girl over the phone. She sneaked a little bit of the stuff out and came up. I took her downstairs to the Jacuzzi and started messing with her on my wedding night while my bride was messing with somebody else.

After three or four hours, Angela finally made it to the suite. She brought her mother, her mother's boyfriend, her brothers, their friends and all the girls. Now she's calling for me.

"What are you doing down there?" she wanted to know when she finally got me on the telephone.

"Why don't you come down here?" I said. We were reduced to playing little kids' games with each other.

"No, you come up here."

"No, you come down here."

The bridesmaid I was with was getting fidgety, but I wouldn't let her leave. I never saw Angela the entire night, my wedding night.

## Chapter 81: Faltering steps

The morning after my wedding, I had to catch an 11 a.m. flight because I had to get to Los Angeles in time to catch another flight for Florida. I had agreed to go to my very first Dodger fantasy camp, which was another reason to clean myself up. If I didn't catch that flight, I wasn't going to make it on time. Everybody was ready in the hotel lobby to leave. Except Angela.

She never came down, so I went to the airport and boarded the plane alone. Another plane was leaving three hours later. I waited for it in Los Angeles, but she didn't get on that one, either. Or the next one or the one after that. She ended up coming in about two in the morning. We flew down to Florida together and got in a day late.

I had as much fun at the camp as I could. It was pretty tough, though. Even in 1985, a black man wasn't supposed to walk into Vero Beach with a blonde. I was uneasy about it, but she was my wife.

Angela had a swell time. They had plenty to drink. She was the kind of person who had to have a drink to wake up with. She was the type who hid bottles under the table, under the sink, on the shelf in the closet, under the bed, between the mattress and the box spring.

Once I got on the field, it felt good to be back in uniform. I was accepted again. And the Dodgers offered me a job with the club. I would be going to spring training.

When we got back from the camp, I went immediately into cleaning up. She did, too. I started urine testing to stay clean. But I didn't know anything about amino acids and the chemistry of the brain. My body chemicals were depleted and you're talking about the dullest life I'd ever lived. The drug was out, but there wasn't anything coming back in. There was no sex now. There was no interest in it.

A big part of recovery is learning to do all the things you want to do without having to drink or use. In those days, I couldn't do anything unless I used. Angela couldn't do anything unless she used, drank and had pills at the same time. She had to have prescriptions for Valium and Quaaludes. I was able to get them. She was my wife, and I said she needed them because she was always hurting, which was true. Sometimes, I bought them on the street, where the pills cost $2 each. Then an eighth of an ounce of cocaine cost $150. So it was $40 for 20 Valium, $150 for the coke, and another $70 on booze. She had to have all three and still it didn't work out for her.

I kept testing for a while and working for the Dodgers, but eventually I blew the job. I wrecked any prosperity and success I was having.

By the time I blew the Dodgers job, I had accumulated $30,000. I had also started collecting my baseball pension, which is a substantial amount, after I turned 50 in 1982. Between the pension and the $30,000, we got through the summer and into the winter. Then I started running out of money. I had always had enough money that I didn't have to steal to get drugs. I didn't have to take from anybody. Everybody took from me. But now I was really running low on cash.

## Chapter 82: Farewell to Fowling Street

By the end of 1986, I was just about broke. To get more money, I had signed over a lien on my Fowling Street house. Finally, the notification came that I was being evicted.

The marshals came to throw us out in January 1987. When they came, Angela and I got into our car with her two parakeets. The marshals had wanted to shoot Charmer, my Doberman, but Charmer came with us.

The marshals had made it clear that once we walked out the door, I could not come back on the premises or my ass was going right to jail. But when we got outside, I realized I had left about a gram and a half of cocaine in a little cellophane bag on the kitchen counter. The marshals and the real estate people who took over the house were inside.

"Screw that," I said when I realized I had left it behind. "I'm going back to get it."

"No! You're going to get in trouble," Angela said trying to stop me.

I walked into the house and right through everybody. They looked at me as if I were crazy. I went to the counter, put the cocaine in my pocket, walked right back through them, got into the car and left.

My furniture, all the antiques I'd collected when I was living the good life, stayed there. I had two weeks to get it out. The people who took over the house had to provide a truck for me to transport the furniture, and they did. I put it in storage. My neighbor paid for the first month of storage. I kept up the payments for a few months after that, and then stopped. The storage place was on the verge of selling the furniture when the Dodgers found out what was happening. I didn't even know about it. I was too messed up to care. So the Dodgers paid the storage company, took the furniture and stored it at Dodger Stadium for me. I didn't find out until about three months later.

I called the Dodgers when I learned what they had done. "You can't lose your stuff, Maury," they said.

When we were evicted, we stayed with a friend, Mark Gallardo, who had a house in Redondo Beach. Mark was not involved in drugs. He told us if there were any drugs involved, we would have to leave. He's the person who eventually took me to Alcoholics Anonymous. He also got me a job selling telephone pagers.

The shock of losing my house helped me clean up again. I had heard a lot of stories about people losing their homes and their families, losing their businesses to the drug. I had always said, "That ain't going to happen to me. I got plenty of money."

Now it had happened to me. I realized that I had to fight the disease.

My pension was coming in. I was selling pagers and doing great. I was selling—leasing actually—100 of them a month. I had 300 policemen throughout the Los Angeles area among my clients. I was making a lot of bucks and I was so proud of myself. The cops were proud of me, too, because they knew I had a problem.

January, February, March and April went by and I was clean as a whistle. Angela was doing well, too. But she had no vocation, and that became a problem. That's when I sent her to the art school and she went to one class and decided the teacher didn't know what he was doing.

We had been sharing the house with Mark and his girlfriend. After a while, they moved out. I took over the rent. That's when things started getting chaotic again.

I started coming home and finding Angela drunk. I remembered that when I lost my first family because my baseball career was more important to me, I had vowed that the next time my family would come first. So I quit my job to stay with Angela and help her.

The Dodgers were having a series of special promotions as part of the 25th anniversary of Dodger Stadium. One of the nights was for Dodger base stealers Davey Lopes and Maury Wills. Angela and I were both clean and it was beautiful. I got all dressed up. My friend, Jon Gallen, came from New York. We were sitting in a booth with Fred Claire and his wife. I was so proud.

I went downstairs for the ceremony and Angela started sneaking out to get something to drink. It took her only one or two drinks and BAM! All of a sudden she's sloppy, her mascara is all over the place, her hair is a rat's nest, her dress is hanging all over, she's slurring her words and she's spilling her drink all over herself.

When I came back, that's how she was. I looked at Fred. Fred looked at me. I could tell Fred felt bad for me. I tried to get Angela to go.

"NO!" she insisted. "Let's go down to the Stadium Club!"

I tried to calm her down, but I couldn't without having her go off on me. I had to back off and let her do what she wanted to do until I got her out of the stadium.

When I got home, I was disgusted and humiliated. I figured I had blown it with my friend, Jon, who had helped my recovery by hiring me to appear at baseball card shows. I thought I'd blown it with Fred and the Dodgers.

I didn't blow it that night, but I did myself in just the same. I went off by myself and got stoned. Later that year, I was supposed to go back to the stadium for MVP night with Sandy Koufax and Steve Garvey. I never showed up. The Dodgers figured I was off somewhere killing myself. They weren't far from the truth.

The Dodgers and Fred Claire never gave up on me, though.

I knew that if I stayed clean I would lose Angela and I didn't want to lose her. I told her that.

"You know one thing, Angela," I said, "it's going to be tough with the both of us being cleaned up. I know damn well if I don't have drugs around, I'm going to lose you."

She didn't disagree. It wasn't difficult for me to start using again. I preferred being an addict with her to being clean and sober without her. That wasn't liking myself very much.

And all the money that I had saved I went through again.

It didn't make any difference. On Aug. 10, 1987, about four o'clock in the morning, Angela left. She had been going eight days non stop smoking that pipe. She had 15 Valium in her, 10 Quaaludes, and three fifths of 151 Bacardi rum. She walked out with the guy who was her connection. She just said she was leaving. I said okay. She left carrying a little Yorkshire terrier under her arm. She was walking, sort of. When she and the guy got into a taxi and drove away, I felt as if 4,000 pounds had been lifted from my shoulders. I never saw her again.

## Chapter 83: Fear of success

I lost the house in Redondo Beach, too. I wanted to stay there, but I had to leave. A developer friend of mine who had lived up the street from me in Playa del Rey let me stay rent-free in a building he had on Queen Street in Inglewood.

It was in a nice-looking stucco building just a block down from the Inglewood City Hall and the Inglewood Police. And it was in the crack center of the universe. You don't want to go down there at night. You don't want to go there in the daylight. There were people there who would mess you up over one little piece of rock. The place is bad, bad, bad, bad. It was so scary that even with my mind altered to its limits, to the point where I'd normally be fearless, I was still afraid.

I had come to that apartment beginning another good period. It didn't last any longer than it took to get the key in the door. I got so altered and so bad I didn't even move my furniture in.

I could clean up for a while, but never for long. I was afraid of success. I would make progress and get to the point where my life began to improve. But success means responsibility. You have to make commitments and keep them.

Peter O'Malley always wrote me a personal invitation to the Dodgers old-timers games. He would send it two or three months ahead of time. That gave me a target date. If the game was July 15, I would say to myself that by July 1, I had to stop and get some rest, eat properly and change my ways so I could be in some kind of condition for the game.

On July 1, I'd put everything down. I'd start getting my rest.

I'd go three or four days and couldn't believe how good I was feeling. I was jonesing the whole time, but I could ward off the desire by staying away from the people who would get me back into that.

A week would go by. Now there was one week to go. I'd persevere. With two days to go, I'm thinking, "I'm going to do it. I'm going to play this year. I'm all set." I'd dig into my belongings and find a pair of shoes and a glove. I'd call the club and tell them I needed a uniform.

Now it's the 14th. I have to leave the next morning for Dodger Stadium to play in the game. That night, the demon would come out and say, "No, you don't."

And I'd go on a binge. I did everything I could to sabotage those two weeks of good feeling I had built up. I'd get loaded all night long. I wanted to go to the game so badly, but something wouldn't let me go. My obsession took over. It was the damnedest thing.

I always said if I could go two days without using I would be over the worst part of the craving. But it's a psychological disease. It was like a voice talking to me. Richard Pryor did a perfect impression of an addict and his pipe. "Where do you think you're going?" the pipe says in the kind of tones your father used when he caught you sneaking out at night. "I let you have those 13 days. I let you get all built up just to shoot you down. Now keep your ass in the house where you belong. Get over here and fire me up." It was just like that.

I've met Richard Pryor since his accident with freebase. I would never ask him about it, though. I don't need to. I know what he went through. He was locked up in his house, too. We weren't unique. Everybody who does it is like that.

I wanted to quit, but I was afraid to. As I continued to fight the disease, it got to the point where all the cocaine I bought was in eight-tracks or eight-balls—eighths of an ounce. I could have had an ounce—that's 28 grams—for $900, but I bought eight balls for $150 each. I'd go to the store to buy baking soda to cook it up with and I'd always buy the smallest box. Then I'd go get 151 rum to smoke it. You soak some cotton in the rum and light that and use it to flame the freebase. Some people use rubbing alcohol. Some use a match. The rum gives you a stronger high and you don't get the poisons from the rubbing alcohol. Richard

Pryor used ether, which is highly volatile and explosive, to light it, and that's what got him so badly burned. But ether gives a stronger high, although that's one thing I never tried. I'd always buy a half-pint of rum—the smallest bottle.

It was all my way of saying, "I'm not going to do all of this stuff. I'm getting out of this." It's like buying cigarettes by the pack instead of the carton because you're going to quit. I did that, too.

I was just bullshitting myself. I ended up using just as much, but I paid twice as much because I was buying in such small quantities.

I moved from Inglewood to Laguna Beach. I thought I could escape my disease by moving down there. I found out the disease is portable.

It never seemed that it was another person doing these things. It was always me. I was always able to maintain one-eighth of me that stayed sane. That was what kept me alive and cognizant of what was going on. It also kept me coming back. I went to several out patient drug programs. In January 1988, I started going to Alcoholics Anonymous meetings. I wasn't well yet, but I persevered because of that smidgen of me that stayed sane.

I had trouble accepting that I am powerless and my life is uncontrollable. Even when I cleaned up, I was still in denial. I ended up going back. I told myself that if I could go several months without using it, I could buy a little and I didn't have to use all of it. I could use just a gram or a half gram a day. It doesn't work that way. What you have is what you're going to use until it's gone. Then you'll get more.

From the day I started in the minor leagues, I was always taught never to give up. The man picks you off, you get in a rundown play. You try to find ways to get out of everything. You're not out until the man tags you with the ball, and even then you look at the umpire.

When I first got into AA, they taught me that first of all I had to surrender. I had never heard of surrender. I was the kind of guy who was never going to be taken prisoner. You would have to shoot me first. But the program said I had to surrender my entire life, give up my ego.

Ego! Ego is what you want to build in baseball. Ego is another word for pride and perseverance and dedication and loyalty and the killer instinct. All of a sudden, I had to give that up.

I spent 22 years as a player and another 10 years as an instructor, teaching guys the art of base stealing, telling them to get off that base and eliminate any fear of failing. Don't give up.

For seven years, I couldn't give up.

But I kept coming back. That's the key. The first time you try to clean up, you get a little bit of clarity back, a little bit of sanity. Now you figure you can go back and drink like other people. You can just have a sip or a cocktail or two and then go on home. Come closing time, you're still sitting in the bar. It's the same with using. A lot of people can drink or use. For people like me, one's too many, and a thousand's not enough.

## Chapter 84: Rock bottom

My final binge lasted five or six months. I don't know for sure. It seems that time goes so fast when you're using drugs, because you have no concept of what day it is, what time of day it is, how much money you have, where the next dollar is coming from. It doesn't matter. It's all just one big piece of time. When you come out of it, three, four, five months have gone by.

I was living in a brand-new two-bedroom apartment in Laguna Beach. I had gotten my furniture back from the Dodgers. I had started 1988 in Alcoholics Anonymous. I was going to the meetings, but I wasn't working the steps of the program. In the spring, I left the program to do, as we say, some more research on my disease.

I was a lost soul. I'd sleep on the couch three or four days at a time. Then I'd wake up and lie there for three or four more days. I got hooked on MTV. I'd lie there and watch it around the clock. My life revolved around the first of the month when my pension check came in.

I'd get the check and I'd go through $3,000–$4,000 in maybe

eight days. It always seemed to be eight or nine days. I could never stretch that out to two weeks. When I was out of stuff and money I'd fall asleep. I'd sleep for three or four days. Then I'd lie there and watch MTV until the 15th of the month. That's when I could get fronted. Getting fronted is the word in the drug scene for credit. That would take me through the next two weeks.

Now it's the first again. I'd pay off my front, buy some more, and start all over again. That was the pattern for three or four months. I never seemed to have any money in my pocket. I didn't care. It all went to drugs. The refrigerator was always empty. But I always had liquor and drugs in the house.

I knew about Len Bias and how he died from an overdose. It didn't scare me at all. I figured Bias didn't do something right. The risk of dying was no reason to quit using. I didn't like myself anyway. The real risk is not of dying, but of being clean and sober without reason to be.

That's the psychological part of the disease. And I was finally running out of reasons to drink and use. I had no more excuses. I wasn't hiding from anything. I was long over the emotional trauma from my failed romance. After that, I had figured I'd use drugs for sex. Then using prevented sex. I was over that.

You never grow to the point of not thinking about it, but you grow to not want it. You never see old coke heads because they die. They die or clean up. Those are the choices. Your body can't handle it forever. It's just a question of time.

My time came in August 1988.

I was lying on the couch not using when it happened. I'd run out of drugs and I was sick and tired of being sick and tired. I didn't want any more. I was lying there numb for three days watching MTV saying, "I can't go any further. I can go get some, but I don't want to."

I had tried everything. I'd been in and out and back. I had exhausted my imagination. I had actually accepted what AA preaches, that I was powerless, my life was unmanageable and I couldn't go on.

I wasn't having any fun and I had run out of fun plans. I was defeated.

I didn't call anybody. I didn't get up. I lay there and waited. Part of the vision, the feeling that I had, was that someone was going to come and get me—*IF* I didn't use. Nobody was going to come for me as long as I continued to use. Yet no one knew whether I was using or not. I was locked in.

I didn't want to make a move because my best thinking got me right there where I was. I couldn't trust my thinking anymore to make a move and get out of it. I had done that often enough. So I stayed on my couch. I stayed there a week.

Then Barbara showed up. She's a good woman, not a user or abuser, who I had met a year or two before. She said she just got a feeling that I needed help and she decided to come and get me. She took me home with her to Hermosa Beach and put me up on her couch. I was finished using.

They say that God works in strange ways. Well, he works in spooky ways, too.

## Chapter 85: One day at a time

Around the first of September, 1988, I did a card show in San Francisco. About the same time I got paid for that, I got my pension check. I had some money in my pocket, and damn, it felt good.

I was feeling good, looking good and Barbara was in my life. Before I knew it, the first of October came around and I still had money. Plus I had a job working for a cellular phone company and had made some money. I felt rich again.

The first of the month was a big psychological hurdle for me. Even during those periods when I had been clean, the first of the month was scary. That's when all my friends feared for me because they knew I had a sizeable amount of money. And when I had money in my pocket, I had to celebrate. I had celebrated by getting high.

But now I had had money in my pocket all month long. When the first came, getting more money wasn't a big deal. I had gotten over the first-of-the-month hang-up. It used to be that if I had

$20 in my pocket in the middle of the month, it was a big thing. I could eat. Now I had $100 in my pocket all month.

I had never wanted to think that for the rest of my life I wouldn't be able to get high again. What a dreadful thought. But as I got serious about AA, I had to learn to think only about now. Just today.

It's easy to quit. What's devastating to an alcoholic or an addict is the thought that for the rest of his life he can't take one drink; he can't take any drugs. But if you think of it as just today, that's easy. You can handle today. Then tomorrow becomes today. The next day becomes today. Before you know it, you have a whole bunch of todays. It's so easy living in the now.

After a while, I didn't even think about it.

I've been talking about the drug, but I stopped thinking about the high of it all. That's the real danger—thinking about the feeling, the mood that it gives you.

## Chapter 86: AA

Testing is a very good behavior-control mechanism. I tested five days a week the first time I went back to work for the Dodgers. I had to test to keep the job. And I stayed clean for three or four months. I couldn't fool that machine. But I got tired of that. I was white-knuckling my way through. Life was no fun anymore.

I had to go through the cycle many times. After a while, I started to turn the cycle around. Instead of my good periods being shorter than my bad periods, my good periods became longer than the bad.

It took Bill W. and Doctor Bob, the founders of AA, three or four years before they became sober. The thing is to keep coming back. It takes a long time to build up enough knowledge and spirituality to make it work. You have to surrender to a higher power. As long as I figured I could do it myself, I was never going to beat it.

I surrendered on that couch in Laguna Beach. You can call the power you surrender to anything you want. I call it God, but it doesn't matter, as long as you have a higher power. Confirmed atheists and agnostics have stopped drinking and using through AA.

When I surrendered to my higher power through AA, I started taking weekly urine tests, but this time it wasn't because I had to take them to keep a job. I took them because I wanted to. If you're forced to do something, it's bitter. When you want to do it, it's so nice.

When you come into AA, you pick a sponsor from among the longtime members, people who have several years of sobriety behind them. In February 1988, I picked Frank C., a garrulous retired postal worker who was born in the south and was part Cherokee Indian. He practiced his disease in Philadelphia and had 20 years in the program.

After I first came to AA, I disappeared for four days. I went on a drinking binge. I was supposed to call Frank C. every day. When I finally did after the binge, I made up a great lie to explain why I hadn't called. It didn't fool him for a minute.

"Let me tell you something, Maury," he said. "When you stepped through the doors of AA, you came in contact with the biggest liars, thieves, cutthroats and bullshitters in the world, so cut the shit and tell me where you've been."

Part of AA is practicing a rigorous honesty in all our dealings, and it starts with the sponsor. I couldn't lie to Frank. You can't bullshit a bullshitter. Everybody in that meeting every morning had been there. Nobody's unique. Maybe some of us spent more money than others because we had more money to spend, but we'd done the same things. We were all wise to the same old excuses.

My word to anyone who's dabbling in drugs or drinking alcohol excessively is to watch out, because you're setting yourself up. Everything may be going along well in your life. You haven't hit any snags yet. But you're due to hit them soon, because even if the snags don't come from normal day-to-day living, you're going to create them. You're changing your disposition and your behavior patterns. You will change them because every time you use you affect your neurochemistry.

I was blessed with great genes. I played hard and I played most of the games every year. I was 29 years old when I stole 104 bases. I was 32 when I stole 95. Most ballplayers have their best years starting around 24 years old. By 32, they're smarter, but they're not as strong and quick as they were when they were 24. I was still in the minors when I was 24. So I was gifted. But going out and getting high and drunk every day I found that my body wasn't so resilient anymore. I was starting to feel the wear and tear. I got the message that I was going to die early if I continued the path I was on.

One morning at my AA meeting in Hermosa Beach, a woman speaking about alcoholics and addicts said, "Isn't it amazing that people who have so much ego can hate themselves so much."

Since I was 17 years old, I projected an aura of confidence, even cockiness. Only much later did I learn that cockiness and confidence are two different things. Cockiness comes from weakness and insecurity; confidence comes from strength.

After I finally made the big leagues at the age of 27 and became a national hero, I used to complain about how tough it was being Maury Wills. I kept complaining for years, and when I was released by the Dodgers in 1972, I actually thought that one good thing about it was that I was through paying my dues. I didn't have to be on stage all the time. I could be myself. I was talking about that one day when somebody heard me and said, "You may as well stop your crying because we pay dues every day of our lives. You will continue to pay dues, so you might as well face it."

That's so true. You have to pay dues for living. That much I learned.

I didn't have 90,000 people screaming in the stands and pulling for me to steal a base, but in my recovery program I had hundreds of thousands of people pulling for Maury to make it. In place of the Coliseum crowd chanting, "GO! GO! GO!" was my AA fellowship yelling, "NO! NO! NO!" AA didn't give me all the answers. But I knew that this time would be different because I hadn't merely stopped using and drinking. I was working my spirituality. A program that provides spirituality teaches you how to live again. AA taught me to seek a power greater than any here on earth in order to restore my sanity.

I was punishing myself because I had failed and I was embarrassed. I felt guilty for not being able to be everything that I said I could be, that I boasted I was. I failed to make a relationship work. I failed by letting the relationship distract me from my managing. I failed because I didn't have the strength to cope with it all. When that happened, I didn't like myself anymore. I didn't want to face the world. I didn't want the responsibility. I felt I was no good.

I was mad at the world because everybody witnessed my failure. I became a man with no vision, and a man with no vision is a lost soul. Fear set in.

I was safe from all that in drugs. There's no responsibility in drugs. There's no commitment. Everything's a lie. I didn't have to get up in the morning. I didn't have to go to bed at night. The only perseverance I had was the perseverance to get the drugs.

I found out in the program that being Maury Wills didn't mean I wasn't human. Drugs or alcohol don't make you a bad guy. They just make you bad while you're abusing them.

I stopped using them. But I learned I would never get well. I'd just keep getting better. And better is good enough.

# Afterword

Alcoholism and drug addiction are devastating diseases. Those who are recovering, who are in recovery, and who are recovered by the grace of God as we understand God can be most instrumental in helping alcoholics and addicts who reach out for help.

In my humble opinion, Maury W. has accepted and surrendered to the disease. He is well on the AA road of being of maximum service to his Higher Power, to himself and to alcoholics and drug addicts who still suffer.

Maury admitted the first step of AA in January 1988. We are helping each other and are very careful not to confuse recovery with cure. "We have a daily reprieve contingent on the maintenance of our spiritual condition."

I met Maury for the first time Feb. 2, 1988, at the Sea Horse Motel in Manhattan Beach, Cal. It was a 12th step call. It was a warm and affectionate meeting of the minds, because I had been where he was.

Maury had given his fans and me many thrills in baseball. But that day he didn't look like the speedy Los Angeles Dodger who broke Ty Cobb's long-standing record by stealing 104 bases in 1962. He looked more like me as I was on Nov. 13, 1970—the day I had my last drink of alcohol and last drug fix.

We are only actors in a play which the Manager directs. God is our Director and the "Big Book" is the script. We learn the script and play the role by getting good direction day by day. Maury and I find this is a simple idea and the keystone to freedom. Look at the past, good and bad. Look at the future. Dream and plan. Do not wallow in the painful past, nor guarantee the future: "Thy will be done." Live today!

We can go on from design to design, add hope to hope and lay out plans for the enjoyment of many years. But what are the external trappings of human dignity, the power of wealth, the dreams of ambition, the pride of intellect or the charms of beauty when alcohol and drugs exact their debt?

We have entered the detox centers, Maury, and have "viewed life stripped of its ornaments and exposed in its natural meanness." By our past we have been persuaded of the utter emptiness of the delusions of a drink or a fix for the alcoholic and addict. When we learn to do sober and clean what we wanted to do drunk and spaced out, our troubles are over. It's a grand and glorious feeling to know where we've been, what we did and who we did it with.

Maury, let us keep trudging the road of happy destiny together. We have the help of our High Power, the miracle of Alcoholics Anonymous, our families and our non-alcoholic friends. For that, Maury, let us be grateful by staying sober and clean one day at a time.

I love you, Maury.

Thank you,
Frank C.
S.W. Alano Club
Hawthorne, Cal.
9/24/89